OCT 7 1993

The Sense of Self

Research and Theory

Alan O. Ross, PhD, has been professor of psychology at the University at Stony Brook since 1967. He did his undergraduate work at City College of New York and earned his PhD degree in clinical psychology at Yale University. He is a Fellow of the Society of Personality and Social Psychology, a Division of the American Psychological Association, and has served on the editorial boards of the *Journal of Consulting and Clinical Psychology* and other publications. A biographee of *Who's Who in America*, Dr. Ross is the author of some 60 articles in scientific journals, 12 chapters in edited volumes, and 10 books, the most recent being the well-received text, *Personality: The Scientific Study of Complex Human Behavior*. In 1982 the Division of Clinical Psychology of the American Psychological Association honored Dr. Ross with its Award for Distinguished Professional Contributions.

The Sense of Self
Research and Theory

Alan O. Ross, PhD

Springer Publishing Company
New York

Copyright © 1992 by Springer Publishing Company, Inc.

All rights reserved

No part of this publication may be reproduced, stored in a
retrieval system, or transmitted in any form or by any means,
electronic, mechanical, photocopying, recording, or otherwise,
without the prior permission of Springer Publishing Company, Inc.

Springer Publishing Company, Inc.
536 Broadway
New York, NY 10012-3955

92 93 94 95 96 / 5 4 3 2 1

Library of Congress Cataloging-in-Publication Data

Ross, Alan O.
  The sense of self : research and theory / Alan O. Ross.
    p. cm.
  Includes bibliographical references and index.
  ISBN 0-8261-7430-2
  1. Self. I. Title
BF697.R6575 1992
155.2—dc20   91-868
                                                                                                       CIP

Printed in the United States of America

To ILSE, JUDY, and PAM

Contents

1	Introduction	1
2	Origins of Self-Concept	5
3	Self-Concept: Content and Organization	20
4	A Model of the Self-Concept	37
5	Self-Awareness and Self-Consciousness	53
6	Self-Perception	73
7	Self-Assessment, Self-Efficacy, and Self-Esteem	94
8	Self-Handicapping	113
9	Self-Attention, Self-Prediction, and Self-Regulation	131
10	Self-Monitoring	152
11	Summing Up	175
	References	178
	Author Index	191
	Subject Index	195

Preface

All of psychology converges and acquires significance in the personality of the individual. All of personality culminates and acquires meaning in the individual's sense of self. That is what endows the sense of self with its importance and fascination.

My purpose in writing this book was to introduce those who share this fascination to the principal current theories and research on such aspects of personality as self-awareness, self-esteem, self-consciousness, and self-monitoring. The importance of these aspects of personality stems from the fact that they influence how we think about, evaluate, and conduct ourselves; affecting not only our own lives but also those of the people we encounter.

This book is addressed to students of personality and others who seek to learn. Its major focus is on theory-driven research. It was my aim to communicate the sense of excitement and challenge that rewards those who investigate topics related to the sense of self. At the same time I wished to highlight and thus credit the ingenuity these scientists bring to bear in surmounting the unique obstacles and difficulties that are inherent in conducting research in this area. To that end I included for each of the topics covered details of at least one representative study together with critical but, I trust, constructive comments.

ALAN O. ROSS

1

Introduction

SELF-CONCEPT
Meaning of Self

Self Is Not an Entity

Strictly speaking there is no such thing as the self—at least not in scientific psychology. That is why the expression "the self" will be found in this book only in quotes from other, less particular writers. In almost all instances when "self" appears it will be followed by a hyphen that links it to a noun, such as concept, awareness, or esteem, to form such compound nouns as self-awareness or self-esteem. In these combinations self assumes the syntactic function it has in such reflexive pronouns as myself, herself, and himself; it refers to the person who is the agent of the action. Self-awareness, for example, means that the person is aware of himself or herself. It does not mean that the person is aware of some imaginary entity, called his or her self.

This insistence that self is not an entity, that it must not be reified, is in line with the usage found in the contemporary research literature on which this book is based.

Evolution of a Word

Self-Denial to Self-Assertion

Self denied. "Self" as a noun is a relatively recent addition to the English language. Baumeister (1986) discovered that it was not used in that form until about AD 1400. In those days self carried the negative connotation of selfishness as in the pledge "Our own self we shall deny, and follow our Lord Almighty."

The ubiquitous hyphen appeared by the end of the sixteenth century when preachers would warn people against such follies as self-praise, self-conceit, self-love, and self-liking. Self-knowledge, self-preservation, self-made, self-pity, self-contempt, and self-interest came into use later, in the first part of the 17th century.

Self asserted. The term *self-consciousness*, in the sense of being conscious of oneself, aware of one's unique identity, did not make its appearance until 1690. By then, so Barfield (1954) reports, the literature also contained compound nouns with positive connotations, such as self-confidence, self-esteem, and self-knowledge. Since that time hyphenated expressions that join self to a noun have increased in number so that a recent edition of *Webster's New Collegiate Dictionary* (1987) lists no fewer than 210 of them.

Democracy and Sense of Self

Baumeister (1986) reports that in German the pattern and dates of the linguistic development traced earlier were approximately the same as in English. In French analogous developments occurred somewhat later. It is unlikely that people can think about concepts before they have words to express them. It therefore would seem that awareness of the individuality and personal identity connoted by self came gradually and relatively recently to the people of Western Europe. Once the notion of self had become available, however, it was possible for these people to assert their unalienable personal rights to life, liberty, and the pursuit of happiness; to speak of being secure in their persons against unreasonable searches and seizures; and for Benjamin Franklin's contemporary, Nathaniel Cotton (1705-1788), to write,

> The world has nothing to bestow;
> From our own selves our joys must flow.

A Definition of Self-Concept

In her two-volume examination of the self-concept Ruth Wylie (1974) observed that "it has recently become widely fashionable and acceptable to write about such hypothetical constructs as the self-concept and self-esteem without seriously attempting to define terms" (p. 316). Let us make such an attempt.

In line with the discussion at the beginning of this chapter, the self-concept is no more than the concept a person has of himself or herself. That concept represents how one thinks and feels about oneself—how one perceives oneself. People acquire a concept of themselves as distinct individuals through their experiences with their physical and social environment. From these they learn who and what they are.

A key to human behavior. One's self-concept influences how one acts and how one acts influences how one perceives oneself. This reciprocal process makes the self-concept a central aspect of the person for it provides her or him with a sense of identity. Knowing something about a person's self-concept helps others explain and predict that individual's actions. The study of people's self-concepts thus provides a key to the study of human behavior.

SENSE OF SELF
Observer and Observed

Reflective nature of self-concept. The perceptions of one's thoughts and feelings about oneself that enter into the self-concept require that one be both the object being observed and the observer making the observation. That does not imply a dualism. Obviously, there are not two people inside the person, one who is being observed and another who is doing the observing. When a man is thinking about his own thoughts he simply shifts his attention from thinking about events in the environment to events transpiring within himself. "The same self performing multiple functions does not require creating multiple selves endowed with different roles" (Bandura, 1989, p. 1181).

Need for objectivity. Nevertheless, the two functions do take place in the same person, and this state of affairs poses a problem for those who wish to engage in the scientific study of self-concepts. In all other scientific investigations of natural phenomena the scientist and the object of study are separate entities. In fact, together with repeatability and communicability, objectivity is one of the essential requirements of science so that scientists must seek to eliminate subjectivity from their research.

Because of the personal, reflexive nature of the self-concept objectivity would be impossible if a scientist were to study her or his own self-concept. Such studies must therefore be conducted on the self-concepts of other people. There, however, the scientist faces another problem.

Validity of self-reports. Because people's self-concept is based on their perceptions of themselves, a way must be found to gain access to these perceptions. One approach would be to ask people to report their self-perceptions. That, however, raises the question whether what they report is what they actually perceive. Even if people were fully cooperative and wanted to tell the truth, it is possible that they do not have accurate perceptions of themselves. Moreover, it could be that certain aspects of themselves are hidden even from them; or if not hidden, some people might be deceiving even themselves. In short, self-reports on such mental processes as self-perceptions raise the question of their validity.

Neglected Topic

Impact of behaviorism. The issue of validity of self-reports explains why most North American psychologists avoided studying self-related topics during a period of some 40 years when behaviorism was their favored approach. As long as only the acts of people were legitimate objects of study, their self-concept had to be ignored.

While behaviorism flourished and the study of self-related topics was banished from the psychological laboratory there flourished the formulations of philosophers such as George Herbert Mead (1934) and psychotherapists such as Sigmund Freud (1953/1974), Erik Erikson (1959), and Carl Rogers (1961). The lone exception to this general reluctance to conduct research on self-related topics was Gordon Allport (1961) who, throughout the decades dominated by behaviorism, studied and wrote about the individual person's self-concept.

Interest in Self Renewed

Not until the emergence of the movement that has come to be known as "The Cognitive Revolution" (Baars, 1986) did psychologists' interest return to such private events as the self-concept. Obstacles posed by the inaccessible nature of self-related processes have begun to be overcome in sophisticated investigations that employ the methods of cognitive psychology. The results of these investigations are providing some tentative answers to such questions about the self-concept as how it is formed and organized, what it contains and how it is manifested, whether it facilitates or hinders social interactions, and whether people can give veridical reports about it.

As we proceed to examine contemporary research on the self-concept and related topics we shall see how and how well present-day investigators deal with the problems posed by science's demand for objectivity, repeatability, and communicability. In the course of this examination we shall come to appreciate the difficulties that are inherent in such research. Again and again we will encounter sophisticated, well-executed research that seems to have established a certain fact only to find that the next study refutes that fact and reopens a question that appeared to have been answered. Such is the painstaking, self-correcting, open-ended nature of research. Patience is essential both in conducting and in reading about it.

2

Origins of Self-Concept

SELF-RECOGNITION

What is the origin of the self-concept? Do infants have a concept of themselves? When does that concept first appear in the development of a child? These questions are difficult to investigate because, like any concept, the self-concept cannot be directly observed. Another person's concepts can only be inferred from his or her verbalizations or actions and, in the case of a preverbal child, only actions are available. It is these that investigators of infants' self-concepts have employed to study their origin and development.

Distinction Between I and Me

Subject and Object

Lewis (1986) points out that in discussing the development of self-awareness it is useful to differentiate between two aspects of the individual. From one aspect the individual is the subject, the "I"; from the other aspect the individual is the object, the "me."

Existential self. Self-as-subject has to do with people's awareness that they exist as individuals, distinct from the objects surrounding them as well as from other individuals. Lewis (1986) refers to this self-awareness as the existential self because it deals with the knowledge that one exists.

Categorical self. Self-as-object has to do with what one knows oneself to be like. This knowledge is acquired over time and includes such characteristics as gender, age, family membership, size, skin color, traits, occupation, and status—with the categories other people use to classify a person and that people use to classify themselves. Lewis (1986) calls this the categorical self. It is much the same as what is usually referred to as the person's self-concept.

Self and nonself. The development of self-as-subject obviously must precede the development of self-as-object. I must know that I am I before I can learn that I am my mother's child. That, indeed, is the course of development. Infants are generally able to differentiate between their mother and other people by the third month of life (Bronson, 1972). It makes sense to assume that the differentiation between self and nonself has its beginnings around this time, and, as Lewis (1986) points out, this differentiation is well established by the time the child is 1 year old.

Recognition of Self

Mirror studies

Mark-directed behavior. It is one thing to know that I and my mother are two distinct entities; it is another to realize that I am I. This self-awareness seems to emerge between 12 and 18 months, and its presence can be inferred when one places a child in front of a mirror. The infant's interest in her or his own reflection will have emerged earlier, but not until then can one observe two distinct behaviors that are interpreted as reflecting self-awareness. One is a kind of coyness or embarrassment that children in this age range display when they see and point to their reflection in the mirror. The other is so-called mark-directed behavior, which can be observed after an infant is 15 months old.

To test for the presence of mark-directed behavior, the examiner surreptitiously marks the baby's nose with a spot of rouge before placing her in front of a mirror. If, on seeing her reflection, a little girl points to the spot on her own nose, one can infer the presence of self-awareness because she must have recognized that the image in the mirror is, in fact, herself and that the mark is located not on the face of the image but on her own nose. (A little boy would be expected to behave in the same fashion.)

The self-recognition that is manifested in mark-directed behavior can also be observed when children point at themselves in pictures. Both show the beginning of an awareness of self-as-object. With the beginning of language, after about 18 months, self-as-object becomes clearly demonstrable in the use of the word "me" and of such categories as girl and boy, brother and sister.

Developmental Principles and Self-Recognition

Individual Differences

There are individual differences in every aspect of human behavior that undergoes the gradual changes over time that we attribute to maturation. This is the case regardless of whether the aspect in question has to do with physical or mental functions. It is also true that such maturation is inevitably influenced by the interaction of biological and environmental factors. Because each of these factors can take many different forms, the resulting individual differences can manifest themselves in that some children develop a physical or mental capability more quickly and some more slowly than others. In addition the quality of each child's performance can differ so that at any given chronological age, some will do things better, some worse than others (Ross, 1977). Moreover, there is little correlation in the rate and quality at which different physical and mental functions develop. Early development of high-quality motor activity, for example, is not necessarily accompanied by early development of good verbal skills or vice versa.

The development of mark-directed behavior and of the self-awareness we infer from it follow the same principles as the development of all other human capacities. There are individual differences in both the rate and the quality in which that capacity emerges, although Lewis (1986) points out that no mirror study has ever reported finding an infant who demonstrated mark-directed behavior before the age of 15 months. Even at that age this manifestation of self-recognition is found in only about 25% of the children studied.

Age-Related Changes

To recognize oneself in a mirror and to know that a spot on the nose in the mirror indicates a spot on one's own nose implies the operation of such cognitive processes as perception, memory, and reasoning. The little girl in our earlier example must have had previous experiences with a mirror from which she learned what her face looks like. To touch the spot on her nose she must then have remembered and recalled her features, compared these with the image before her, and realized what it was about her reflection that was different from what she remembered herself to look like. It is remarkable that children as young as 18 months are able to do all that.

We know that there are individual differences in the rate and quality in which such functions as perception, memory, and reasoning develop. It is therefore not surprising that research has shown a positive relationship between a variety of cognitive measures and self-recognition. One of the measures used in studies of this relationship is a test of object permanence that entails knowing that an object continues to exist even when it is out of sight (Piaget, 1952).

Self-Recognition and Object Permanence

To test for object permanence the examiner shows the child a toy that is then covered with a cloth or pillow. If the child retrieves the toy she or he is said to have reached the developmental stage of object permanence. Bertenthal and

Fischer (1978) investigated the development of self-recognition in relation to the development of object permanence. They report the fairly high correlation of .84 between the respective tests.

Gradual development. The Bertenthal and Fischer (1978) study also documented that the capacities a child demonstrates in the rouge task do not appear to emerge all at once. They have antecedents in more primitive capacities that develop earlier.

These investigators observed 48 infants (24 boys and 24 girls), in six groups of eight children each, aged 6, 8, 10, 12, 18, and 24 months. All of these children were placed in front of a mirror and given a series of increasingly difficult tests. These ranged from simply touching some part of the mirror to the rouge test described earlier. Intermediate tasks required that the child reach over his or her head for a hat or a toy that was reflected in the mirror. The task with the hat was easier because the hat was fixed over the infant's head so that it moved with the movements of the child. The toy, however, hung on a string so that its movements were independent of the child's movements. The investigators had predicted that success on this range of tasks would follow a developmental sequence such that all children would succeed on the easiest task, whereas only the oldest could handle the most difficult.

The results showed that the performance of 46 of the 48 children followed such a sequence. Only the children in the 18- and 24-month groups were able to succeed on the rouge task, the first to reflect true self-recognition.

Limitation

A cross-sectional study such as the one just described has the limitation that although it can demonstrate what capacities children have at different ages, it cannot show how these capacities change over time. To study that one would have to conduct a longitudinal investigation in which the same children are repeatedly examined during a period of months or even years. Such research is time-consuming and difficult to carry out with families who tend to be as highly mobile as the parents of very young children. It is probably for that reason that no longitudinal study on the development of self-recognition could be located.

Variables in Development of Self-Recognition

As pointed out earlier, the development of self-recognition, as the development of all human characteristics, is more rapid for some, less so for other infants. Any statement that children of a specific age are able to perform a particular task inevitably refers to a group average, rarely applies to every child in that group, and hardly ever to one specific child. The reasons for these individual differences in development are difficult to uncover. They probably lie in a complex

Origins of Self-Concept

interaction of environmental and constitutional factors. We thus cannot point to what it is that makes some children develop self-recognition earlier or later than others. It is instructive, however, to ask about the relationship of this development to other variables that play a role in the child's early life.

Features in the social environment. Several variables immediately come to mind as conceivably related to the age at which an infant's self-recognition develops. Among these are the family's socioeconomic status, the mother's educational level, the infant's gender and birth order, and the number of other children in the family. Each of these demographic variables has been investigated, but none was found to bear a relationship to the onset of self-recognition (Lewis, 1986). This makes it all the more intriguing that a variable that has to do with mother-infant interaction has been found to be related to the development of self-recognition and that this relationship is of a wholly unsuspected nature. The variable in question is attachment behavior.

ATTACHMENT BEHAVIOR

Before we can examine the relationship between self-recognition and attachment behavior we must describe what attachment behavior is, how it develops, and how it is measured.

Development of Attachment Behavior

Around 2 or 3 months after birth the infant develops the capacity to discriminate among individuals: between father and mother, between strangers and members of the family. Just about this time there also emerges the beginning of what appears to be a preference for one specific caregiver, ordinarily but not inevitably the mother. A little later, usually during the second half of the first year, the infant begins to organize a series of already available behaviors into a cluster that is directed at this specific caregiver. These behaviors are smiling, looking, visual following, and vocalizing. A little later clinging and physical following are added to this list. Because all of these actions serve to establish and maintain physical proximity or psychological contact with the caregiver Bowlby (1969) called them attachment behaviors or simply attachment.

Functions of Attachment

Because attachment is found among humans, other mammals, and many birds it is thought to be a genetically based, inborn tendency that has been selected in the course of evolution. What could have greater survival value than an infant's tendency to stay close to the adult caregiver who can provide food and protection against predators?

In addition to its role in the survival of the individual and hence the species, attachment also serves the crucial function of permitting the young to explore and thus learn about the environment. Here the caregiver with whom the infant has developed attachment serves as a secure base from which to set forth and to which to return when the newly discovered becomes too great a threat (Ainsworth, 1979).

Reciprocal Relationship

It would be a mistake to assume that attachment is something the infant develops to the caregiver for it is a two-way street, a reciprocal relationship between the mothering person and child. Smiling, vocalizing, and looking would do the infant little good if there were not a mother who responded to these smiles, looks, and sounds by engaging in behaviors that provide the secure base from which the child can set out to explore the environment (Ross, 1987). Viewed in this light, attachment is not an attribute of the child but a quality that permeates the interaction between two individuals. Sroufe (1979) has stressed that attachment is the product of earlier caregiver-infant interactions for if the infant is to be secure in attachment he or she must previously have experienced the caregiver as a reliable source of comfort—someone who is available, sensitive, and responsive to the infant's needs and signals.

Assessment of Attachment

The Strange Situation

The quality of interaction between infant and caregiver is typically assessed by a laboratory method, the "Strange Situation," that was developed by Mary Ainsworth and her associates (Ainsworth, Behar, Waters, & Wall, 1978). This situation is strange in the sense that it is unfamiliar to the 1-year-old infant whose reactions are unobtrusively observed in a series of standardized episodes. Four individuals participate in this procedure. They are the mother, her infant, a woman who is a stranger to the infant, and an examiner who briefly introduces the situation that takes about half an hour to complete.

Procedure. The examiner leaves mother and infant alone in a room that contains several age-appropriate toys and some magazines. The stranger then joins the two, briefly engages the mother in conversation, and seeks to interact with the infant. At that point the mother quietly leaves the room so that stranger and infant are alone. The mother reenters after 3 min. and the stranger departs so that mother and infant are alone once again. Mother now seeks to interest the infant in one of the toys. Once the infant seems comfortably occupied, she rises, says "bye-bye," and leaves the infant alone in the room. After 3 min. the stranger comes back into the room and, unless the infant is engaged in solitary play, tries to interact with him or her. The stranger, 3 min. later, again exchanges places with the mother who greets and picks up the infant for some spontaneous interaction that lasts for another 3 min. Throughout all this trained observers behind a one-way mirror watch and record the infant's movements, posture, looking, crying, smiling, and vocalizing. Should the infant become unduly upset during any of the mother-absent episodes, that condition is immediately terminated.

Observations. The observations primarily focus on the infant's reactions to the entrances, exits, and absences of the mother and the stranger. It is these reactions, especially those to the reunion with the mother after the two separations, that enabled Ainsworth and her fellow investigators to identify three major classes or groupings of attachment; they named these *secure attachment, resistant attachment,* and *avoidant attachment* (Waters, Vaughn, & Egeland, 1980).

Because the focus of the observations on which these groupings are based was on the infant's behavior it is easy to forget that the form attachment takes is not a characteristic of the infant but a quality of the mother-infant interaction. Phrases such as "a securely attached infant," which one occasionally encounters, thus tend to be misleading. It is important to remember that such an expression is merely a short way of speaking of a child who participated in a mother-infant interaction that fostered secure, resistant, or avoidant attachment.

Three Forms of Attachment

Secure attachment. During the strange-situation episode before the first separation infants whose behavior reflects secure attachment will have used their mother as a secure base from which to explore the room. When the stranger enters, they may scurry back to the mother as if seeking the safety of her proximity. Such attachment behaviors as crying, clinging, vocalizing, and looking greatly increase following the separation episodes, during which exploration is reduced and distress becomes likely. In the reunion episodes, such infants seek contact with and proximity to the mother or at least interaction with her. Once reunited with their mother, they quickly recover from the distress shown during separation and display no negative emotions, such as anger.

Resistant attachment. In this form of attachment the infants show signs of anxiety even while they are with their mother in the episode before the first separation. They become intensely distressed by the separation and are difficult to quiet on reunion. Although they will seek proximity to the mother when she returns, they resist her attempts to initiate contact and interaction with them. They will kick, hit, and squirm to be put down, or push away a toy that is offered to them. Because of these characteristics, this form of attachment has sometimes been referred to as "insecure-ambivalent" (e.g., Hetherington & Martin, 1986).

Avoidant attachment. Unlike the infants in the other two groups, those classified as showing avoidant attachment rarely cry during the separation episodes or on reunion. What particularly distinguishes them, however, is that they will actively avoid their mother when she reenters the room. They will ignore her and look away, actually turning their back to her when she seeks to establish contact or interaction with them. Occasionally these infants may make abortive approach responses, but throughout the remaining period they fail to resume active exploration. When reunited following the second separation episode, these infants display the same or even greater avoidance of their mother.

Stability Over Time

The pattern of attachment behaviors displayed by individual infants in the Strange Situation when they were 1 year old has been shown to remain stable for at least 4 years. Waters (1978) reevaluated a group of these children when they were about 2½ years old and reported that they still displayed the secure, resistant, or avoidant attachment pattern they had shown 18 months earlier.

Behavior related to that pattern was still evident when Arend, Gove, and Sroufe (1979) asked the teachers of these children to rate them when they were 5 years old. Those who had earlier been classified as securely attached were now described as spontaneous, enthusiastic, resourceful, curious, self-reliant, and able to maintain appropriate control over their impulses, wishes, and desires. Those, on the other hand, who had been assigned to the avoidant or resistant categories of attachment—collectively referred to as insecurely attached—had difficulty with self-control. The children from the avoidant group were described as maintaining too tight a control over their impulses so that they were rigid and lacked spontaneity, whereas those from the resistant group had too little self-control so that they tended to act impulsively and to be unable to delay gratification.

Note of Warning

At this point a note of warning or explanation seems in order. We just cited a study that had found that children, who as infants had been classified as avoidant, were described as overcontrolled, rigid, and nonspontaneous when they were 5 years old. That finding, based as it is on a correlational study, must not be interpreted as saying that avoidant attachment causes later rigidity. Nor should one conclude that every rigid and nonspontaneous 5-year-old had experienced avoidant attachment in infancy. Far too little is known about the causes of human characteristics to justify such generalizations. It should also be stressed that the research findings about 5-year-olds' behavior are based on data gathered on groups and that they do not necessarily apply to every child in that group. Moreover, an individual 1-year-old girl, who fails to run toward her mother who is coming home from a party or looks away and ignores her, does not necessarily reflect avoidant attachment, nor is she inevitably doomed to become a rigid, nonspontaneous 5-year-old.

We began this discussion of attachment because we had asked how this important phase in the development of human interaction relates to the development of self-recognition. We can now return to that subject.

Attachment and Self-Recognition

Assumption

One might assume that from the point of view of the development of the child's self-concept early emergence of self-recognition is a positive sign. Given what has been reported about the relationship between the quality of early mother-infant attachment and the child's competencies in his or her later years, it would seem that secure attachment is the most positive of the three forms of attachment that have been identified. This should lead one to assume that securely attached children would develop self-recognition earlier than children whose attachment is of the avoidant or resistant qualities.

Assumption Tested. The preceding assumption was tested in an investigation reported by Lewis, Brooks-Gunn, and Jaskir (1985). As part of a longitudinal study of children's social development that spanned 9 years, these investigators examined 37 infants when they were within a month of being 1 year, 18 months, and 2 years old. At the first stage of this study, the quality of the infants' attachment behaviors had been observed in the Strange Situation, which had been modified by eliminating the use of a stranger and having the mother depart and return only once. As in the attachment studies discussed earlier, the mother-infant attachment was classified as secure, avoidant, or resistant (which Lewis et al. call "ambivalent"). Secure attachment was manifested by 27 of the infants; the remaining 10 (7 avoidant and 3 ambivalent) were classified as showing insecure attachment.

When they were 18 months old, and again at 24 months, the behavior of each of these children was observed in front of a mirror to evaluate the development of their self-recognition. As Lewis et al. (1985) describe their procedure, the infant was placed in front of a mirror and observed for 20 to 30 sec. After this the mother wiped the child's nose, surreptitiously applying an odorless red dye that had been shown not to cause children to touch their nose or to pay undue attention to it. With the nose so marked, the child was again placed in front of the mirror and observed for another 20 to 30 sec.

As in other self-recognition studies in which the mirror procedure had been used, the investigators scored their observations for the presence or absence of mirror-directed and mark-directed behavior. Mirror-directed behavior generally develops before mark-directed behavior. As the child gets older mirror-directed behavior decreases, and mark-directed behavior increases.

Unexpected results. Figure 2-1 displays the results of the Lewis, Brooks-Gunn, and Jaskir (1986) study. It reveals that, counter to the assumption, the securely attached children did not develop self-recognition earlier than the children classified as insecurely attached. Instead, infants who had been classified as insecurely attached at age 1 developed the presumably more mature, mark-directed behavior earlier than the infants who had been classified as securely attached.

Lewis et al. (1985) report that the mirror-directed behavior, which precedes mark-directed behavior in development, was exhibited by 70% of the securely attached children at 18 months. As expected, that behavior decreased with maturation and only 22% of the securely attached were still showing it at 24 months. Only 40% of the insecurely attached infants were displaying mirror-directed behavior when they were 18 months old, and by 24 months only 20% of them were still engaging in that relatively immature behavior. The more mature, mark-directed behavior, on the other hand, was already present at 18 months for

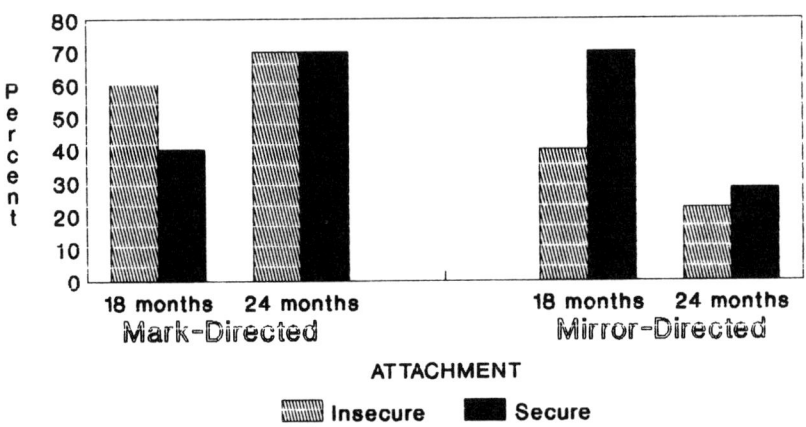

FIGURE 2-1 Self-recognition at 18 and 24 months as a function of attachment at 12 months.

Redrawn from Lewis, M., Brooks-Gunn, J., and Jaskir, J., 1985. Individual differences in visual self-recognition as a function of mother-infant attachment relationship. *Developmental Psychology*, 21, 1181-1187. Copyright 1985 by the American Psychological Association. Adapted by permission.

60% of the insecurely attached. At that age only 40% of the securely attached displayed that behavior. By 24 months 70% of both groups were displaying mark-directed behavior. As Lewis et al. (1985) sum up their findings, the insecurely attached group of children produced more appropriate self-recognition behaviors at an earlier age than the securely attached.

Attempts at an explanation. Given the repeatedly established relationship between secure attachment and competence in various aspects of personal and social behavior, the earlier development of self-recognition by insecurely attached compared with securely attached children is a surprising finding. How can it be explained?

The first point to be made in looking for an answer to this question is that the development of self-recognition for the securely attached infants in the Lewis et al. (1985) study followed the sequence of development that was expected on the basis of results from earlier studies (Lewis & Brooks-Gunn, 1979). It is not that the securely attached were delayed; it was the insecurely attached who were early.

Is early development of self-recognition a form of prematurity that, rather than being a welcome development, is in fact a sign that something may be wrong? Yes, say Lewis et al. (1985).

Implications of Early Self-Awareness

Self-recognition manifested by the mirror task, we must recall, is used to evaluate self-awareness. Self-recognition reflects self-awareness. Early self-recognition therefore reflects early self-awareness. In the study just discussed the insecurely attached children, 7 out of 10 of whom showed avoidant attachment, thus manifested early self-awareness. Why should these insecurely attached children develop self-awareness earlier than securely attached children?

Recall how infants who are classified as showing avoidant attachment behave in the Strange Situation. During their mother's absence they rarely cry either when she leaves or when she returns. On reunion with the mother these children actively avoid her, ignore her, look away, and turn around when she attempts to establish contact or to initiate interaction. It is difficult not to think of these children as saying, "Never mind, I don't need you. I can't rely on you. I can take care of myself."

Self-Recognition and Self-Concept

Self-reliance. Attachment, we said earlier, provides the infant with a secure, protecting base from which to explore the environment and to which to return when threat is encountered. When that base is not strong and reliable, as it appears to be in the case of insecurely attached children, the exploring infant would have to be more self-reliant and more alert to potential dangers. Indeed, specialized measures show insecurely attached infants to have a higher level of attentional ability than those classified as securely attached.

Early self-recognition, so Lewis (1986) concluded, may be a reflection of insecurely attached children's need to rely less on their mother and more on themselves, to be wary and vigilant, and to act on their own. That seems to make early self-recognition a desirable sign from the view point of the developing self-concept. Drawing on other studies conducted in his laboratory, however, Lewis (1986) reports that by the time they are 6 years old children who had been early self-recognizers tend to have a less positive image of themselves than those whose self-recognition developed later. That would suggest that the early emergence of self-recognition is not a positive event.

What self-recognition reveals. When, at 18 months of age, a girl looks in a mirror and touches a red spot that has been placed on her nose we can infer that she is aware that what she is looking at is an image of her own face and that something about that face is different from what she knows to be her face. She thus indicates that she knows who she is—that she is aware of herself. That demonstration of self-awareness, however, can tell us nothing about what that girl thinks about herself or of herself; it tells us nothing about what concept she has about herself, nothing about the content of her self-concept.

FROM SELF-AWARENESS TO SELF-CONCEPT
Beyond Infancy

During infancy and early childhood attempts to study the development of the self-concept are limited to observations of behavior, such as those that focus on infants' reactions to seeing their reflection in a mirror. As we have seen, such observations make it possible to draw inferences about the infant's self-awareness, but the nature and content of the self-concept remains hidden. Only with the advance of children's verbal skills does it become possible to explore their ideas and thus their concept about themselves.

Verbal Procedures

Asking questions and studying the answers thus obtained may seem simpler and more fruitful than surreptitiously placing a colored spot on an infant's nose, putting her in front of a mirror, and hoping that she will look at herself. Studying the answers to questions asked about a person's sense of self is no simple, straightforward procedure, however, because it requires that one make several assumptions.

Necessary assumptions. My self-concept consists of my thoughts about myself—about who, what, where, how, and maybe why I am. I have acquired this body of self-knowledge over time as a result of the experiences I have had and the observations I have made of myself in the context of my social and physical environment. Among the assumptions a research investigator makes in asking me to talk about my self-concept are that I had such experiences, that I observed them, that I was able to organize them in some fashion, and that I stored them in memory. In short, the investigator must assume that I have the cognitive abilities to think and reflect about myself as an object. In addition there is the assumption that I am willing and able to retrieve that self-knowledge from memory and that I am willing to reveal it without distortions, deletions, or fanciful additions. Should any of these necessary assumptions not be met, the true nature and content of my self-concept would remain inaccessible to an investigator who relies on my self-reports.

Who Are You?

Social exterior. Inquiries about children's self-concept reveal a developmental trend in that the focus of their answers gradually shifts from external characteristics to internal traits and qualities. In the preschool years (ages 3 to 5) children respond to questions about their self-concept by describing what Rosenberg (1983) calls their "social exterior." They will give their name, their gender, their age, and their address. Prodded to say more, most will add statements about their family; their pets and other prized possessions; physical attributes such as body build, hair, and eye color; what they are good at; and what they enjoy doing. Note that all but this last category are matters that others can observe or easily verify. What a child enjoys doing is private knowledge that others can only infer from observations or learn about from the child's statements.

Psychological interior. A statement about what one likes and enjoys is about an inner state and foreshadows descriptions of the "psychological interior" that become more and more prevalent as the individual moves from childhood to adolescence.

Earlier we said that the body of knowledge on which the self-concept is based was acquired over time through experiences the person has had in the context of his or her social and physical environment. It is easy to imagine how a 3-year-old learned her name, her address, and that she is a tall, thin girl with brown hair and brown eyes, who is good at throwing a ball, and has a baby brother named Daniel. In all likelihood somebody told her these facts. How did she come to know, however, that she likes ice cream? How, for that matter, did any of us learn to label our internal states, whether that be a stomach ache, anger, jealousy, or being partial to ice cream?

Learning to label internal states. One answer to this, based on the self-perception theory of Daryl Bem (1972), is that the labels for private states are learned in the same way as the labels for public conditions and concrete objects. Just as Sarah's mother or father taught her to say her name and to learn her address and telephone number, and told her that she is 3 years old and has brown hair, one of them probably saw her consume with gusto a dish of ice cream and said, "My, you sure like ice cream, don't you?" In such a manner, according to Bem's theorizing, did she learn to label the inner states of likes and dislikes, loves and hates, fears and hopes. A study by Wylie (1990) of the interactions of mothers and their 2½-year-old children tends to confirm this view.

Self-Concept and Language

A series of studies, reviewed by Rosenberg (1983), has demonstrated that younger children identify themselves in terms of publicly observable categories, whereas older children, and adolescents in particular, tend to describe themselves more and more in such private terms as attitudes, beliefs, values, wishes, traits, and feelings. This developmental trend from a focus on external characteristics to one on internal states parallels, is in fact dependent on an increasing capacity and disposition to think about one's own thoughts and feelings, to introspect. Adolescents, at least in Western culture, are well known for spending a great deal of time and energy exploring their own thoughts and feelings, and in speculating about the thoughts and feelings of those around them. Alongside this introspective emphasis there develops a tendency to view and describe oneself in relation to others, such as someone who is popular, makes friends readily, and is easy to get along with. Table 2-1 shows some examples of statements children at different ages produced when Montemayor and Eisen (1977) asked them to write 20 answers to the question "Who am I?"

The changes in the answers these children gave to this question reflect not only the larger and more sophisticated vocabulary they acquire as they grow older, but also their gradual acquisition of abstract concepts. Note that the 9-year-old boy's concept of himself is largely concerned with such external, objective characteristics as how old he is and where he lives. He displays only a limited ability to write about more internal, introspective aspects of himself when he tells us that he loves food, fresh air, and school. It is also worth noting that the children had been instructed to produce 20 statements and that this boy turned to these introspective statements only at the very end of his list.

Look now at the answers given by the 11½-year-old girl. After stating her name, which is a public label, she immediately employs an abstract concept (human being). Shortly thereafter she adds that she is a truthful person. That is an internal characteristic, a personality trait, and the fact that she is able to produce it so early in her listing reflects her developing ability to think about her inner life, to introspect.

TABLE 2-1 Answers Written by Children at Different Ages to the Question "Who am I?"

A Boy Aged 9
My name is Bruce C. I have brown eyes. I have brown hair. I have brown eyebrows. I'm nine years old. I LOVE! Sports. I have seven people in my family. I have great! eye site. I have lots! of friends. I live on 1923 Pinecrest Dr. I'm going on 10 in September. I'm a boy. I have a uncle that is almost 7 feet tall. My school is Pinecrest. My teacher is Mrs. V. I play Hockey! I'm almost the smartest boy in the class. I LOVE! food. I love freash (sic) air. I LOVE School.

A Girl Aged 11½
My name is A. I'm a human being. I'm a girl. I'm a truthful person. I'm not pretty. I do so-so in my studies. I'm a very good cellist. I'm a very good pianist. I'm a little bit tall for my age. I like several boys. I like several girls. I'm old-fashioned. I play tennis. I am a *very* good swimmer. I try to be helpful. I'm always ready to be friends with anybody. Mostly I'm good, but I lose my temper. I'm not well-liked by some girls and boys. I don't know if I'm liked by boys or not.

A Girl Aged 17
I am a human being. I am a girl. I am an individual. I don't know who I am. I am a Pisces. I am a moody person. I am an indecisive person. I am an ambitious person. I am a very curious person. I am not an individual. I am a loner. I am an American (God help me). I am a Democrat. I am a liberal person. I am a radical. I am a conservative. I am a pseudoliberal. I am an atheist. I am not a classifiable person (i.e., I don't want to be).

From Montemayor, R., and Eisen, M., 1977. The development of self-conceptions from childhood to adolescence. *Developmental Psychology, 13*, 314–319. Copyright 1977 by American Psychological Association. Reprinted by permission.

The 17-year-old adolescent's answers to the who am I question are almost entirely of an introspective nature. She describes herself as moody, indecisive, ambitious, curious, and liberal, using words and concepts that few 9-year-olds would have in their vocabulary. Note, incidentally, that this girl's answers manifest the *identity crisis* ("I don't know who I am") that Erik Erikson (1959) described as central to adolescence. The differences among these self-descriptions strongly suggest that the development of the self-concept depends on the development of language.

Like other self-report procedures, asking children to give 20 answers to the question "Who am I?" entails all of the assumptions previously outlined. There is no way of knowing whether the answers thus obtained represent a valid picture of these young people's self-concept. Fortunately, the study of the self-concept is not limited to asking people to talk or write about themselves. Psychologists also have other methods. Some of these we shall encounter in the following chapter.

3

Self-Concept: Content and Organization

INFORMATION PROCESSING
Self-Schema
A Conceptual Tool

Miller, Galanter, and Pribram (1960) are generally credited with providing psychologists with the conceptual tools with which to approach the study of such internal events as the formation and maintenance of the self-concept. Within that frame of reference, one's self-concept is an organized representation, a schema one holds of oneself in relation to one's environment: a self-schema. (Self-schema and self-concept are often used interchangeably.)

In the view of many personality psychologists the self-schema is the frame of reference by which people evaluate all perceptions that have to do with their social environment. Whether we see another person as young or old, rich or poor, tall or short, for example, is largely a function of where on these dimensions we see ourselves positioned. We shall want to look at some studies that have explored the self-schema, but to do so we first have to know something of the concepts and methods that are used by those who conduct these studies.

Memory
Stored Representations

The formulation advanced by Miller et al. (1960) served not only to legitimize the study of mental life, so long excluded from the psychological laboratory, but also pointed the way to how that study might proceed. If people build an organized representation of themselves and their world to form a self-schema they must be doing so on the basis of their experience. Moreover, that representation must be stored somehow if it is later to be used in evaluating social and other situations.

Stored representation is another word for memory, and memory has been an object of psychological research ever since the days of Hermann Ebbinghaus (1850-1909), one of the founders of psychology as a science. The tools for the study of memory have long been available, and these are the tools cognitive psychologists are bringing to bear on such questions as how people attach meaning to the stimuli they encounter in their world and within themselves. The influence of computer technology led to these stimuli being viewed as information and making sense of that information as a way of processing it. It is thus that the storage and retrieval functions of memory came to be referred to as information processing.

Methods for Studying Memory

Memory processes and research on memory are topics that fill many volumes. For our purposes a rudimentary introduction will have to suffice. We need thus not become involved with such intricacies as the distinction between sensory memory, short-term memory, and long-term memory. It is the long-term aspects of memory that play the principal role in the formation and maintenance of the self-schema.

Recall, Recognition, and Relearning

Recall. Of the several well-established methods for studying memory the most obvious is the method of recall. If one wants to know whether a man remembers what people in the United States celebrate on the Fourth of July all one has to do is ask him. If he replies, "Independence Day" one can conclude that he had been keeping this fact somewhere and was able to retrieve it. Moreover, one can infer that at some earlier time this man had been exposed to this information, and theorize that it had been stored, presumably in his brain, as something we call memory.

Recognition. Similar to the method of recall is the method of recognition. Here one would show the man a list of various holidays and ask him to pick the one that is celebrated on the Fourth of July. In effect, this is a multiple choice test that makes the man's task somewhat easier than the open-ended recall test that is more like an essay or fill-in examination.

Both these methods require a criterion against which to check the correctness, that is, the validity of the elicited answer. This limits the usefulness of these methods in the study of such self-related concepts as a person's self-schema where independent validity criteria do not exist.

In addition, there are problems involving the interpretation of the responses obtained with these methods. Let us return to the example of the man who was asked about the Fourth of July. Suppose he answers or, in the case of a recognition test, points to Memorial Day. Can we conclude from this that his memory is defective? It could be, but it could also be that he had once been given the wrong information or that, for reasons of his own, he wants the questioner to think that his memory is defective and gave the wrong answer intentionally.

Let us now assume that his answer was "I don't know." Again we cannot know whether he is telling the truth, but let us assume that he is. In that case we are left with two possible explanations. He may never have had a chance to acquire the knowledge called for by the question or, having once acquired it, has since forgotten. It is not easy to get into a person's head to find out what it contains, especially if he or she does not want others to know. This situation often tends to be the case with matters relating to oneself.

Because of problems such as those just enumerated psychologists who study memory rarely employ the methods of recall and recognition with information the subject already possesses. In laboratory studies of memory, volunteers (who, one hopes, do not intend to deceive the experimenter) are given entirely new information that they could not have previously encountered. This information has traditionally been a set of three-letter, consonant-vowel-consonant combinations, such as ZOK, WUK, LUN, or KOR, so-called nonsense syllables. The subject's task might be to memorize a list of such nonsense syllables or to learn them in pairs, trying to remember that ZOK goes with KOR and LIN with WUK, for example.

When subjects have mastered such a list, either perfectly or to some preestablished criterion of accuracy, the experimenter knows that they have learned the material, and can plan to test their ability to retrieve it by recall or recognition after a given period. When subjects now give a wrong answer or say "I don't know" the possibilities of their never having learned it or having learned it incorrectly need not be entertained.

Relearning. At this point a third method for testing retrieval from memory can be mentioned. It is the method of relearning. Assume that a year after first having learned a list of nonsense syllables a man is called back to the laboratory and asked to recall the list. Chances are that he will remember very few, if any, of the syllables, but when he is then given the task of learning the list again it is very likely that it will take him less time than he had needed for the original learning. Something has been saved, and this gives another indication of the workings of memory.

Measures of Memory

The methods used in testing a person's memory just outlined make it possible to talk about memory in quantitative terms, to measure memory. A list of nonsense syllables has a certain length so that one can talk about the capacity of someone's memory in terms of the number of syllables recalled after a stated period such as a week, a month, or a year. Moreover, one can compare how long it took the person to learn the list originally with how long it took her or him to relearn it.

Because of their objectivity and universality measures that employ units of time are particularly favored by investigators of memory. Take, for example, a person whose task it was to learn which nonsense syllable goes with ZOK, which with WUK, and so on. It is called *paired-associate learning*. One measure of this person's memory is the number of pairs correctly recalled, but another is the time it took her to respond with WUK when ZOK was presented. On the basis of the length of this *reaction time*, students of memory draw various inferences, depending on the theoretical viewpoint from which they approach their research. Investigators who approach memory research in the framework of information processing use reaction time to assess the accessibility of information that they suppose to have been stored and to speculate about where in memory this storage might have been located.

Library analogy. Analogies are rarely perfect, but at the risk of distorting how memory is deemed to operate imagine yourself at the circulation desk of a large library. To obtain a book at this library one has to fill out a call slip and hand it to one of the librarians who then goes to the stacks to retrieve that book for you. Only librarians are permitted in the stacks; you therefore do not know the location of the book for which you asked. You can, however, make a reasonable guess as to how far the book is from the circulation desk by timing how long it takes the librarian to return with it. You might even strengthen your confidence in this guess by repeating this observation on different days and with different librarians (but with the same book). Were you to patronize this library long enough and made enough of such observations with many different kinds of books, you might eventually be able to draw an imaginary map of the stacks, showing where various subject matters might be shelved. Students of information processing use observations similar to these in their attempts to find out about and to map human memory.

Memory and Self-Schema

Encoding, Storage, and Retrieval

Those who approach the study of memory from the standpoint of information processing differentiate among three basic stages: encoding, storage, and retrieval.

In encoding, the constellation of sensory stimuli that has been given some meaning by the perceptual process is put into a code suitable for storing in memory. That code may be a complex image, a combination of sounds, or even ideas involving characteristics and attributes of an event. Accordingly, one speaks of acoustic, visual, and semantic codes. For our purposes semantic coding is the most interesting because it is the type of coding that is relevant for a discussion of the self-concept or, to use the term investigators in this area prefer, the self-schema.

What is stored? By and large, people encode and remember general ideas or meanings, and relatively few specific details. Studies have shown that when people are asked to recall a list of words they had memorized a week or so before they often substitute synonyms for words that had actually been on the list. If the list had contained the word car, for example, they may recall automobile. Alternatively, they may incorrectly recall "kitchen" as having been on a list that contained only the words pot, spoon, pan, knife, oven, stove, and sink.

Common experiences can also attest to the fact that general ideas are more readily retrieved than specific details. Thus, instead of remembering the exact date of a relative's birthday we know that it is around Christmas. Alternatively, having heard only last week the exact salary of our congressional representative, we can only recall that it more than doubles our own.

These examples relate to another aspect of long-term memory. It is easier to learn (that is, to store for later retrieval) material that is related to information already in memory than it is to acquire entirely novel information that has nothing to do with anything ever before encountered.

Imagine, for example, that in this morning's newspaper you read of two people. One named Kennedy, the other Czartoryski. Unless you happen to be familiar with Polish surnames you are far more likely later to recall the first than the second of these names. To be familiar with Polish surnames is, of course, another way of saying that you already have that kind of information in your memory when you read about Mr. Czartoryski. In the language of those who study such matters, you find it easier to process that person's name if you already possess a schema for Polish surnames.

ORGANIZATION OF SELF-CONCEPT
Information Processing and The Self-Schema

The self-schema can be viewed as an organized cluster of all the information people possess about themselves: their characteristics, attributes, features, skills, social standing, occupation, family status, and gender—in short, all of their ideas about who and what they are.

This self-schema has been assembled over time and is the product of the person's experience in relation to his or her physical and social environment. As such, people's self-schema is an aspect of their long-term memory so that everything we said about long-term memory applies to the self-schema. It is, for example, easier for people to store and retrieve material that has personal relevance to them (as in the example about congressional salary). Similarly, people can more readily make sense of new information if they can relate it to something that has significance for them; if it fits into their self-schema.

A familiar experience can again serve to illustrate the point just made. We may be talking to someone in a large and noisy crowd, concentrating on what that person is saying, when suddenly we hear a voice from another part of the room mention our name, our occupation, or our hometown. Any of these references to an aspect of our self-schema stands out above the noise. We notice these single words, they demand our attention, although we can hear nothing else the person who uttered them is saying. The self-schema acts as a screen through which incoming information is sifted and encoded.

An appeal to a personal experience, however, no matter how common, cannot serve as evidence supporting the statement about the role of self-schema in the screening of information. For that one has to be able to cite controlled research.

Me or not me. Several studies cited by Markus and Smith (1981) have shown that people more quickly and more easily process information for which their self-schema contains relevant material. Thus, Sentis and Markus (1979) asked subjects to respond with "me" or "not me" to a series of adjectives that are used to describe people. They found that subjects who had identified themselves in an earlier survey as seeing themselves as independent responded more quickly to words related to independence (such as "assertive" or "individualistic") than to words that have to do with dependence (such as "conforming" or "obliging"). The exact reverse was true for subjects who had earlier described themselves as dependent.

There are, of course, people for whom the dimension of dependent-independent is relatively unimportant, in whose self-schema that dimension does not play a central role. As predicted, these so-called aschematics (Markus, 1977) did not differ in their reaction times to either kind of word.

The subjects in the Sentis and Markus (1979) study were later tested for the recognition of the adjectives that had been on the original list. This revealed that the schematics (those whose individual self-schema involved independence or dependence) recognized words relevant to this dimension more quickly and more accurately than did the aschematics for whom the dimension had no relevance. Data such as these demonstrate the importance of the self-schema to the way in which people process information.

Storage, Retrieval, and Self-Schema

In discussing memory storage we employed the image of a library and suggested that by observing how long it takes librarians to retrieve certain books one could eventually speculate about the layout of the stacks without ever having had access to them. Markus and Sentis (1982) attempted something like this with respect to the self-schema.

Serial search. The studies by Hazel Markus, just mentioned, had shown that schematics responded more quickly to words related to their self-schema than to those not so related. In addition, it emerged that schematic subjects pressed the "me" button more quickly and with more confidence than the "not me" button. This finding suggested to Markus and Sentis (1982) that the information in a self-schema must be organized in such a way that a search can stop and the "me" report made as soon as confirming evidence has been located but that, when confirming evidence is not found, all of the stored information must be searched before "not me" can be reported. If this formulation is correct it implies that when we seek to retrieve from memory information that has to do with the self we employ what Saul Sternberg (1969) referred to as a *serial search* in which the stored information is examined one item at a time.

Self-perception theory. Why should it take a person longer to arrive at the "not me" answer than at the "me" answer? Here the self-perception theory of Daryl Bem (1972) may provide an explanation. According to that theory, when people are asked whether a word like "assertive" is or is not descriptive of them, they search their memory not for that word but for an instance in the past when they behaved assertively. As soon as they find such an instance, they can say "yes," or press the "me" button in one of the Markus experiments. When an appropriate instance of assertive behavior is not found, however, the search continues (thus taking longer) until the person is sufficiently convinced that no such instance exists. At that point the "not me" response can be made.

Sources of Uncertainty

Individual differences. The results of experiments such as the one by Sentis and Markus (1979) are almost always reported in terms of group statistics. If one were to examine the scores of each individual participant in the study one would find that many had scores that were higher or lower than the reported averages. Such individual differences do not negate the results of a study; the experimental design and statistical procedures take these differences into account. When one is interested in the study of an individual's self-concept, however, the analysis of group statistics is not very helpful.

Take, for example, the point made earlier that the search for an instance of assertive behavior continues until the person is sufficiently convinced that no such instance exists. How soon a person is sufficiently convinced depends on a variety of factors. People differ in how meticulous, how persevering, how honest, and how cooperative they are. While participating in an experiment, some will take their task very seriously, whereas others may be bored, pressed for time, tired, or distracted. None of these individual and situational differences can be gleaned from the results of studies when only group statistics were gathered and reported.

Fallibility of judgments. In addition to the uncertainty contributed by individual differences there is another factor that beclouds the conclusions one can draw from studies in which people are asked to make judgments about themselves. It is the correctness of the research participants' responses. What the subjects in the "me," "not me" studies were essentially required to do was to judge whether an adjective like assertive was or was not descriptive of them. Human judgment, however, is remarkably fallible. In making judgments we often use misleading mental shortcuts or rules of thumb; Tversky and Kahneman (1974) call them *heuristics*.

Availability heuristic. One such rule of thumb is the availability heuristic, which leads people who are faced with a choice to select the alternative that is most readily available. Asked to judge whether assertiveness is or is not descriptive of me, for example, my response would depend on how readily I can recall an instance of assertive behavior. Asked to indicate "me" or "not me" to the word "assertive," I would be likely to pick "me" if only yesterday I politely objected when someone attempted to get in front of me at the supermarket check-out line. Conversely, the availability heuristic would lead me to choose "not me" if an instance of my asserting myself did not readily come to mind. It should be stressed that people are not aware they are using such a heuristic. They are not distorting their responses on purpose, although that also happens when people are asked questions about themselves, which further contributes to the difficulty in interpreting data based on self-reports.

Organization of Self-Schema

As pointed out earlier, Miller et al. (1960) had introduced the notion of an organized representation of the environment that they conceived as the mechanism that permits humans to make sense of their experiences and enables them to respond to these experiences in an adaptive fashion. Following that frame of reference we have seen that self-schema can be construed as the organized representation of those aspects of people's experiences that have to do with themselves and their interaction with the environment.

One question that students of self-schema have asked and investigated with the methods of information processing is how that particular representation of the environment might be organized. We shall take a look at the results of some of these investigations in a moment, but to do so a review of that research method and its conceptual basis is in order.

Semantic Categories

In an influential series of studies Eleanor Rosch and her colleagues (Rosch, 1975; Rosch & Mervis, 1975; Rosch, Mervis, Gray, Johnson, & Boyes-Braem, 1976) employed the model of semantic categories.

Categories. Nature does not come in categories; it is people who, looking at nature, assign what they see to such categories as animals, plants, or minerals. People speak of things that possess life and things that do not, when life begins and when it ends, and when they encounter ambiguity on such points they can get into heated arguments. By and large, however, people are in general agreement on how the phenomena of nature are to be conceptualized and categorized. As a result it is easy to get the impression that categories are provided by nature. We speak of natural categories, forgetting—as Gergen (1985) and others remind us—that categories are based on a social consensus, and that the world could be conceptualized or construed in any number of other ways.

Categorical hierarchies. Because the categories people employ in their communications with each other are expressed in words, one speaks of semantic categories. These, according to Rosch (1975), are concise mental representations of similar objects. Many of these categories contain different levels or hierarchies, some higher, some lower than others. It is customary to speak of superordinate levels, basic levels, and subordinate levels.

Take, for example, the category "eating utensils." It is superordinate to the basic level forks, to which the category dessert forks would be subordinate. If you were shown a picture of a dessert fork and asked to name it you would be most likely to say, "fork," not "eating utensil" or "dessert fork." This preference for the basic level of categorization was demonstrated in a study by Rosch et al. (1976).

There are, of course, all kinds of forks: pitch forks, fish forks, tuning forks, lobster forks, garden forks, and salad forks. We also speak of forks in the road, and use the metaphor forked tongues. Each of these is an instance of the category fork, and each instance is composed of attributes that determine its membership in the category. What are the attributes these instances have in common so that we call all of them forks?

Prototypes

This question brings us to the concept of prototype, for category membership is based on prototypicality. The prototype of a fork, the prototypical fork, is an object with four slender pointed parts (we call them prongs or tines) that stick out from a base, that is mounted on a handle roughly twice as long as the tines. Any given instance of the category "fork" shares some of these attributes. An object may have a longer handle and as few as two prongs and we still call it a fork, but there are no one-pronged forks, nor forks without handles.

There is a fairly wide range of instances that are entitled to membership in the category fork, but if you are a city dweller and asked to think of a fork, it will undoubtedly be the prototypical dinner fork that immediately comes to mind. "Immediately" is the key word because the first instance of the category we tend to think of when we hear the word fork is its prototype.

Prototypes and reaction time. This brings us back to our discussion of memory and the use of reaction time as a method for exploring where in memory a given item might be stored. The research of Rosch and other investigators has shown that the prototype of a category is produced more quickly (with a shorter reaction time) than any other instance of the category. If you live in a city, it will take you longer to think of pitch forks than of dinner forks. This is another way of saying that our memory storage is so organized that we can access and retrieve the prototypical exemplar more readily than less prototypical instances.

We know, of course, that what we store in memory is a function of our past experiences. As a result not everyone shares the same prototypes; hence, the earlier stipulation that you live in a city. A farmer might think of pitch fork more quickly than of dinner fork, and someone who lives in a city and habitually uses chopsticks may take a long time to respond with either word. This phenomenon has enabled investigators to explore the prototypes held by different individuals.

Study of Prototypes

The typical procedure for studying prototypes is to instruct people to answer "true" or "false" as quickly as possible to a series of statements, such as

A canary is a bird.
An ostrich is a bird.
A penguin is a bird.
A chicken is a bird.

Most English-speaking people would no doubt answer "true" to each of these statements, but their reaction time to ostrich, penguin, and chicken would probably be longer than to canary. Moreover, if these same people were asked to make a list of birds, canary would probably appear earlier on the list than ostrich, penguin, or chicken.

By using either of these approaches one can conclude that people consider a canary the most "birdish" of the birds on the list, that the canary is closer to the prototype of bird than any of the others. Moreover, by using a long list of birds and a large number of people of similar background, it is possible to determine that the prototypical bird is characterized by the ability to sing and to fly.

Self-Schema as Prototype

Not only is it possible to use the method pioneered by Rosch (1975) to investigate people's prototype for a semantic concept like bird, one can also employ it to explore an individual's prototype of a given concept including his or her self-schema.

The logic underlying the use of Rosch's method for studying the self-concept runs as follows (Ross, 1987). Just as people acquire concepts about forks, or birds, or trees from their exposure to various instances of these categories (either firsthand or by learning about them from others), so have they acquired a concept about themselves—their self-concept—by virtue of the fact that they have been constantly in their own company, and able to observe their own actions and the reactions of other people to them. These observations begin in the first year of life when the infant finds out whether people can be relied on and whether it is safe to explore one's environment. Since then, the individual will have continually observed his or her successes and failures, strengths and weaknesses, likes and dislikes. Storing all that in memory, the person forms a schema of himself or herself: a self-schema.

This schema or concept that a woman, for example, formed about herself can be viewed as a prototype, analogous to her prototypes of fork, or bird, or tree. If these prototypes can be explored with the reaction-time method, why not explore her prototype of herself in the same way?

Just as one can present people with a list of birds and ask them to say as quickly as possible whether each is or is not a bird, so one can present people with a list of adjectives and ask them to indicate as quickly as possible whether or not each is descriptive of them. Differences in reaction time should then help the investigator to determine which of the adjectives are a part of a given person's self-prototype. That, of course, was the principle Sentis and Markus (1979) had employed in the "me," "not me" studies mentioned earlier.

T. B. Rogers (1981) reported a series of studies in which he explored people's self-prototype using the Rosch method. He reports that his subjects responded more quickly to adjectives that described them than to those that did not. What is more, when these people were asked to recall which adjectives had been on the list presented to them earlier, they recalled the self-descriptive adjectives more quickly than the others. Rogers (1981) concluded from his studies that "the self is a prototype that contains a collection of features the person sees as describing him or her" (p. 196).

False-alarm effect. The recall task Rogers (1981) had used also threw light on the earlier question about what it is that we store in memory. Do we store specific items like individual words, or do we store superordinate concepts? Asked to recall the adjectives that had been presented to them, Rogers's subjects would often include not the word itself, but a synonym of the one that had been on the list. For example, if the original list had included "jealous," a man who had indicated it as descriptive of him might on the later recall task report that "envious" had been on the list even though it had not. Students of memory refer to this as a "false-alarm effect." It strongly suggests that what is stored in memory are not the specific words, but the concepts or categories to which these words belong.

TRAITS

Personal Characteristics

The adjectives investigators such as Rogers (1981) or Markus and Sentis (1982) used in studying people's self-concepts describe pervasive response tendencies, personal characteristics that are usually called traits. According to a count reported long ago (Allport & Odbert, 1936) there are close to 18,000 trait-related words in the English language. Only relatively few of these are required to describe ourselves and others because many of these words, such as cowardly and timid, denote roughly the same concept, whereas others, such as pusillanimous, have fallen into disuse. Moreover, whenever two words are mutually exclusive antonyms, such as honest and dishonest, only one of them is needed in a description of a given individual. In practice, about thirty words suffice to characterize a person in terms of his or her traits.

Traits and Factors

Direct Experience

For anyone not familiar with the concept of traits and with the organization of these traits into factors a personal experience can be a fruitful means of introducing these ideas that we shall have occasion to refer to repeatedly in the following chapters.

Instructions. Figure 3-1 contains an alphabetical list of 30 words that represent personality traits. The first word is adventurous. Opposite that word is a circle. Fill in that circle if adventurous describes you. If it does not describe you, if you consider yourself to be more cautious than adventurous, leave that circle empty and go to the next word on the list, proceeding in this manner to the end. For the moment ignore the letters (E, A, C, S, and I) on top of the columns of circles. We will take these up later.

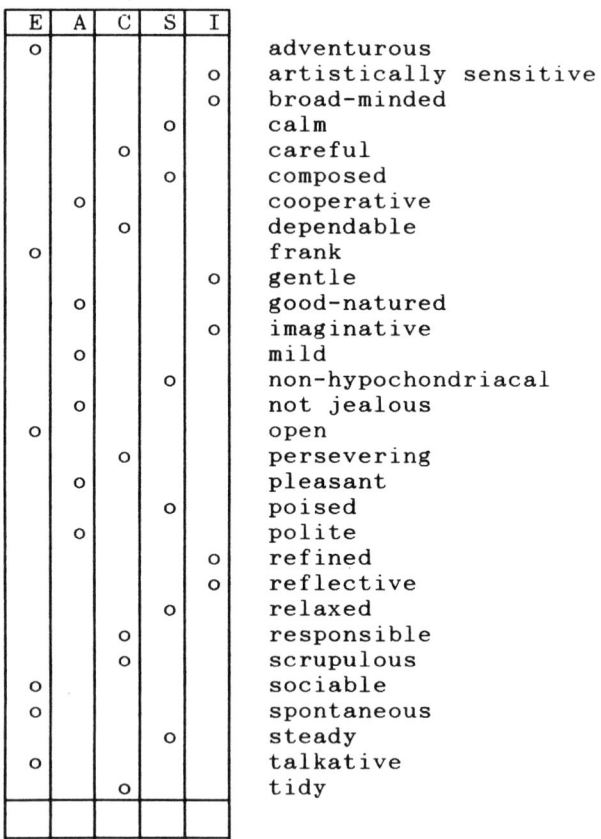

FIGURE 3-1 Checklist of traits.

Implications

As you worked your way down this list of traits you may have noticed that each term has an opposite that does not appear on the list; it is implied. If adventurous does not describe you, cautious probably would. With terms like adventurous you may have wished that the choice had not been between filling in the circle or leaving it empty. You may have wanted to qualify your response by writing "well, occasionally," or "more or less" because you see yourself as neither totally adventurous nor completely cautious.

Self-Concept: Content and Organization

Bipolar continuum. The reason for your discomfort with the forced choice between accepting or rejecting adventurous as describing you is that adventurous, like all other words on the list, represents an extreme on a line that runs from "cautious" to "adventurous." Few people are correctly described by one or the other of these extremes.

All trait labels are end points on a bipolar continuum, and most people fall at a point somewhere between the two poles. Those who design and use a checklist like the one shown in Figure 3-1 are aware of this and assume that an endorsement of a trait reflects on which side of the midpoint on that continuum the person's disposition tends to fall.

Thus, if you accepted adventurous as descriptive of you by filling in the circle on the top line you indicated that you see yourself as more adventurous than cautious; not that you are adventurous and daring in everything you do, and never cautious and circumspect about anything.

Clusters. There is another observation you may have made as you went down that list of traits. It is that several of them are related; they "go together" or form clusters. Look at "calm," for instance. If you filled in the circle next to that word, you probably also filled in the circles next to "composed," "poised," "relaxed," "steady," and maybe "nonhypochondriacal." Conversely, if you left blank the circle next to "calm," you probably did the same with the circles next to these other five words. You may discover similar relationships among other clusters of words and notice that the circles for such clustered words also are all in the same column. Now we are ready to consider the meaning of the letters E, A, C, S, and I that head the five columns.

Factors. When you and others who worked on the list of traits in Figure 3-1 consistently fill in the circles next to "composed," "poised," "relaxed," and "steady," it shows that these traits are related. The degree of such a relationship can be assessed by the statistical method of correlation and expressed by a number, the correlation coefficient.

When a large group of people has recorded their responses on a trait measure like our checklist one can use the method of correlation to discover for each trait with which other traits it is linked and to which it is weakly or not at all related. Once all these correlations have been calculated it is possible to examine them statistically for the existence of the kind of clusters we recognized in noticing that calm, composed, poised, and relaxed were related. Such clusters are called *factors*, and the statistical method used in identifying them is *factor analysis*.

The Big Five

Using a list of traits similar to the one shown in Figure 3-1, Norman (1963) asked 622 college students to rate each other. He then subjected the intercorrelations of their responses to a factor analysis from which five factors emerged. These he labeled extraversion, agreeableness, conscientiousness, emotional stability, and culture or intellect. These five factor labels, represented by the letters E, A, C, S, and I, head the columns in our checklist of traits (Figure 3-1).

Trait Labels

The names given the five factors are somewhat arbitrary because the statistical technique of factor analysis only identifies their existence; the investigator has to label them. Thus, extroversion has sometimes been called sociability, agreeableness conformity, conscientiousness will-to-achieve or orderliness, emotional stability adjustment, and culture intellect or openness. Whatever their name, however, the existence of these five factors, which Fiske had identified in 1949, have now been found in many different studies, by different investigators using different measures, and different groups of subjects of different ages and different backgrounds (Goldberg, 1990: Peabody & Goldberg, 1989). This led Digman (1989) to speak of these factors as the Big Five personality dimensions.

Traits and Self-Concept

Just as each of the traits in Figure 3-1 represented one end point of a bipolar continuum, so is each of the Big Five a pole at one end of a bipolar dimension. The exact terms are again open to debate, but the following pairs will serve to illustrate this point:

Extroversion-Introversion
Agreeableness-Disagreeableness
Conscientiousness-Carelessness
Emotional stability-Emotional Instability
Culture-Coarseness

You might now take another look at the circles you filled in when you worked with the checklist of traits. For each of the five columns count the circles that are filled in and write that number in the box at the bottom of the column. Now ask yourself whether you are more of an introvert than an extrovert, more agreeable than disagreeable, more conscientious than careless, more emotionally stable than unstable, and more tending toward culture than toward coarseness. You will probably find that the magnitude of the sums for each column roughly corresponds with your self-concept with respect to the Big Five personality dimensions.

For example, if the sum for column E is 6, you probably view yourself as an extrovert. If it is zero or 1, you may be considering yourself an introvert. If it is 3, you probably feel that neither extrovert nor introvert is descriptive of you—that you fall somewhere in the middle, in a range sometimes referred to as ambivert. The same principle holds for the other columns. The larger the sum, the more likely you are to consider the column heading to represent you and vice versa.

Knowledge of Oneself

This exercise should have demonstrated several points. One is that traits are not some esoteric quality that only psychologists can detect, but that most people are able to describe their own personality characteristics. Whether these descriptions agree with those other people might provide is a question we shall leave for later. Funder (1991), for one, asserts that the person is in a relatively poor position to observe his or her own traits and that peer report is the single best method for assessing traits. That, however, does not negate the importance of the individual's self-perceived personality characteristics, which are revealed in conscientious responses to self-report measures.

Another point that our exercise demonstrates is that a person's self-perception confirms what the statistical technique of factor analysis has revealed: Traits can be organized in five dimensions. Moreover, these five dimensions are not only a means for classifying people; they also reflect something about the content and organization of their self-concept.

PUBLIC SELF AND PRIVATE SELF

Public Traits and Private Traits

Working with the 30 traits listed in Figure 3-1 will have revealed that some of them have to do with how people relate to the world around them, whereas others deal with matters that only concern the individuals themselves. Dependable, polite, and talkative, for example, are adjectives that have relevance only in terms of how the individual interacts with others. To a hermit they would be irrelevant. Artistically sensitive, imaginative, and reflective, on the other hand, are characteristics that people may have quite apart from how they relate to others. These traits would be as relevant to a hermit as to anyone else. One could thus say that some traits are public traits, whereas others are private.

Differential Observability of Traits

Note that public traits, such as dependable or talkative, directly manifest themselves in behavior affecting those who come into contact with the person. Others are thus able to judge the presence or absence of these traits, and to record their judgments on instruments such as rating scales. Private traits, such as reflective or artistically sensitive, conversely are known only to the individual who possesses them. Others have no direct access to these traits and are therefore not in a good position to judge their presence or absence. Investigations of private traits are thus largely restricted to self-report instruments or to inferences drawn from observed actions that are thought to be manifestations of such traits.

Self-Image

We have seen that traits and their labels can be used to describe and define the image one has of oneself; one's self-image. Inasmuch as there are public and private traits, the self-image can be viewed as composed of public and private aspects. Thus, one can speak of a public self and a private self.

People can shift their attention between their public self and their private self so that at different times they are more aware of one than of the other aspect of themselves (Scheier & Carver, 1983). The two aspects of the self-image are, in part, a function of how one sees one's own traits, but other people's judgment of these traits and how they act and react to one also contribute to the formation of that image. In fact, Cooley (1902) proposed long ago that a major, if not the only, source of the image we have of ourselves is our observation of how other people react to us.

Changes in Self-image

Others, as we said, judge a person's public traits on the basis of the behavior they are able to observe and that may directly affect them. They see a woman act in what they consider to be a polite manner and consequently judge her to be polite. That judgment may be erroneous, however, because a person can behave politely without necessarily possessing the trait of politeness. One may thus be aware that others attribute a trait that one does not possess. This may lead to a change in one's self-image.

A man, for example, might be widely thought of as sociable, although he sees himself as shy. His acquaintances, having judged him to be sociable, will then base their behavior toward him on that judgment. This man's public self thus differs from his private self, and his public image differs from his private image. Other people's expectations and actions, however, can exert a powerful influence on one's behavior. The man in our example, knowing that others expect sociability of him, may act sociably; the others, confirmed in their judgment, may then communicate to him that they see him as a sociable person. This feedback may eventually convince this man that he is indeed a sociable person and result in his bringing his private self in line with that public self.

We shall have more to say about the public-private distinction as we familiarize ourselves with the concept of self-consciousness in chapter 5. First, however, we turn to a more detailed examination of stability and change in the way people perceive themselves. We do so in the context of presenting an influential theoretical model of the self-concept.

4

A Model of the Self-Concept

MODELS IN THEORY BUILDING

In the development of a theory the construction of a model can be a useful step in that it depicts the postulated relationships among different aspects of the phenomenon whose operation the theory seeks to explain.

In the previous chapter we employed the analogy of a library in discussing how measures of reaction time are used in drawing inferences about the organization of memory. We suggested that a regular user of a library might eventually be able to imagine a map that shows the presumed layout of the stacks. That map might simply show where books on various subject matters are stored, or it could go into greater detail, representing how these books are categorized, and whether they are arranged alphabetically, by year of publication, or by some other method. Such a map would be a model of the stacks that helps our imaginary library patron to develop a theory about how the library is organized and functions.

Models can take the form of verbal descriptions, mathematical formulas, or graphic displays such as block diagrams or flow charts. Like the theories they serve, models are judged by their ability to organize available data and to generate testable hypotheses. To serve these functions a model need not be correct if by correct we mean that the proposed units and their relationships actually exist. The model should be open to modifications and revisions on the basis of new observations for it is first and foremost a scientific tool and not a definitive statement.

MODELS IN PERSONALITY THEORY

Some theorists who study the self-concept have proposed models that show how the various aspects of the perceptions people have of themselves might be interrelated. One possible model is to view the self-concept as a unitary entity composed of various features. Rosenberg (1983), for example, speaks of the self-concept as a body of self-knowledge that encompasses such features as self-esteem and self-consciousness. Another conceptualization in the form of a model was offered by Shavelson, Hubner, and Stanton (1976). It proposes that the self-concept is organized in a multidimensional and hierarchical fashion. Because it lends itself to a discussion of several important issues, we shall examine this model in some detail.

MULTIDIMENSIONAL MODEL
Levels of Self-Concept

Shavelson's multidimensional model, applied to a hypothetical 16-year-old high-school student, is shown in Figure 4-1. Examining this representation we find a general self-concept at the top of the hierarchy. At the next level the general self-concept is shown to have two components: one has to do with academic matters; the other with the nonacademic, social, emotional, and physical aspects of this young person's self-concept. Subareas of these self-concept components are found on the next lower level. They are the areas of endeavors and relationships that constitute the academic and nonacademic areas of this student's experience.

Below that level and not further identified in the model are even more specific aspects that enter into this adolescent's self-concept. Under science, for example, one might find biology and chemistry; under physical ability, swimming and softball playing. At the very lowest level of the hierarchy would be this person's experiences in and reactions to specific situations. Here one might find the student's taking various quizzes and exams in biology class, and playing softball on different days or against different teams.

Individual Differences

The conceptualization depicted in Figure 4-1 makes it clear that the components of Shavelson's model will differ for different individuals. The self-concept is, after all, a very personal matter. Thus, the picture just described would not fit a student who plays soccer, not softball, or who is taking physics, not chemistry. Moreover, the academic-nonacademic bifurcation of the self-concept that makes up the second level of the hierarchy for this hypothetical high school student would not

A Model of the Self-Concept

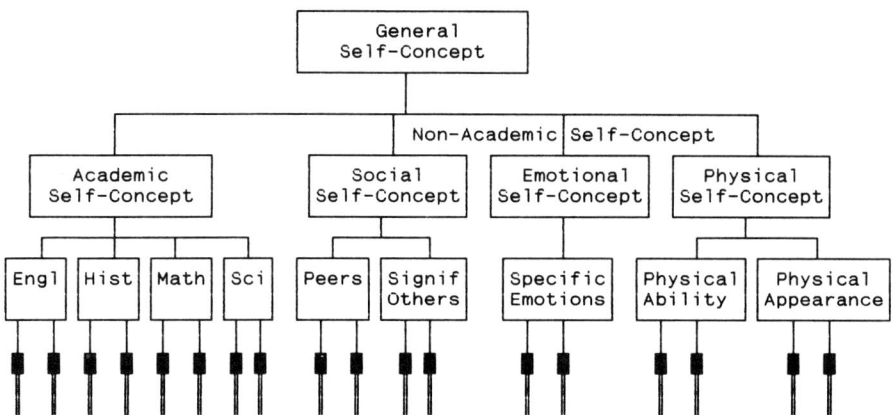

FIGURE 4-1 Hierarchical multidimensional model of self-concept applied to hypothetical high-school student.

Adapted from Shavelson, R. J., Hubner, J. J., and Stanton, G. C., 1976. Self-concept: Validation of construct interpretation. *Review of Educational Research, 46,* 407–441. Copyright 1976 by American Educational Research Association. Adapted by permission of the publisher.

be relevant for a working adult whose occupation and family life might be the most prominent components of the self-concept.

Self-Evaluation

Another important feature of the self-concept as conceptualized in the multidimensional model is that it is entails evaluation. Take the aspect of the academic self-concept that has to do with the student's experience in chemistry. The student will evaluate that experience and come to such conclusions as, "I like it," or "I find it interesting." After a few quizzes and exams she might add, "I'm good at it," or "I'm better at Chem than most other kids." Self-evaluative statements like these then enter into a self-concept such as, "I'm the kind of person who likes chemistry and is good at it." If this leads to the self-statement, "I'm pleased with myself for being such a good student" we have arrived at that aspect of the self-concept that is generally referred to as self-esteem.

Stability of Self-Concept

When the self-concept is conceptualized in the fashion Shavelson et al. (1976) suggest, it is possible to view the general self-concept at the top of the hierarchy as relatively stable. The subsidiary self-concepts, however, may be modified by the specific situations and experiences on which they are more and more dependent the lower on the hierarchy they are located. As we shall see in the following example, such modifications might be quite temporary because subsidiary self-concepts are under the influence of self-concepts at higher levels on the hierarchy. For a change at the top of the hierarchy to occur the individual may have to encounter many situation-specific experiences that are inconsistent with the general self-concept.

Let us suppose that the hypothetical student whose self-concept is depicted in Figure 4-1 maintains, as part of her general self-concept, the view that she is successful. That aspect of her self-concept would not be challenged by her receiving a failing grade on a chemistry examination or placing last in a swimming meet. In all likelihood her positive self-concepts around science and physical ability would also not be challenged by such isolated experiences, which she would probably rationalize as being due to an unfair examination or a cold on the day of the meet. Only after repeated failures would one expect this student's self-concepts to become modified, and then only those around chemistry and swimming; if she continued to be successful in soccer and biology, there would still be no reason for her self-concepts around science and physical ability to undergo a change.

Carrying this example to the next higher level on the hierarchy, a change in this girl's academic self-concept would require prior changes in most of the subareas of English, history, math, and science that would have come about by repeated failures in the specific subject matters subsidiary to these. But even if her positive academic self-concept were to change to that of being a poor student, her general self-concept of being successful need not be modified as long as she continued to excel in the areas that feed into her non-academic self-concept.

Differential weights. There is yet another feature of the multidimensional model that contributes to whether and under what circumstances a person's self-concept undergoes change. It is that the various dimensions of the self-concept may be differentially weighted. For one person the academic dimension may be extremely important; for another it may count for very little. For some physical appearance is central to the general self-concept, for others it is hardly taken into consideration. It stands to reason that a limited number of disconfirming experiences relevant to a heavily weighted dimension is more likely to occasion a change in self-concept than would the same number of such experiences in a dimension that the individual views as of little importance.

Research Based on the Multidimensional Model

It follows from the multidimensional model that questions about a person's self-concept can be framed in general or specific terms. That is, one might ask our hypothetical high school student about her general self-concept ("How do you feel about yourself?") or about her physical self-concept ("How do you feel about yourself as an athlete?"). To each of these and other possible questions the student might give different answers. She might, for example, feel "great" about herself overall but "not so hot" about herself as an athlete.

Academic Self-Concept

With these considerations in mind, and in line with the model of Shavelson et al. (1976), Marsh and Parker (1984) investigated the determinants of students' academic self-concept. The results were published under the intriguing subtitle, "Is it better to be a relatively large fish in a small pond even if you don't learn to swim as well?"

Size of Pond

Marsh and Parker (1984) started from the premise that school children form their self-concept with respect to academic abilities by comparing their own perceived abilities with the abilities of other students in their school or class. Assume that two students, Arthur and Bernard, have the same level of academic ability, but that Arthur's classmates are higher in average ability than Bernard's classmates. In that case Arthur would be likely to have a lower academic self-concept than Bernard because Arthur's basis for comparison, his frame of reference, is more demanding. Using the fishpond metaphor, Arthur sees himself as a small fish because he is in a large pond, whereas Bernard, in his small pond, sees himself as a large fish.

Marsh and Parker (1984) found support for this intuitively reasonable hypothesis in a study they conducted on some 300 students in the sixth grade of five different schools in Sidney, Australia. These children's academic self-concept was indeed influenced by the level of academic ability of their classmates. If confirmed by other research, this finding would have important implications for policy decisions regarding the placement of underachieving students into classes or schools where the achievement level is average or above.

Attempted Replication

For this and other reasons, having to do with the way Marsh and Parker (1984) had defined and measured the schools' level of academic achievement, Bachman and O'Malley (1986) sought to replicate the Australian findings. They approached this task by analyzing data from almost 1,500 10th-grade public school students in the United States. These data had been gathered in the context of an extensive longitudinal study, labeled Youth in Transition, that had been conducted some years earlier by Bachman, O'Malley, and Johnston (1978).

Multiple bases of comparison. Bachman and O'Malley (1986) reasoned that by the time they are in high school, students compare their academic ability not only with that of their classmates but also with that of their siblings and friends who attend other schools, and with that of their parents and other adults. All of these comparisons would contribute to the formation of the students' academic self-concept. In addition, however, young people receive feedback about their abilities from other sources, such as their parents, coaches, employers, and standardized tests.

These considerations led Bachman and O'Malley (1986) to predict that "To the extent that any of these factors influence self-concepts, groups of students who are above average in actual ability will also tend to be above average in self-concepts of scholastic ability, in which case there will be a positive correlation between school mean ability and students' self-concepts of ability" (p. 36).

Results. In the Bachman et al. (1978) inquiry, school mean ability had been measured with three well-known aptitude tests. Academic self-concept had been assessed with a rating scale on which the students compared their overall school ability, their reading ability, and their intelligence with those of other students their age. When Bachman and O'Malley (1986) analyzed these data, leaving individual ability uncontrolled, they found low positive but statistically significant correlations, thus confirming their prediction and seeming to contradict the findings of Marsh and Parker (1984).

We say "seeming to contradict" because a closer look at these two studies reveals that they really are not comparable. It is instructive to take that closer look not only because it helps to understand how two studies of the same question can arrive at different results but also because it highlights a difficulty we shall repeatedly encounter in the chapters to follow: the difficulty—peculiar to the behavioral sciences—of repeating an earlier study and reproducing its results.

Differences Between Two Studies

Both Bachman and O'Malley (1986) and Marsh and Parker (1984) had asked whether students' academic self-concept is a function of the academic level of the school they are attending. Beyond that, however, the two studies differed in their approach.

One of the differences is that in the Australian study a school's academic level had been inferred from the socioeconomic status of the area served by that school, whereas in Youth in Transition that index was based on the mean of three tests of academic ability administered to a small sample of students attending that school.

Another difference lies in the measures employed to assess the key variable, academic self-concept. Marsh and Parker (1984) had used the sum of three rating scales: one for reading; one for mathematics; and one for "all school subjects" on which the students had indicated their ability, their enjoyment, and their interest. These academic scales had been embedded in the 62-item Self-Description Questionnaire (SDQ) (Marsh, Relich, & Smith, 1983) that also covered sports, physical appearance, peer relations, and relationship to parents. Bachman and O'Malley (1986), on the other hand, measured the self-concept of academic ability by means of the following three questions:

1. How do you rate yourself in school ability compared with those in your grade in school?
2. How intelligent do you think you are compared with other boys your age?
3. How good a reader do you think you are, compared with other boys your age?

The 6-point scale provided for making these ratings ranged from "far above average" to "far below average" (Bachman, 1970).

Other differences between the two investigations that make comparison difficult were that Marsh and Parker (1984) studied 305 6th-grade children attending five coeducational elementary schools in a city near Sidney, Australia, whereas the subjects in the Bachman and O'Malley (1986) study were 1,487 male students attending the 10th grade of 79 predominantly white public high schools in various parts of the United States. There were, moreover, differences in the statistical methods used to analyze the results of the two studies.

Given these many differences the fact that the two studies led to different conclusions is hardly surprising. As Marsh and Parker (1984) pointed out, "results [of studies] depend on the unit of analyses, the sampling procedure, the type of analysis used, and the component of self-concept that is examined" (p. 227). Why, one might ask, did Bachman and O'Malley (1986) not follow more closely the procedure of the earlier study? There are several answers to this question, but the most obvious one is that they limited themselves to data gathered years earlier and for a different purpose. That limitation, however, did not prevent them from conducting analyses that contribute new insights into the fishpond question.

Size of Pond Is Unimportant

Influence of school. To enable them to compare their results with those of the Australian study Bachman and O'Malley (1986) had not controlled for students' individual ability. Having made that comparison they proceeded to test what they considered an important prediction. It is that there will be an inverse relationship between school mean ability and individual self-concept when one takes individual ability into account. This prediction is based on the assumption that relative to the influences on the students' academic self-concept of factors outside of school, within-school comparisons play a minor part in forming these concepts.

Their data analysis confirmed this prediction. There was a low but statistically significant, *negative* correlation between students' self-concept and their school's ability level. This indicates that the academic level of the school a student attends has relatively little impact on his or her self-concept of academic ability. In the fishpond metaphor, the size of the pond has little to do with how the fish feel about themselves. If not the school environment, what does predict how students feel about themselves?

Personal Ability and Achievement

In addition to the data evaluation just described, Marsh and Parker submitted the longitudinal data from the Youth in Transition study to a computer-assisted analysis known by the acronym LISREL (Jöreskog & Sörbom, 1979, 1984), which stands for *l*inear *s*tructural *rel*ations. It is a statistical model that estimates the causal relationships among measures of constructs by comparing their intercorrelations. This approach, sometimes called causal modeling, was employed by Bachman and O'Malley (1986) to ascertain the relative contributions to the students' academic self-concept that had been made by academic performance, academic ability, the academic level of the school, and the family's socioeconomic status.

This analysis again revealed the minimal effect the academic level of the school had on the students' academic self-concept. The strongest effect on academic self-concept was exerted by the student's own academic ability and academic performance (a total effect of .74), whereas the academic level of the school (the fishpond variable) had only a negligible effect (−.09).

Educational Attainment and Self-Esteem

The data Bachman and O'Malley (1986) had available also permitted them to examine the relationship among academic self-concept, educational attainment, and global self-esteem. Educational attainment, ranging from high-school dropout to some graduate study beyond the bachelor's degree, was known because the boys on whom the data were based had been followed from 10th grade until they were 23 years old (Bachman et al., 1978). These longitudinal data also included a 10-item measure of global self-esteem that had been administered at the end of the 11th grade.

Self-esteem. The causal modeling approach mentioned earlier revealed that global self-esteem is strongly influenced by academic self-concept, which, as we learned earlier, is affected by academic ability and performance. The socioeconomic status of the family and the academic level of the school have no influence on global self-esteem, nor does self-esteem have any direct connection to academic ability and performance. These make their impact only indirectly through their effect on the academic self-concept.

Educational attainment. Regarding the question of which variables contribute to how far a young man pursues his education (educational attainment), we learn from the causal model of Bachman and O'Malley (1986) that, listed in order of effect size, the major impacts are brought by academic performance, the family's socioeconomic status, and academic ability. Minimal contributions to educational attainment are made by the global self-esteem and academic self-concept the students had recorded in high school.

That people with good grades, high test scores, and educated parents with high-status jobs who live in comfortable homes that contain many books—all of which enter into the assessment of socioeconomic status—are more likely to go to college than to drop out of high school should come as no surprise. That these relationships emerge from a statistical model, however, serves to enhance the confidence with which one can view the following statement with which Bachman and O'Malley (1986) end their report:

> Our findings indicate that the dimension that really matters for self-concept of ability is not school climate but actual ability. What is more important is that the dimension that really matters for long-range educational attainment is also actual ability, not self-concept. So if we want students to do better academically, little is likely to be gained by placing them in schools with more limited classmates. A more promising approach would be to help them maximize the use of their aptitudes and thus actually raise their abilities. For what it is worth, that would also raise their self-concepts. (pp. 45–46)

Relationship of Constructs: A Reminder

When we spoke earlier of studies that assessed the relationship of academic ability to academic self-concept, for example, we omitted an important qualifying phrase for the sake of smoother exposition. Every reference to such constructs should have been preceded by the words "measures of": for example, measures of academic ability on measures of academic self-concept.

Constructs, we must remind ourselves, can neither be directly observed nor directly measured, hence, they cannot be directly compared, or have their relationship or influence directly assessed. In every instance what we are assessing or comparing are measures or tests that *presumably* reflect the construct in which we are interested.

In the Bachman and O'Malley (1986) study, for example, academic self-concept was represented by the ratings with which students had responded to the three questions we cited. Academic performance was expressed by the grades students received in their courses, academic ability was represented by scores on achievement tests, and the academic level of a school was defined as the mean of the test scores of the students in that school. Finally, statements about socioeconomic status, another construct or latent variable, were based on a combination of the father's occupation, the parents' level of education, a checklist of possessions, the number of books, and the ratio of rooms per person in the home.

In each of these instances one could ask such questions as, "Do scores on achievement tests *really* reflect academic ability?" or "Do the number of books in the home *really* say something about the family's socioeconomic status?" That is, questions about the relevance of the measure to the construct. Those who raise such questions, however, would have to be prepared to say how they would measure these constructs, for ultimately constructs are defined operationally—by the measures we use to assess them. As we have seen, different investigators use different measures—hence, different definitions of the same construct.

Limits of Correlational Studies

We have examined two studies that investigated whether students' academic self-concepts depend on whether the schools they attend have a high or low level of academic achievement. In conducting these studies the investigators had used the correlational method. Essentially, they measured students' academic self-concepts and examined the relationship of these to measures of the achievement levels of the schools they were attending. For various reasons the contradictory results of these two studies were difficult to reconcile; however, even if they had been entirely consistent with one another, correlational data often provide ambiguous answers to such causal questions as whether the demands of a school environment influence the self-concepts of the students who are exposed to it. Only a well-controlled experiment in which the same individuals' experience changes in the demands their environment makes on them can provide a clear-cut answer to the question whether the nature of the environment affects people's perception of themselves. A study that approximates such an experiment was conducted by Marsh, Richards, and Barnes (1986). We turn to it next.

STABILITY AND CHANGE IN SELF-CONCEPT
Effects of Intervention

Limits of Experimentation

In the strictest sense, an experiment requires the random assignment of a representative sample of individuals to at least two groups. One of these, the experimental group, will then be exposed to the intervention the experimenter has planned, whereas the other, the control group, is not exposed to it but to an experience that is similar to that of the experimental group in all aspects except for that aspect whose effect the experimenter is seeking to test.

By this rigorous criterion few, if any, studies of the impact of meaningful real-life experiences on human behavior can qualify as experiments. In fact, one can argue that the more relevant a study is to the effect of real-life experiences, the less rigorous it is in its method and design (Ross, 1981). It is well-nigh impossible to collect a representative sample of the entire human population or of those living on the North American continent. Because of this it is usually not possible to say whether the results of a given experiment apply to people other than those who participated in the study or the group from whom they were drawn. Similarly, it is hardly ever feasible or even permissible to assign people at random to experimental and control groups for the purpose of testing the effect of meaningful and realistic events that the experimenter is in a position to manipulate. The best that experimenters interested in the effects of such events are usually able to do is to study the impact of naturally occurring events or of those to which people are voluntarily exposing themselves. The latter was the road taken for an intervention study that Marsh et al., published in 1986.

Outward Bound

Demanding Experience

Originated in Britain during World War II, Outward Bound schools now operate in more than 15 countries. Their programs are designed to help participants recognize and understand their own weaknesses, strengths, and resources so that they can develop the means to master difficult and unfamiliar situations. Much emphasis is placed on rigorous outdoor activities such as rock climbing, cross-country runs, canoeing on swiftly flowing rivers, and survival exercises. In addition to physical fitness, initiative, and perseverance, the programs seek to develop and strengthen self-confidence, self-reliance, and self-awareness, as well as cooperation with, awareness of, and responsibility for others. A course usually lasts 26 days, and is both physically and psychologically a very demanding experience. One might expect that such an experience would have an impact on the participants' self-concept and that is what Marsh et al. (1986) decided to examine.

Two Compromises

In line with our earlier discussion of the limitations on the requirements of the experimental method, it is obvious that no investigator could sample the general population and randomly assign half of this sample to participation in Outward Bound and the other half to a control group. Participants in such programs are inevitably either self-selected volunteers or recruits in one of the armed services who, in peacetime, are also self-selected. Given this constraint, whatever the results of a study based on this self-selected sample might turn out to be they may apply only to people who voluntarily expose themselves to such rigorous experiences and not to those who would avoid them at all costs.

Another compromise with the requirements of the experimental method that a study on the effects of a program like Outward Bound must make has to do with the use of a control group. Even if it were possible to permit only half of the people who apply to an Outward Bound school to participate in the program, whereas the other half is kept out to serve as a control group, there would be the question of how to make sure that whatever effect is found is indeed due to the rigors of Outward Bound and not to such extraneous variables as the participants' expectations, the excitement at having being accepted, the high-protein food consumed, or the friendships formed among the participants.

The usual method for controlling for variables such as these is to us a placebo control group. This group is led to believe that they are receiving the same treatment as the experimental group; however, in reality, they are undergoing an experience that is identical in all respects except that it lacks the aspect of the intervention that the investigator suspects of being the "active ingredient." It is of course not possible to devise a 26-day program that would lead its participants to believe that they are taking part in Outward Bound when what they are actually experiencing is only a placebo. For that reason Marsh et al. (1986) opted for a research design in which each participant served as his or her own control.

Interesting Dilemma

Marsh et al. (1986) point to what they call an interesting dilemma that investigators of the self-concept must face. It is that the notion of a self-concept would not be very useful if it were not a relatively stable aspect of an individual's enduring personality. At the same time many intervention studies focus on changes in self-concept. Marsh et al. (1986) wonder how the self-concept can be perfectly stable when it is also responsive to dramatic life events or systematic interventions. Their Outward Bound study, which was conducted in the framework of the multidimensional model, offers an answer to this seeming dilemma for it showed that some of the component facets of the self-concept can change, whereas others are left essentially unaffected.

Effects of Outward Bound

Participants

The participants in the study Marsh et al. (1986) conducted were 361 people between the ages of 16 and 31 who completed the Outward Bound program in 10

A Model of the Self-Concept

different 26-day courses held over a period of 7 months at one of two different locations in Australia. Of the 27 groups of participants, 15 were all male, 3 all female, and the rest had participants of both sexes, with from 50% to 69% of the group being male.

Measures

To assess the effect of participation in an Outward Bound program on a person's self-concept Marsh et al. (1986) used a self-report instrument, the SDQ, which had previously been shown to meet high psychometric standards. In line with Shavelson's model, the SDQ is composed of 13 scales, each of which consists of 10 or 12 statements that the respondent rates on an 8-point scale from "definitely false" to "definitely true." Marsh et al. (1986) describe these scales as follows:

1. Math: I have good mathematical skills/reasoning ability.
2. Verbal: I have good verbal skills/reasoning ability.
3. General academic: I am a good student in most school subjects.
4. Problem solving: I am good at problem solving/creative thinking.
5. Physical ability: I am good at sports and physical activities.
6. Appearance: I am physically attractive/good looking.
7. Relations with same sex: I have good interactions/relationships with members of the same sex.
8. Relations with the opposite sex: I have good interactions/relationships with members of the opposite sex.
9. Relations with parents: I have good interactions/relationships with my parents.
10. Religion/spirituality: I am a religious/spiritual person.
11. Honesty: I am an honest, reliable, trustworthy person.
12. Emotional stability: I am an emotionally stable person.
13. General self: I have self-respect, self-confidence, self-acceptance, positive self-feelings and a good self-concept.

Discriminative validity. Note that built into the SDQ is a check on its discriminative validity in that it contains some items that the experiences in the program might change and other items that they should leave unaffected. An instrument that has discriminative validity should reflect this difference in its results.

Recall that the focus of Outward Bound programs is on strenuous physical group effort in rugged outdoor settings, and that they seek to enhance self-reliance, perseverance, initiative, cooperation, and responsibility for self and others. Mathematical and academic skills would not be likely to change as a result of this experience, nor would one expect it to have an effect on a person's religious beliefs or spiritual attitudes. Any changes in one's relationships with members of the opposite sex would obviously depend on whether one is experiencing the program's rigors in a mixed group or in one composed only of members of one's own sex. As we shall see, the data analysis confirmed all of these expectations, thus attesting to the discriminative validity of this measuring instrument.

The SDQ was administered to all Outward Bound participants on three occasions: approximately 1 month before the start of the course when the applicants were in their own home, at camp on the first day of the course, and on the last day of the course before leaving camp.

Results

Home to camp. The first comparison of interest is the one between the first and second administration of the 13 self-concept scales. Here, Marsh et al. (1986) found a small increase (improvement) in the scores on the Emotional Stability scale and mostly small decreases on the scales assessing the participants' perception of their verbal and academic skills, problem-solving abilities, and physical appearance. A large decrease was found for physical ability. On the whole the self-concept scores remained relatively stable, and the changes can probably be attributed to the different settings in which the two administrations had occurred.

For the first administration, the participants had received the questionnaire in the mail and filled them out in their own homes together with other application material. The second administration of the scale occurred when the participants had just arrived at camp and were, understandably, apprehensive of what lay ahead and afraid of being found wanting. This seems most clearly reflected in the large decrease in the scores on the physical ability scale.

Beginning to end. For an evaluation of the effect of Outward Bound on various aspects of the participants' self-concept a comparison of their questionnaire responses from the first and last day at camp is of greatest interest. Here Marsh et al. (1986) report statistically significant increases in mean scores on all 13 scales. The size of these increases varied, however, the smallest (less than half that for the mean of the other scales) being found for the scales where little or no impact had been expected: mathematics, academics, and religion. The scale on relations with the opposite sex was also among these less affected scales, but, as expected, this was found only in the groups that had both male and female participants.

Twenty-seven replications. A particularly important feature of this study was that the Outward Bound procedure was experienced by 27 different groups, in two locations, during varying times spread across 7 months. In a sense, this represents 27 replications of the study. The fact that the results were consistent across these groups strongly supports the conclusion that the participants' self-concepts had remained relatively stable from the first to the second administration of the SDQ were then selectively modified in particular dimensions by the experience in the Outward Bound program.

Two Questions

Two questions remain. One is whether the changes in the scores from the second to the third administration of the SDQ validly indicated a change in the participants' self-concepts or whether they merely reflected the elation these people probably felt when they had come to the conclusion of their demanding 26-day group experience.

The second question follows from the first. If the changes in SDQ scores did indeed reflect changes in self-concept, were these merely temporary or could they still be detected after the participants had returned to the routine of their daily lives?

Marsh et al. (1986) argue against the interpretation that their data might be due to what they call "post-group euphoria." They point out that it is unlikely for the effect of such euphoria to have been as selective with respect to the 13 SDQ scales as their data demonstrated. Elated participants might be expected to feel as great about their mathematical skills as about their honesty. The data, however, showed that after completing Outward Bound the participants viewed their mathematical ability to have changed relatively little, whereas they perceived themselves as far more honest, reliable, and trustworthy.

Similarly, postgroup euphoria might have led participants indiscriminately to report feeling great about their relationships with members of the opposite sex regardless of whether or not they had been in a mixed-gender group. Again the data show specificity in the way the scores changed. Significant improvement in their perception of their relations to the opposite sex were reported only by those participants who had been assigned to mixed-gender groups.

Follow-Up

The systematic and logical pattern of the results thus argues for accepting the changes in SDQ scores as reflecting real changes in self-concepts. Another, and stronger, argument comes from the answer to the second question. Evidence for the changes recorded on the last day of the Outward Bound experience could still be found 18 months later when Marsh and his colleagues conducted a follow-up in which they again administered the SDQ. In a footnote to their 1986 article they report finding no statistically significant changes since the previous administration of this test in the scores on 8 of the 13 scales, modestly lower scores on 3 (scales 9, 11, and 12), and modestly higher scores on 2 (scales 5 and 8).

Conclusions

Returning then to the question whether the self-concept, conceived as multi-dimensional, remains stable over time or is capable of change, the answer appears to be both. That, of course, is what the multidimensional model would predict.

Given a stable environment, the self-concept remains fairly stable, but specific dimensions of the self-concept can be changed by environmental influences that are relevant to that dimension. The question of its malleability is so central to the notion of a self-concept that we shall encounter it several more times in later chapters.

Before leaving this discussion it bears noting that the Outward Bound study, in addition to contributing an answer to the question about the malleability of the self-concept, also represents a long overdue step in the direction of establishing the construct validity of the SDQ and, by extension, of similar self-report measures of self-concept. That alone would make it a milestone in the study of personality.

5

Self-Awareness and Self-Consciousness

DEFINITIONS

We previously pointed out that both self-concept and self-schema denote self-perception so that they can be used interchangeably. As we continue our discussion of self-related processes we will encounter other terms that are either synonymous or have very similar meaning. This can be confusing, particularly because different writers sometimes use the same term to denote different concepts, whereas others use different terms to denote the same concept. It therefore becomes necessary to define some of these terms and to establish some consistency in their usage.

Self-Awareness

Self-awareness simply means being aware of oneself. Self-awareness is a situational variable because both its focus and its magnitude vary as a function of the situation in which the person happens to be at the moment. A young woman, for example, might show more self-awareness—be more aware of such aspects of herself as her looks, her dress, or her actions—when she is about to meet a blind date than when she is at home with her parents. In personality theory one differentiates between traits and states. Traits are more or less permanent characteristics of a person—they have been referred to as pervasive response dispositions (Ross, 1987)—whereas states are more transitory reactions to given situations. Because self-awareness is a situational variable it is more like a state such as fear than a trait such as sociability.

Self-Consciousness

The dictionary tells us that "self-conscious" has two meanings. In one sense it means ill at ease; uncomfortably aware of being observed or discussed. That is how that term is typically used in everyday language. The second meaning has to do with being conscious of oneself as an individual and aware that what one does and how one feels are part of or originate in oneself. We shall be using self-conscious in that second sense.

Unlike self-awareness, which is a situational variable and thus similar to a state, self-consciousness is a dispositional variable, similar to a trait. A trait, as we said, is a pervasive personal characteristic. When such a characteristic is measured, as we did with the trait scale in chapter 3, some people obtain high and others low scores, reflecting the degree to which the characteristic is descriptive of the individual. Thus, just as people can manifest much or little of a trait, they can manifest much or little self-consciousness. They can thus have high or low scores on a scale that measures that characteristic.

Given this distinction between self-awareness and self-consciousness, it bears pointing out that the two can interact. Thus the presence of a mirror (which focuses attention on oneself) has been shown to make a person with high self-consciousness more readily self-aware than a person with low self-consciousness (Carver & Scheier, 1978).

Self-Assessment and Self-Evaluation

Self-assessment and self-evaluation are closely related concepts. Both have to do with taking stock of oneself. Self-assessment entails a person's view of his or her own capacities and abilities, whereas self-evaluation has to do with judging the quality of these capacities and abilities. People generally engage in self-assessment before they undertake a task, as by asking themselves, "Will I be able to do this?"; self-evaluation occurs after a task has been completed by asking, "How well did I do?" (Strube & Roemmele, 1985). Self-assessment and self-evaluation feed into a person's *self-esteem* which, as we saw earlier, is expressed in the answer to "How do you feel about yourself?"

Self-Monitoring

To monitor means to observe and regulate. Snyder (1974, 1987), who originated the concept, conceived self-monitoring as the operation of comparing, checking, and adjusting of one's own behavior against an external or internal standard. The external standard or norm usually involves the expectations or reactions of other people, whereas the internal standard is one's own concerns and values (Baldwin & Holmes, 1987). A great deal of research has been devoted to self-monitoring, and we shall review much of it in chapter 10.

Self-Attention and Self-Focus

We shall be using self-attention and self-focus interchangeably. Both connote that the person's attention is directed to or centered on himself or herself. This attention can be on any aspect of oneself; on one's actions, thoughts, appearance, or achievements. It therefore follows that one must focus one's attention on oneself before one can be self-aware or self-conscious, and before one can engage in self-assessment, self-evaluation, or self-monitoring. All of these previously defined concepts thus presuppose and imply self-attention or self-focus.

SELF-REPORTS

Validity

Like the self-concept we discussed in the previous chapter, all of the constructs we just defined are private events that cannot be directly observed and must be inferred from the person's statements or actions. The usual way these self-related constructs are studied is by requesting people to respond to checklists, questionnaires, scales, or inventories that ask them questions about themselves. When such a self-report instrument is used the question inevitably arises whether the responses people give to it truly reflect those private aspects of them that the instrument is intended to measure—in other words, whether the instrument is valid.

It is a regrettable reality that the measures used in studies on self-related constructs have rarely undergone a rigorous test of validity. An exception of this is the demonstration of discriminative validity of the SDQ developed by Marsh et al. (1986), which we presented in the previous chapter.

Reliability

To ask about the reliability of a measuring instrument is to ask whether it is consistent from one time to the next in the information it is expected to provide. This poses a problem for investigators of self-related constructs because to demonstrate test reliability they must be able to assume that the characteristic being measured remains stable from one administration of the test to the next. Yet, as we saw in the case of the self-concept, some self-related aspects are stable, whereas others are subject to change.

Suppose an investigator has developed a test of the situational variable, self-awareness, and finds that this test leads to different answers when it is administered to the same person on different days. Does that mean that the test lacks reliability or that the person's self-awareness fluctuates?

Yet another source of difficulty stems from the fact that people vary in the degree to which they attend to their own feelings, reactions, traits, and similar characteristics (e.g. Turner, 1980). That being the case, it would stand to reason that these variations will affect the reliability of the responses people give on self-report inventories. Those with a high degree of self-attention should be able to be consistent in their reporting, whereas those with low self-attention might give different reports from one time to the next. In that case the test might be reliable, but the people who respond to it are not consistent in the way they respond to it.

All of these potential sources of uncertainty will have to be kept in mind as we review studies that relied heavily on measures of self-report.

SELF-CONSCIOUSNESS
Dilemma and Solution

Self-consciousness, like other theoretical constructs, was initially postulated to explain observed behavior. The construct therefore has merit only if it can be shown that it varies with that behavior in a predictable manner. A test of this would consist of an experiment in which self-consciousness, as the independent variable, is systematically varied while one observes the effect this manipulation has on behavior, the dependent variable.

That procedure poses the question of how to vary self-consciousness. Self-consciousness, as we pointed out, is a traitlike, pervasive response disposition so that a research participant would arrive at the investigator's laboratory with that characteristic well established. It is therefore extremely difficult, if not impossible, to manipulate a subject's self-consciousness in the course of a laboratory session. How then is one to study self-consciousness with the experimental method?

To answer this question we must recall that self-consciousness is conceptualized as a dispositional variable, whereas self-awareness is viewed as a situational variable. As we stated earlier, the two constructs are related in such a fashion that self-awareness is more readily heightened in people who have a high rather than a low level of self-consciousness.

A reference to the relationship between hostility and anger may clarify this matter. Hostility, like self-consciousness, is a dispositional (trait) variable; anger, like self-awareness, is a situational variable. It is well established (e.g., Berkowitz, 1989) that people who score high on measures of hostility are more readily made angry by laboratory manipulations and more likely to behave aggressively than are those with low hostility scores. Similarly, then, those high in self-consciousness should be more readily made self-aware than those low in self-consciousness.

Following this reasoning, an experimental study of self-consciousness can be based on a manipulation of self-awareness, and that, as many studies have shown (Carver & Scheier, 1981), can be accomplished by exposing research subjects to the presence of mirrors, television cameras, or live observers.

References to high and low levels of self-consciousness imply that self-consciousness can be measured. How is that done?

Measure of Self-Consciousness
Self-Consciousness Scale

In 1975 Fenigstein, Scheier, and Buss published an instrument they had developed, the Self-Consciousness Scale (SCS). This scale consists of 23 items similar to those shown in Table 5-1. People who respond to this scale are asked to indicate for each item the degree to which it is characteristic of them. For this purpose they are provided with a 4-point scale that ranges from 0, "extremely uncharacteristic," to 4, "extremely characteristic." Statistical analyses have established that this scale is composed of three subscales that are labeled *private self-consciousness, public self-consciousness,* and *social anxiety*. For the purposes of the present discussion only the first two of these subscales need concern us here.

Self-Consciousness and Self-Reports

In our discussion of reliability we mentioned that some people are more reliable in reporting about themselves than others. Does the level or type of self-consciousness play a role in this? Nasby (1989) reported two studies that bear on this question.

The instruments Nasby (1989) used were two versions of Jackson's (1984) Personality Research Form (PRF), which is a self-report personality inventory, and the SCS of Fenigstein et al. (1975). In the first of his studies Nasby administered to a group of college students the private self-consciousness subscale of the SCS and one form of the PRF. Approximately 2 months later these students completed a second form of the PRF. The results revealed that the PRF

TABLE 5-1 Typical Items on the Self-Consciousness Scale

Items reflecting private self-consciousness
  I am always trying to figure myself out.
  I am often the subject of my own fantasies.
  I am alert to changes in my mood.
  I am constantly examining my motives.

Items reflecting public self-consciousness
  I am concerned about the way I present myself.
  I usually worry about making a good impression.
  I am concerned about what other people think of me.
  I am usually aware of my appearance.

Adapted from Fenigstein, A., Scheier, M. F., and Buss, A. H. 1975. Public and private self-consciousness: Assessment and theory. *Journal of Consulting and Clinical Psychology, 43,* 522–527. Copyright 1975 by American Psychological Association.

scores from first to second administration were far more consistent for individuals high in private self-consciousness than for those low in private self-consciousness. This led Nasby (1989) to conclude "that individuals high in private self-consciousness report more reliably about the self across time than do individuals low in private self-consciousness" (p. 952).

There is the possibility that individuals who are low in private self-consciousness are able to report more reliably about themselves under conditions that raise their self-awareness. To test this hypothesis Nasby (1989) conducted a second study in which he employed the experimental method.

Using a new group of subjects he again had them complete one of the forms of the PRF, but this time half the participants did so while sitting in front of a nonreflective surface, whereas the other half faced a large mirror that reflected an image of the face, neck, and shoulders. The presence of the mirror was meant to increase subjects' self-awareness. The pronoun test (Davis & Brock, 1975), designed to assess self-awareness, revealed that it did indeed accomplish this goal. Before the session ended, all subjects filled out the SCS to assess their level of private self-consciousness.

About 8 weeks later the subjects again completed the SCS, the pronoun test, and an alternative form of the PRF. The analysis of these results revealed that even under conditions of raised self-awareness the self-reports of subjects with low private self-consciousness failed to be consistent from one time to the next. Conversely, the self-reports of subjects high in private self-consciousness, maintained their test-retest reliability regardless of the induced level of self-awareness. The dispositional, traitlike characteristic of private self-consciousness thus appears to provide the individual reliable access to his or her self-concept or self-schema, which is independent of the level of the statelike self-awareness.

The studies reported by Nasby (1989) demonstrated that people differ in their knowledge of themselves, depending on their scores on the SCS. Are there other differences that correlate with these scores?

Correlates of Self-Consciousness

Four Distinct Groups

As the statements in Table 5-1 suggest, private self-consciousness involves the tendency to be aware of the inner aspects of oneself, whereas public self-consciousness has to do with an awareness of oneself as a social object that is perceived by others.

Research cited by Scheier and Carver (1983) has shown that private and public self-consciousness are relatively independent characteristics and not simply two ends of the same continuum. This means that a person who possesses a great deal of one of these tendencies need not necessarily have little or none of the other. People's scores on the SCS can therefore identify four distinct groups.

One group is highly cognizant of the private self but inattentive to the public self; we shall refer to them as high private-low public. The attention of another group, the high public-low private, is focused on aspects of the public self, whereas the aspects of the private self are ignored. A third group is composed of people who are highly aware of both aspects of self: the high private-high public. Lastly, there is a fourth group. It is made up of those for whom neither aspect of self is particularly salient. We shall refer to them as the low private-low public.

These four groups differ not only in the way they respond to the items on the Self-Consciousness Scale, but also on a variety of other dimensions.

Self-Description

High-private individuals. When we discussed self as a prototype in Chapter 3 we pointed out that when people are asked whether a trait label, such as "jealous," is or is not descriptive of them, they will respond with "yes" more quickly than with "no." Investigators have concluded from this that self-descriptive adjectives are more readily accessed from memory storage than adjectives that are not self-descriptive.

Suppose one were to administer the SCS to a group of people and then compare the high private with the low private on a test of self-descriptive adjectives; what would one expect to find? If people high on private self-consciousness are those who are highly aware of the inner aspects of themselves and think a lot about what they are like, one would expect that they can more readily access words that describe these aspects than can people who are low on private self-consciousness. That, indeed, is what several research studies have found (e.g., Turner, 1980).

High-private individuals not only have more ready access to self-descriptive terms than low private persons, the high private also remember these terms better and with greater accuracy, consider them more important, and can list more of them (Scheier & Carver, 1983).

High-public individuals. If such self-descriptive trait labels as calm, imaginative, and refined are judged as important by high-private individuals, what sort of words are deemed important by high-public people? According to research cited by Scheier and Carver (1983), the answer is words that describe physical features, such as height, hair color, and shape of chin, that are readily apparent to another person. Furthermore, just as the high private are faster than the low private at judging whether a personality trait describes them, so are high public faster than low public at deciding whether or not they possess a particular physical characteristic. Furthermore, compared with low-public people, high-public individuals are better at predicting what impression they will make on others, seem better at adjusting their behavior to suit the social context, do more to prepare their appearance before a social encounter, and are more sensitive to the reactions of others.

Self-Consciousness and Interpersonal Behavior

Conformity

The relationship between public and private self-consciousness also affects how a person behaves with respect to others. There is a well-known social psychology demonstration of conformity showing that most people will modify their opinion when they are under group pressure (Asch, 1956).

Minority of one. Typically, the subject in such a study is placed in a small group with people who are all confederates of the experimenter. The group is instructed to judge the relative lengths of a series of vertical lines, to count the number of metronome clicks heard over earphones, or to make some other, relatively easy decision. The subject usually gives a correct response, whereas the confederates, whom the subject believes also to be subjects, give different, incorrect responses. Because of this ostensible disagreement, the experimenter asks the group to repeat the process, and after a few such repetitions the real subject is the only one who maintains his or her original (and correct) response. Left thus exposed as a minority of one, most people capitulate and conform to the majority view.

One might predict that people high on private and low on public self-consciousness, people who are highly aware of and value their own feelings and opinions while caring little about how they appear to others, would be among those who refuse to give in to the majority view or who, at the very least, hold out the longest. Conversely, people who are high on public and low on private self-consciousness should quickly join the majority view because they are concerned about the impression they make on others and pay little attention to their own feelings and thoughts.

How many clicks? This prediction was tested in a conformity study conducted by Froming and Carver (1981). Here the task was to count sets of metronome clicks that the subject heard over earphones. Over these earphones the subject could also hear the voices of three other people, allegedly other subjects, who were working on the same task in another part of the building. In fact, both the clicks and the voices had been prerecorded and the subject heard only an audio-tape. With this arrangement, whenever the subject reported how many clicks she or he had heard, the other "subjects" could be heard to report their count. They were always unanimous; sometimes they were correct, at other times they were off by either one or two clicks. The real subjects were thus in the position, typical of conformity experiments, of having their judgments run counter to those of the majority. Would they stick by their guns or change their judgment to bring it in line with that of the other people? And if they did conform, how was that related to the level and direction of their self-consciousness?

Resistance or capitulation?   As the experimenters had predicted, the higher people's level of private self-consciousness, the less likely they were to bring their judgment in line with that of the majority. This was true regardless of whether the subject's count and the count reported by the three other voices were one or two clicks apart. For public self-consciousness, conversely, the results were the exact opposite. Here, the higher people's level of public self-consciousness, the more likely they were to make their judgment conform to that of the majority, *but only when the discrepancy between their count and that of the others was two clicks*. How is that to be explained?

Scheier and Carver (1983) suggest that people who focus their attention on the public self are sensitive to how they appear to others. When they are then placed in a situation in which they must reveal their judgment to others (or are led to believe that they are doing so), they seek not to offend them by disagreeing with their judgments. They may be able to tolerate a mild disagreement, such as differing by one click, but when the disagreement is more substantial (two clicks) they are concerned that others will view them as being relatively extreme in their deviation from group norms. Hence, they conform.

Before leaving this point, it is important to recall that both the SCS and the theoretical framework to which it is related consider every person to have both private and public aspects of self-consciousness, and that these can vary independently. Thus, as we pointed out, there can be four distinct types of self-consciousness: high public-low private, low public-high private, high public-high private, and low public-low private. Froming and Carver (1981) did not apply this fourfold classification in their data analysis. We can thus only speculate on the possibility that in the click-counting study those classified as high-public stuck by their judgment when they differed from others by only one click because this satisfied the needs of some muted private aspect of their self-consciousness. Their stronger public self-consciousness, however, became the determining factor when the discrepancy rose to two clicks. Here it is also worth considering the fact that the subjects had to announce their judgments in public (or thought they were doing so) and that this is a situation that tends to focus one's awareness on the public aspects of oneself.

Attitudes and Opinions

We have seen that the direction in which their attention is focused, whether on the private or the public aspects of themselves, plays a role in whether individuals change their judgment to make it conform with that expressed by others. A similar relationship has been found in the case of attitudes and opinions.

Coercive communications. In conformity studies, subjects are simply exposed to the divergent judgments of others. No one attempts to convince them to change their opinion. There are many occasions in our lives, however, in which others explicitly set out to do so. The entire advertising industry is devoted to that goal, and before an election we are bombarded by messages intended to influence the opinions we hold about parties and their candidates. Psychologists refer to such messages as coercive communications.

Opinion Change

Resistance and reactance. Research has shown that resistance to coercive communications is related to the level and type of self-consciousness. In a study reported by Carver and Scheier (1981), subjects had been given the biographical sketch of a purported candidate for an appointive public office in which the candidate was presented in a favorable light. The subjects were asked to rate this person's suitability for that office. Afterward the subjects were exposed to a coercive communication, designed to change their opinion about the candidate. They were then asked to rate the candidate's suitability for the office once again. As the experimenters had predicted, subjects who were high in private self-consciousness resisted the coercive communication, in fact they displayed what social psychologists call reactance. Not only did they fail to comply with the content of the coercive message; they actually shifted their attitudes in the direction *opposite* to the one the message had advocated.

The results of this study were less clear-cut with respect to public self-consciousness. Here, only those low in public self-confidence reversed their opinion; those high in public self-confidence were unresponsive. Scheier and Carver (1983) speculate that this was due to the subjects' having been led to expect a series of messages about the candidate so that the highs did not want to commit themselves after hearing just one message, fearing that further messages would lead them to a different conclusion so that they would appear to others as vacillating and inconsistent.

Attitude Change

Scheier (1980) reports yet another study that demonstrated how people's behavior differs depending on whether they focus their attention on the private or the public aspects of themselves. The participants in this study had been given an anonymous questionnaire on attitudes toward punishment. They filled it out in a group setting, and one can assume that under these impersonal circumstances the subjects had no need to moderate or otherwise disguise their true attitudes.

Consistency or disparity? Later each participant attended a session in a smaller group. There the subjects were told that they would be asked to express their attitude toward punishment, first in the form of an essay and then in a free discussion with another subject. Given these instructions, the investigator expected that the participants would be more circumspect in expressing their attitudes, knowing that whatever they privately committed to writing would later have to jibe with what they would say in the public discussion. Actually, no discussion took place because the purpose of the study had been to find out how the attitudes the subjects had expressed in the anonymous questionnaire corresponded with those they revealed in the essay they had written in anticipation of a later discussion.

The comparison between the questionnaire responses and the content of the essays revealed that whether or not a subject changed his or her expressed attitude as well as the direction of any change depended on the nature and level of the subject's self-consciousness. The consistency between the questionnaire and the essay responses was highest among people with low public and high private self-consciousness. Among subjects with low public self-consciousness, those who had initially indicated a favorable attitude toward punishment wrote essays reflecting more favorable attitudes than did those who had initially been against punishment. Subjects who were high in public self-consciousness, on the other hand, expressed in their essays moderate attitudes that were unrelated to the attitudes they had indicated in the questionnaires.

The fact that only the high-private-low public group remained consistent in their attitudes, regardless of where and how they were expressed, showed once again that these individuals not only have an accurate awareness of their beliefs but that they are also little concerned about the impression they make on other people.

Given these results it is worth asking how the high-private-high public group reacts to other people. Here a study reported by Shaffer and Tomarelli (1989) offers some intriguing results and provocative interpretations.

Self-Disclosure

Revelation of intimate material. Self-disclosure is the tendency to reveal relatively intimate material about oneself in the course of a conversation. The exchange of self-disclosures between two newly acquainted people contributes to the sense of trust that forms the basis for the formation of eventual friendship (Derlega & Chaikin, 1976).

A Study of Self-Disclosure

Shaffer and Tomarelli (1989) sought to relate mutual self-disclosure between people who had just met to public and private self-consciousness.

Procedures. College students who had earlier filled out the SCS were asked to participate in an investigation that was ostensibly designed to study how people get acquainted. When a participant appeared for the study, he or she was introduced to a purported fellow subject of the same gender who was actually a confederate of the experimenters. The two were instructed to take turns volunteering personal information to get acquainted with one another. They were cautioned that some of the exchange might cover very private matters.

After the experimenter had left the room the confederate began discussing the first of four preselected topics. These were "things in my past or present of which I am ashamed," "aspects of my personality that I dislike," "my disappointments with the opposite sex," and "aspects of my body with which I am dissatisfied."

In one condition to which the experimental subjects were exposed the confederate made highly intimate self-disclosures connected with the topic under discussion. In another condition the discussion dealt with the same topics, but the confederate's self-disclosures were of a low level of intimacy. In both conditions the actual participant was expected to follow the confederate with his or her discussion of the same topic, and then the confederate would move to the next topic; the two would take turns until all topics had been covered.

Predictions. The investigators had predicted that, compared with people who scored low on public self-consciousness, those scoring high would be more inclined to imitate the confederate's intimacy level of self-disclosure. Thus, they would respond to highly intimate material with equally intimate material of their own while remaining at a less intimate, more general level when the confederate's self-disclosure had been circumspect. Conversely, so Shaffer and Tomarelli (1989) predicted, subjects who scored high in private self-consciousness would be less inclined to reciprocate the intimacy level of the confederate's self-disclosures than would people who scored low. The results of this study turned out to be more complicated than the investigator's straightforward prediction.

Results. Recall that the SCS identifies four combinations of the private and public aspects of self-consciousness. We spoke of four groups that, for ease of further discussion, we will here identify by capital letters, as follows:

A. High public–high private
B. High public–low private
C. Low public–high private
D. Low public–low private

In the first of two studies Shaffer and Tomarelli (1989) conducted they found that participants who had scored high on one aspect of self-consciousness and low on the other (Groups B and C) reciprocated the confederate's level of intimacy, whereas those who had scored either high or low on both aspects (Groups A and D) were not influenced by the intimacy of the confederate's disclosures. How, the investigators asked, might one account for this pattern?

To find an answer to this question Shaffer and Tomarelli (1989) conducted a second study. In this they used essentially the same procedure as in the first study, but in addition they measured response time and collected difficulty ratings. The self-disclosure results essentially replicated those from the first study. Again, participants in Groups B and C self-disclosed on the level of intimacy that had been used by the confederate. When the confederate revealed highly intimate material, the participant did likewise; when the confederate revealed no intimate material, the participant remained equally noncommittal. The self-disclosures of subjects in groups A and D, in contrast, were not affected by the intimacy level used by the confederate. They revealed moderately intimate material regardless of whether the confederate's revelations were of little or great intimacy.

Explanation of the Results

Desire to please. In discussing their results Shaffer and Tomarelli (1989) point out that the primary concern of high public–low private subjects is with the impression they make on others. They focus relatively little on their own needs and feelings. In the self-disclosure situation with a new acquaintance these subjects could therefore be expected to want to make a good impression on their partner by following his or her lead on how the discussion should be conducted. This is exactly what the results of the two experiments showed. When the confederate revealed little intimate material, these subjects did likewise; when the confederate revealed a lot, they did the same. Moreover, in their own discussion they referred significantly more frequently than members of the other groups to the content of their partner's discourse. Aware of what one *should* do to make a good impression, they aimed to please the other person.

Proper behavior. The participants in the low public–high private group (Group C) also reciprocated their partner's level of self-disclosure but for a different reason. These are people whose self-consciousness is focused primarily on their own thoughts and feelings. In an interpersonal situation they would want to protect these thoughts and feelings by avoiding shame and embarrassment. They would therefore do the socially correct thing, do what one *ought* to do, so as not to be shamed or embarrassed. In conversation with a new acquaintance, they know that the socially correct thing is to be agreeable and polite, to respond in kind to the social overtures of the other person. This is exactly what the subjects in Group C did; they politely permitted the confederate to take the lead and imitated the degree of intimacy of that person's self-disclosure.

Assumption. Although the interpretation for the behavior of the people in Group C sounds reasonable, we should be aware of the fact that it hinges on the correctness of an assumption. We categorized people as high in private self-consciousness on the basis of their having indicated that certain items of the SCS are characteristic of them. These items, however, tell us only that these people think a lot about themselves, and are attentive to their thoughts, feelings, motives, and moods. They tell us nothing about the content of their thoughts or the nature of their feelings, moods, and motives. We therefore do not know whether they are motivated to be agreeable and polite. Thus, when we follow the lead of Shaffer and Tomarelli (1989), and assume that high private subjects are strongly motivated to be agreeable and polite, we do so in the absence of direct supporting evidence. Indirect support for these inferences comes from studies like those of Froming and Carver (1981), cited earlier, which had demonstrated that people who are high in private self-consciousness have a strong tendency to agree with other people's judgments.

Practice of "doing their own thing." Turning now to the behavior of Group D, those with low-public and low-private levels of self-consciousness, we find it easy to explain. Unconcerned about the impression they make on others and unlikely to pay much attention to their own motives and feelings, they have no need to reciprocate their partner's disclosures. Their own disclosures thus remain unaffected by the degree of intimacy the confederate displays.

The puzzling high-high group. This leaves the behavior of the high public–high private (Group A) to be explained. As mentioned, in their second experiment Shaffer and Tomarelli (1989) had gathered not only self-disclosure data but also some additional information. One was the length of time it had taken a subject to begin self-disclosing after the confederate had concluded his or her contribution to the discussion. The other was a rating of the level of difficulty the subjects reported as having experienced in deciding what to say when it had been their turn to talk about themselves.

On both these measures the participants with high-public–high private self-consciousness scores (Group A) were significantly different from those in the other three groups. Not only had they taken almost twice as long to begin their part of the discussion, but they had also experienced considerably more difficulty in deciding what to say.

The performance of this group is puzzling. One should imagine that people who have a great need to make a good impression on others (high-public self-consciousness) and who are also sensitive to internalized social norms (high-private self-consciousness) would be doubly motivated to reciprocate a new acquaintance's manner of discourse. Yet the subjects in Group A did just the opposite in both the first and second experiments. Like the low public–low private group they remained unaffected by the confederate's disclosures, but they also took longer to begin their own discourse and reported having been unsure about what to say. What could have been going on?

One interpretation. Shaffer and Tomarelli (1989) offer the interpretation that people who focus at one and the same time on their public impression and on their private concerns divide their attention, "thereby reducing the extent to which either of these motives guided their self-presentation" (p. 774). "The end result of these competing attentional foci," they write, "may be a state of uncertainty or confusion about how to best serve two social motives—a state that is sufficiently disruptive as to undermine the disclosure reciprocity of subjects scoring high in both public and private self-consciousness" (p. 771).

Alternative interpretation. Competing foci of attention, as between attention to public and private self, may well be the explanation for the unexpected behavior of the subjects in Group A, but it does seem strange that people should experience difficulty deciding what to say when both public and private self call for the identical response—to disclose at the same level of intimacy as the other person. Might there be other interpretations of the puzzling results reported by Shaffer and Tomarelli (1989)?

What Does SCS Measure?

Let us go back to the scale used to assign the research participants to four groups according to the focus of their self-awareness, the SCS of Fenigstein, Scheier, and Buss (1975). Doing so we find that each of the seven items that makes up the subscale labeled "public self-consciousness" deals with the respondent's concern about his or her impression on others: how I present myself; the way I look; the impression I make; what people think of me; my style of doing things; and my appearance. Individuals who rate all or most of these items as being characteristic of them and thus obtain a high score on public self-conscious are concerned about their public impression. The focus of their self-awareness is on what they *should* do to look good in the eyes of others.

Looking at the ten items that make up the subscale labeled "private self-consciousness" one finds no such specific focus. Five of these items deal with introspection in general—involving a general awareness of oneself, trying to figure oneself out, reflecting about oneself, scrutinizing oneself, and being the subject of one's own fantasies. Three items have to do with attentiveness to inner feelings, examination of one's own motives, and alertness to one's mood. The remaining two items refer to an awareness of the workings of one's own mind while solving a problem and having the feeling of watching oneself from somewhere else.

These items are far more heterogeneous and far less specific than those on the subscale that measure public self-consciousness. Where the latter point to a single-minded concern with one's impression on others, the private self-consciousness items refer to a variety of thoughts, feelings, motives, and moods of which the individual might be aware. Moreover, the content or nature of these thoughts, feelings, motives, and moods is not specified. About these one can only speculate, and one speculation is as valid as the next, as long as it fits the data.

What Are They Thinking?

At the end of their experiment Shaffer and Tomarelli (1989) had asked their subjects, "How concerned were you about being polite and responding in kind to that which your partner had to say?" The high-private participants reported more such concern than the low-private participants. On this basis these investigators speculated that the subjects in their high-private self-consciousness group had been concerned "about being appropriately polite to their partners or about following social reciprocity norms that govern interactions among new acquaintances" (p. 771). Being concerned, however, can mean that they had been troubled, worried, or distressed about it—that it had been on their mind. It does not necessarily mean that they had been highly motivated to be polite and reciprocating.

Take, for example, a young woman who indicates on the SCS that she is highly attentive to her thoughts, motives, and feelings and let us assume that these have to do with, what Shaffer and Tomarelli (1989) call, "well-ingrained norms" (p. 771). Let us further assume that these norms say that it is improper to talk about intimate matters with a relative stranger *and* that it is important to be polite to such a person. Suppose further that this young woman has a high score on the public self-consciousness scale, which tells us that she is concerned about the impression she makes on others.

We now place this woman into the Shaffer and Tomarelli situation in which a confederate (who is also a woman) starts discussing the topic, "things in my past or present of which I am ashamed." Under this topic she talks about a highly intimate sexual experience. Then it is our young woman's turn to discuss the same topic. At that point her public self urges her to make a good impression on the new acquaintance by being agreeable and talking about a similar experience. Her private self, on the other hand, demands that she be polite (which would also make a good impression), but in addition it insists that it is not proper to talk about such intimate things. The woman is in conflict. What is she to say? It is a difficult decision to make, and difficult decisions take time.

The data reported by Shaffer and Tomarelli (1989) fit this speculation as well as they do their own. The high-public–high private (Group A) subjects took longer to begin their discussion, reported difficulty in deciding what to say, and agreed that they had been concerned about being polite by responding in kind to their partner's discussion. One wonders what these subjects would have said had they been asked how they felt about the propriety of intimate self-disclosure.

Self-Consciousness Reexamined

Self-Consciousness or Dependency?

As we saw, the results of the study conducted by Shaffer and Tomarelli (1989) pose some difficulty in interpretation. When such difficulty arises the fault can sometimes be found in the design or execution of the study, but a careful reading of the report of Shaffer and Tomarelli (1989) reveals that this is not the case in their work.

Formulation. Could it be that the source of the difficulty lies with the original formulation of public and private self-consciousness (Buss, 1980; Fenigstein et al., 1975)? A critique of that formulation, entitled "The Fallacy of the Private-Public Self-Focus Distinction" (Wicklund & Gollwitzer, 1987) suggests that possibility.

Wicklund and Gollwitzer (1987) make the point that by defining the direction of self-consciousness (public versus private) solely in terms of either the scores on a self-report scale or by an experimental manipulation (e.g., reaction to mirror presence), Fenigstein et al. (1975) neglected to relate the construct to underlying psychological processes. That does not seem a vital criticism, however, for such an operational definition can be found for many useful psychological constructs. In fact, investigators who work in the objectivist tradition do not find this at all objectionable (for a discussion of this issue see Baars, 1986).

Scale. More damaging to the concept of self-consciousness than their meta-theoretical argument is Wicklund and Gollwitzer's (1987) review of the studies that have accumulated around it. This body of research strongly suggests that the public self-consciousness scale does not measure self-consciousness but "a kind of social dependency or readiness to abide by social demands" (p. 509). That being the case, so these authors argue, one could rename that scale a social dependency scale leading to the tautological finding that dependent people tend to act in a dependent manner. Such a discovery would hardly rate as a contribution to knowledge.

Laboratory procedure. Wicklund and Gollwitzer (1987) also raise the question whether the laboratory manipulations designed to raise public self-awareness (their synonym for public self-consciousness) do indeed increase subjects' awareness of self. In reviewing the relevant studies, they conclude that these manipulations merely create a concern with one's relation to a specific other person or audience, and that the research subject responds to the explicit or implied pressure of that social environment. Self-awareness, so these writers point out, has little or nothing to do with that response.

State of Being Autonomous or Appearing Autonomous?

The critique of public and private self-consciousness that Wicklund and Gollwitzer (1987) had developed was followed by an experiment of Schlenker and Weigold (1990) who raise a fundamental question about how the scores on SCS are to be interpreted.

Individuals who score high on the public self-consciousness scale "have been depicted as chameleon-like impression managers who base their public conduct on social contingencies, not personal convictions" (Schlenker & Weigold, 1990, p. 820). In contrast, those who score high on the private subscale of the SCS have been characterized as autonomous and independent, authentic, truthful, and unconcerned about how they appear to others. Schlenker and Weigold (1990) refer to this as "social obliviousness" (p. 82), but wonder whether this is really the basis of the way these people behave in public.

As an alternative hypothesis Schlenker and Weigold (1990) propose that, rather than having the predisposition to be authentic and truthful, people who are privately self-conscious are just as concerned about how they appear to others as their publicly self-conscious counterparts are said to be. The difference between the two, so these authors suggest, lies in the type of impressions they most want to convey.

The privately self-conscious "may prefer to create an identity as someone who is autonomous, independent, and forthright, both in their own eyes and in the eyes of others" (Schlenker & Weigold, 1990, p. 821). "[I]t is not that they are oblivious to the social matrix; rather, their desired identities call for a different set of self-presentational strategies—ones that identify them as sovereign and authentic" (p. 821). The publicly self-conscious, in contrast, may prefer an identity of cooperation and dependence, of being a team player who gets along by going along.

Two Hypotheses

Focusing on the individual with high private self-consciousness, Schlenker and Weigold (1990) set out to examine whether subjects who are privately self-conscious are more influenced by *being* autonomous or by *appearing* autonomous. To this end they juxtaposed two hypotheses. One, the *social obliviousness* hypothesis, makes the traditional prediction that privately self-conscious subjects will express their attitudes regardless of how they appear to an audience. The other, the *autonomous identity* hypothesis, predicts that such subjects will try to appear autonomous, even if it means changing their publicly reported attitudes to do so.

Test of hypotheses. To investigate which of these hypotheses is supported by data, Schlenker and Weigold (1990) conducted an experiment that consisted of two sessions. From a pool of subjects to whom the SCS (Fenigstein et al., 1975) had been administered the investigators selected 47 men and 47 women who had scored in the upper and lower quartiles on private self-consciousness. Their scores on public self-consciousness had also been recorded.

In the first session, the subjects responded in private to questionnaires that dealt with their attitudes on numerous topics. Before the second session the subjects were "led to believe they would discuss several attitude topics with a partner who supposedly had formed the impression that they were either independent or dependent" (Schlenker & Weigold, 1990 p. 823). In addition, they were led to assume that if they expressed the attitudes to which they had committed themselves during the first session, they would appear to be either extremely similar or extremely dissimilar to the modal student at the university where the study was conducted. Similarity would make them appear socially dependent; dissimilarity would make them seem independent.

Privately Self-Conscious and Publicly Aware

The results of this experiment and of two correlational studies reported in the same article (Schlenker & Weigold, 1990) clearly reveal that, contrary to the traditional conception, privately self-conscious people are neither oblivious to the social implications of their conduct nor indifferent to the impressions they make on others. In keeping with the traditional formulation they do indeed see themselves as independent and are concerned about the personal rather than the social factors of their identity. In their attempts to construct and protect the identity of an autonomous person, however, these individuals will publicly report attitudes that differ from their private beliefs.

The privately self-conscious are thus no different from the publicly self-conscious; both seek to manage the impressions they are making on others. The difference between the two lies in the type of impression they seek to create. The privately self-conscious want to appear autonomous; the publicly self-conscious want to appear conforming. "In either case, the behavior represented a sensitivity to social contingencies and the desire to construct and maintain a particular type of identity" (Schlenker & Weigold, 1990, p. 826). "What distinguishes high privates from high publics is . . . the nature of the identity one is trying to construct" (p. 821).

The results of these studies make it clear that there is a difference between the private and the public types of self-awareness, but that difference does not seem to lie in the concern these two kinds of people have for the reactions of others. As symbolic interactionists like Cooley (1902) and Mead (1934) maintained long ago, we can best know ourselves by the impressions we make on the people around us. From this it follows that the more we care about ourselves, the more we are likely to manage these impressions. In that sense most of us are chameleons, regardless of our scores on the SCS.

6

Self-Perception

PERCEPTION OF SELF AND OTHERS
Actor and Observer
Different Attributions

We now return once more to the topic of traits that we first encountered in Chapter 3. Traits, so Jones and Nisbett (1971) observed in an oft-cited paper, are "things other people have" (p. 92). By this they meant that we tend to attribute our own behavior to external, situational causes, but when we try to explain the behavior of others we attribute it to such internal causes as personality traits and attitudes.

Limited support for this contention can be found in a study by Nisbett, Caputo, Legant, and Maracek (1973, Study III). These investigators presented their subjects with a list of 40 trait terms arranged in bipolar pairs, such as energetic-relaxed; lenient-firm; and quiet-talkative. Both for themselves and for four other people the subjects were either to indicate for each of these pairs which members of the adjective pairs applied, or to check "depends on the situation."

The results showed that the subjects were significantly more likely to select the depends-on-the-situation option for themselves than for the other persons. Conversely, they used trait adjectives more often when they rated the others than when they rated themselves. Although this does not confirm that "traits are things other people have," it does demonstrate that as observers of other people's behavior we are more likely to attribute their actions to traits than when we, as actors, judge the basis of our own behavior.

Our most frequent companion. This divergence in perspective is hardly surprising when one considers that each individual has the opportunity to be the best informed observer of his or her own behavior. Unlike others, who see us only some of the time, we are constantly in our own presence and thus able to amass a vast store of information on how we behave in a great variety of situations. Asked whether I am energetic or relaxed, I am likely to say, "that depends on the situation" because I know that I am energetic on the tennis court but relaxed when reading a novel in my living room. My tennis partner, however, who sees me only when I am on the court is likely to describe me as energetic.

Ambiguous response. There remains the question whether it is correct that, as Nisbett et al. (1973) speculated, "each individual may view every other individual as possessing more personality traits than he himself possesses" (p. 160). Their subjects, it will be recalled, were faced with a forced choice on each of 20 word pairs. They had to decide, for example, whether their best friend was lenient or firm, or whether it depended on the situation. They faced the same limited choice when they were judging themselves. Although, on average, the subjects chose trait labels more often for their friends than for themselves, this cannot be interpreted to mean that they viewed their friends as having more traits than they themselves. For that conclusion to be possible the subjects would have had to be able to indicate that either both or neither of a given word pair were applicable. The ambiguous "depends on the situation" is difficult to interpret for it could mean that both trait labels are pertinent.

Contrary Findings

The question whether we attribute more traits to others than to ourselves was addressed more directly in experiments by Monson, Tanke, and Lund (1980), and by Sande, Goethals, and Radloff (1988). Both groups of investigators arrived at conclusions that are the opposite of the one Nisbett et al. (1973) had reached. The reason for this can be found in the different methods these investigators used to assess their subjects' trait judgments.

Different questions, different answers. Monson et al. (1980) presented their subjects with a list composed of each of the 40 trait terms that had been presented in pairs by Nisbett et al. (1973). First the subjects were asked to pick from among these 40 traits those that applied to themselves, and then they were instructed to pick those that applied to an acquaintance of the same sex. The depends-on-the-situation option was not available. This approach showed that subjects selected more of the traits as characteristic of themselves than of their acquaintance.

Sande et al. (1988) proposed that when people are given the opportunity to express themselves freely they will reveal that they perceive themselves as multifaceted, "as having a richness and depth of personality that confers on them the capacity to act flexibly and appropriately" (p. 13).

Regarding the perception of others, Sande et al. (1988) predicted that people would attribute fewer traits to them than to themselves. Using cooperation and competition as an example, they reasoned that one can perceive oneself capable of cooperation in one situation and of competition in another, whereas the other person would more likely be seen as either cooperative or competitive, not both.

In the first of four experiments Sande et al. (1988) provided their research participants with a bipolar trait measure, similar to the one used by Nisbett et al. (1973). Instead of insisting that the subjects choose among two traits and "depends on the situation," however, they asked them to rate the degree to which they and an acquaintance possessed each of 21 traits. A typical question on the bipolar scale would read:

To what extent would you describe yourself as quiet versus talkative?
quiet _____ talkative

Subjects were to place a slash at that point on the line where they saw either their own or their acquaintance's characteristic to fall.

This bipolar scale was similar to the one used by Nisbett et al. (1973), except that instead of a dichotomous choice the subjects were able to indicate the degree to which the traits applied to them or their acquaintance. By checking the midpoint a subject could therefore indicate that he or she felt that both traits applied. Sande et al. (1988) viewed this as tantamount to selecting the depends-on-the-situation option.

In addition to these bipolar rating scales the participants in the experiment by Sande et al. (1988) were given a set of 21 trait scales on which each of a pair of related traits could be separately rated. For the quiet-talkative pair the trait-scale item would read as follows:

To what extent would you describe yourself as:
  a. quiet
not at all _____ very much
  b. talkative
not at all _____ very much

Again, a slash through the line was required to indicate where the person being rated (self or acquaintance) fell on each of these dimensions.

Self and Other

As Sande et al. (1988) had predicted, their results showed that when subjects used the bipolar scales they rated themselves closer to the midpoint than they did their acquaintance. By itself, that finding would seem to support the conclusion of Nisbett et al. (1973) that people see themselves as having fewer traits than they see others as having. The results from the trait scales, however, show that the opposite is true for on these scales the subjects described themselves as possessing significantly more traits than they assigned to their acquaintances.

On the quiet-talkative pair of the trait scale, for instance, a female subject might describe herself as both quiet and talkative by placing the slash close to "very much" for both terms. Describing her acquaintance, on the other hand, she might select "talkative" as not at all applicable, whereas she might check "quiet" as very much to the point. The dissimilar results obtained with these two instruments clearly show that the answers people give—hence, the conclusions that are drawn from these answers—depend on how the questions are framed and what form the answer is permitted to take.

Dispositions or Capabilities?

When a woman checks both talkative and quiet as being characteristic of a friend she obviously does not consider these adjectives in the way the psychologist did who constructed the trait scale on which they appear. To a psychologist a trait such as serious, for example, is a pervasive response disposition, a manner that is characteristic of a person in a variety of different situations. Is that what lay people mean when they check "serious" on a self-report inventory, or would they, if asked, explain "I am capable of being serious, but I am not a serious person for I can also be carefree"?

The second experiment reported by Sande et al. (1988) throws light on this issue. Members of a new group of participants were asked to describe themselves and an acquaintance using a list of 11 pairs of adjectives, such as serious-carefree, cautious-bold, and quiet-talkative. Next to each pair were the words "both" and "neither." The subjects were instructed to circle one adjective in each pair, or "both," or "neither."

After they had completed this instrument, which Sande et al. (1988) call a trait scale, the subjects were asked to indicate the likelihood that, in a "typical" situation, they would behave in the manner characterized by each of the 22 traits on the list. For example, the first question was: "In a typical situation, how likely is it that you would act in a serious manner?" The likelihood was to be expressed as a percentage estimate from 0% to 100%.

The results of this experiment again showed that people perceive their own response dispositions as more varied and flexible than those of others. Not only did the subjects circle "both" significantly more often for themselves than for their acquaintance, but they also saw their own behavior as less predictable than that of the other person.

The remaining two experiments reported by Sande et al. (1988) investigated whether the results they had obtained in the first two were due to subjects assigning to themselves the more desirable and less readily observed characteristics (they were not) and whether people assign more trait characteristics to those they know well and like than to those they know less well and dislike (they do). In view of the latter finding it should not be surprising that we assign more traits to ourselves than to others for we are more familiar with ourselves than with anyone else, and most of us are quite fond of ourselves.

Flattering picture. There is another point Sande et al. (1988) make that is worth noting. It is that the more "traits" one possesses—that is, the wider the variety of behaviors one has in one's repertoire—the more versatile one is and the better equipped one is to deal with the various circumstances one may encounter. In other words, it is more desirable to be flexible and adaptive than rigid and nonadaptive. We thus are painting a more flattering picture of ourselves when we say, "I can be quiet when the situation calls for quiet and talkative when that is appropriate" than if we said, "I am talkative under any and all circumstances." A flattering picture of oneself may make one feel good, but is it accurate? We shall turn to that question in a moment.

Traits and the Lay Person

As mentioned, psychologists view traits as bipolar, mutually exclusive features of personality that they construe as pervasive response dispositions that lead persons to behave in a similar manner in a great variety of situations. Given this frame of reference they are surprised when their subjects indicate that they are both quiet and talkative, serious and carefree, cautious and bold. Sande et al. (1988) declared, "the lay person's view of what a trait is, and how it influences behavior, is quite different from what many psychologists mean when they talk about traits" (p. 19). What is the lay person's view?

What the subject saw. Before entering the first of the four experiments by Sande and colleagues the subjects, who were students in introductory psychology classes, had been told that the investigators were "interested in how people describe their acquaintances and themselves using common personal characteristics and traits" (Sande et al., 1988, p. 14). What they saw when they were given the test booklets, however, were not "traits," but such common English words as serious, carefree, energetic, relaxed, lenient, firm, cautious, and bold. They saw adjectives that one might use every day to describe behavior, and they were asked to use these adjectives to describe themselves and one of their acquaintances. Describing oneself as sometimes relaxed and sometimes energetic is a far cry from stating that one "has" or "possesses" either of these characteristics as a trait.

It is very likely that the subjects looked at the adjectives on the experimenters' "trait scales" as qualities they were capable of displaying, depending on the particular situation in which they might find themselves. Having seen ourselves in many different situations in the past it stands to reason that we check more of these adjectives as applicable than we do for a person who is, according to our instructions, "more of an acquaintance than a friend" (Sande et al., 1988, p. 14).

Regrettable Custom

The source of much of this misunderstanding, which has also been pointed to by Allen and Potkay (1981), lies in a regrettable but probably irreversible custom that is particularly pervasive in the study of personality. Unlike other scientists, who when not coining entirely new words ("quarks") employ terms of Greco-Latin derivation ("ribosome") to denote narrowly defined constructs, psychologists have adopted words from the ordinary language ("sociable"), often without bothering to spell out just what that term connotes. A lone attempt (Cattell, 1966) to give the study of personality its own technical vocabulary with such words as "premsia," "parmia," and "threctia" had relatively limited reception. Little wonder that confusion results when psychologists present their subjects with a list of what they think of as traits and the subject responds in an unexpected or confusing manner.

ACCURACY OF SELF-PERCEPTION
Self-Evaluation

Assessment of Accuracy

All of a person's attributes may be the object of self-evaluation. A person might thus evaluate his or her physical condition, emotional state, aptitude, skill, strength, endurance, intelligence, or any number of other self-perceptions. How accurate are these self-evaluations? The accuracy of some of them are easily checked, whereas with others it is more difficult; when it comes to those aspects of the self-concept that have to do with moods and emotions their private nature makes a direct check impossible.

When a man reports his judgment of a physical dimension, as when he says that he has a fever, we can use a universally accepted, standardized measuring device, a thermometer, to check the accuracy of his judgment. Not so when he reports on a mood or an emotion, as when he says that he is happy. There is no objective measure of happiness with which to check that assertion. What we usually do is to compare a person's self-evaluative judgment with our own judgment or the combined judgments of others. Because such judgments are based on inferences from how that person looks and acts they are subjective attributions that may be far from accurate.

Because of these difficulties investigators seeking to study the accuracy of self-evaluations typically resort to laboratory research that involves highly constrained and artificial situations and frequently focuses not on moods or emotions but on cognitive or motor skills. One way of assessing peoples' evaluations of their own skill, for example, is to have them perform a task and to give them no feedback or false feedback regarding the quality of their performance. The subjects are later asked to judge how well they did on that task and, knowing how well they actually did, the investigator can assess the accuracy of these self-evaluations.

Reality

Both in the preceding paragraphs and those that follow we are skirting a philosophical issue that should be recognized though it cannot be resolved. It is the matter of reality.

When a man declares that he is happy and we ask whether he is *really* happy we ask, in essence, whether the reality of his state is correctly described as happiness. That question, as we have said, may be impossible to answer. Phenomenologically oriented psychologists (e.g., Rogers, 1959) would argue that this man's own reality is all that matters. As far as that individual man is concerned this may well be the case, but for a science of human behavior the question whether what people say about themselves is reliable and valid is not that easy to shrug off.

Aside from the issue of personal reality there is also the age-old, but recently renewed question (e.g., Gergen, 1985; Watzlawick, 1984) about reality as such. Is there, it is asked, a knowable reality "out there" that can ultimately be ascertained or is what we call reality the malleable product (construction) of the consensus of the people living at a given place in a particular time?

From the viewpoint of investigating the accuracy and distortion of people's self-perceptions it does not matter whether the criterion with which these perceptions are compared exists in an objective reality or in the social consensus. In our culture the search for the way things are, for truth or reality, can be pursued in two ways and both have been used in studies of self-perception. One of these approaches is exemplified by controlled laboratory studies in which objective measures are inspected; the other by jury trials in which a group of observers is asked for its verdict. Both are legitimate means for establishing reality though some might consider one of them more trustworthy than the other.

Distorted Self-Perceptions

Illusions

From psychological experiments, dating back to the classical studies of Luchins (1942) and Asch (1955, 1956), it has long been known that we humans are subject to distort our beliefs and perceptions. In addition, as the work of Kahneman and Tversky (1973; Tversky & Kahneman, 1974) has demonstrated, we are prone to predictable and systematic biases in our predictions and judgments. It is therefore not surprising that biases and distortions also enter into beliefs, judgments, and predictions that involve our self-perceptions. Taylor and Brown (1988) speak of these distorted perceptions as illusions.

Self-serving illusions. These illusions usually have the effect of making us appear more skilled, more intelligent, and more moral than we really are. They are self-serving. Alicke (1985), for example, has demonstrated that in rating our own personality we judge positive traits to be overwhelmingly more characteristic of ourselves than negative traits. Moreover, we judge positive personality attributes to be more descriptive of ourselves than of the average person, whereas we see negative personality characteristics to be less descriptive of ourselves than of the average person. Note that it is logically impossible for most people to be better than the average person! This, as Taylor and Brown (1988) point out, is evidence for the unrealistic and illusory nature of the self-evaluations furnished by the college students who are typically the subjects in studies of this kind.

Distortions of memory. In their review of the relevant literature Taylor and Brown (1988) cite studies showing that people recall positive information about themselves more readily than negative information and that they are more likely to attribute positive rather than negative outcomes to themselves. It has also been shown (Conway & Ross, 1984) that people distort their memory of the past to find support for an invalid view of themselves and that erroneous self-assessments are maintained over time even in the face of evidence to the contrary (Lepper, Ross, & Lau, 1986). When subjects' self-ratings were compared with the ratings others made of them the illusory nature of positive self-perceptions again emerged (Campbell & Fehr, 1990; Lewinsohn, Mischel, Chaplin, & Barton, 1980). Note, however, that there is no way of knowing whether the ratings others had made represented the true state of affairs.

Healthy Distortions. Biases, distortions, and illusions about oneself might be thought to be undesirable and even unhealthy. The preponderance of available evidence, however, suggests that the opposite is true. It is the healthy, well-adjusted individual who holds positively biased illusions about the self, whereas realistic self-evaluations tend to be characteristic of people with low self-esteem (Campbell & Fehr, 1990) or of those in subjective distress such as depression (Lewinsohn et al., 1980). A review of the literature on self-perception and psychological well-being led Taylor and Brown (1988) to conclude, that

> contrary to much traditional psychological wisdom, the mentally healthy person may not be fully cognizant of the day-to-day flotsam and jetsam of life. Rather, the mentally healthy person appears to have the enviable capacity to distort reality in a direction that enhances self-esteem, maintains beliefs in personal efficacy, and promotes an optimistic view of the future. These three illusions, as we have called them, appear to foster traditional criteria of mental health, including the ability to care about the self and others, the ability to be happy or contented, and the ability to engage in productive and creative work. (pp. 203–204)

Critical Self-Reflection

If it comes as a surprise to learn that it is conducive to mental health to maintain some illusions about oneself, it is even more astonishing to discover that critical self-reflection can be counterproductive. This, however, is what the results of a study by Batson, Fultz, Schoenrade, and Paduano (1987) would seem to indicate. Specifically, that study explored the effect a critical examination of one's own motivation can have on the perception of one's altruism.

Puzzle of Altruism

Altruism is defined as an unselfish concern for the welfare of others that manifests itself by taking personal risks in helping strangers without expecting or receiving a reward. Such behavior is difficult to explain from the standpoint of psychology (Hoffman, 1981) because it seems to be an exception to the hedonistic principle of behavior according to which everything people do results either in an increase of pleasure or a decrease of pain. In that sense, behavior always serves a function.

What function does altruism serve for altruists? One might say that altruism is its own reward, that the altruistic act fills a need on the altruists' part, that it makes them feel good, or that it keeps them from feeling guilty. This line of reasoning, however, defines altruism out of existence. If altruism is something other than an unselfish act from which the altruist derives no benefit, it ceases to be altruism.

Research on Altruism

Batson et al. (1987) suggested that individuals who critically examine their motivation for altruistic acts may arrive at a similar conclusion. They reasoned that if altruists were to discover that their helping behavior makes them feel good, that it maintains or enhances their self-esteem, they may cease to be altruistic.

Several studies had found that self-perceived altruistic behavior, performed without extrinsic pressure, is reduced when such behavior can earn monetary reward, when it follows having been helped by the person now in need, or when there is a strong expectation to help (Batson, Coke, Jasnoski, & Hanson, 1978; Thomas & Batson, 1981; Thomas, Batson, & Coke, 1981). In view of these findings, Batson et al. (1987) assumed that seeing oneself as an altruistic person is intrinsically rewarding, and they set out to investigate what happens when the altruist engages in critical self-reflection and discovers that his or her altruism is motivated by self-reward.

Logical conflict. Batson et al. (1987) point out that there is a logical conflict between the self-statements, "I am a selfless, altruistic person" and, "I want to see myself as selfless and altruistic because that makes me feel good about myself." The recognition of this conflict may lead the helper to conclude that he or she helped to get the self-rewards that come from seeing oneself as altruistic. That recognition weakens or removes the self-rewards thereby undermining the self-perceived altruism and leading to the cessation of helping behavior.

Effects of Critical Self-Reflection

To test this reasoning Batson et al. (1987) conducted two experiments on the effects of critical self-reflection. In the first experiment 69 college students who served as subjects were randomly assigned to three conditions. All were instructed to engage in a memory exercise by writing a short description about an event in their past. Those in the helping condition were asked to recall and describe a situation in which they had voluntarily helped someone at considerable cost to themselves without expecting any material or social rewards. When they had completed this task, the subjects in the helping/self-reflection condition were asked to write an honest and accurate description of why they had helped. Those in the helping/no-reflection condition were merely asked to write about why they had moved to their current residence.

Following these memory exercises a measure of self-perceived altruism was administered to all subjects. This consisted of two questions to which the answers were to be given on a 9-point scale that ranged from "not at all" to "extremely." The questions were: "To what extent do you generally help others for selfish reasons?" and "To what extent do you generally help others for unselfish reasons?" Low scores on the first, and high scores on the second item were defined as reflecting self-perceived altruism.

Results. The data confirmed the investigators' predictions. The subjects who had recalled a helpful act and had then reflected on their reason for performing that act (the helping/self-reflection condition) rated themselves as less altruistic than did the subjects who, having recalled a helpful act, did not reflect on their reason for doing so (the helping/no-reflection condition). As expected, subjects in the helping/no reflection condition rated themselves as less selfish (more altruistic) than did subjects in the control group who had been asked to recall the move to their present residence before responding to the measure of altruism.

Their findings led Batson et al. (1987) to conclude that "recalling one's helpfulness increased self-perceived altruism but critical self-reflection undermined this self-perceived altruism. Subjects who reflected on their reasons for helping rated themselves as no more altruistic than did subjects who did not focus on helping at all" (p. 598).

The second study. Permitting research participants to recall a situation in which they had helped another person increases the realism of the study but introduces many unknown sources of variance. The helping situations are clearly different if one person recalls running into a burning house to rescue a stranger's child, whereas another remembers letting a woman with a crying baby cut into the line at a check-out counter.

To control for this and other weaknesses of their first study, Batson and his colleagues (1987) conducted a second experiment in which the helping situation was the same for all participants. This time they tested the predictions "that critical self-reflection and its effects on self-perceived altruism should be most apparent (a) when the self-rewards for helping are salient and (b) among individuals who place more value on honest self-knowledge than on showing concern for others" (p. 597).

As before, the subjects were students in Introductory Psychology who participated to fulfill a research requirement for that course. They were ostensibly taking part in a study that required their completing several personality questionnaires. While a subject was still reading an introduction to the study the experimenter interrupted to explain that a graduate student was badly in need of subjects and asked whether the student would be willing to help out by also participating in that study, although no additional credit could be earned for doing so. The experimenter stressed that the decision was entirely up to the student.

To manipulate the salience of self-reward, the low-salience group of the subjects who agreed to help was then given a perfunctory acknowledgment ("That's great. She'll appreciate it. I'll go get her"). The subjects in the high-salience group were extensively praised, assured that they had reason to feel good about themselves, and told "You've certainly done your good deed for the day."

The graduate student who was of the sex opposite to the subject then entered with his or her other study, and indicated that it had to do with decision making. To manipulate critical self-reflection the subjects in the no-reflection condition were asked to identify and describe the most recent decision they had made. The experimenter accepted whatever response the subject offered. The subjects in the self-reflection condition, however, were induced to describe and think about their decision to help out with this graduate student's own study.

Following this all subjects were given a questionnaire that asked them to describe their decision, the alternatives available, and the reasons for their choice. When the subject had completed that questionnaire and turned it in to the "graduate student" the original experimenter returned and administered a measure of self-perceived altruism. On this the subjects rated themselves on 20 personality traits that included helpful, sympathetic, compassionate, generous, responsible, cooperative, and considerate. A further questionnaire assessed the relative importance the subject placed on the two values, honest self-knowledge (e.g., being self-aware) and concern for others (e.g., showing kindness).

The results of this experiment replicated those of the first. Critical self-reflection reduced self-perceived altruism. This effect was most apparent among subjects who placed a higher value on honest self-knowledge than on showing concern for others and also had the self-rewards for helping made salient. No such effect was found among subjects who placed a lower value on honest self-knowledge than on showing concern for others and did not have the self-rewards for helping made salient.

Effects of Self-Reflection

Recall that Batson et al. (1987) had proposed that perceiving oneself as altruistic serves as an implicit reward for helping behavior. They had cited other research, showing that this implicit reward can be vitiated by such extrinsic pressures as being offered money for helping.

The studies just presented demonstrate that self-reflection reduces self-perceived altruism. What has not been shown, however, is that a reduction in self-perceived altruism reduces a person's readiness to help others. It is conceivable that one can perceive oneself as not altruistic but still engage in selfless helping behavior when an occasion for such behavior arises. Whether that is the case remains for future research to explore.

Research into the effects of self-reflection has considerable relevance for efforts that seek to provide people with a better understanding of their motivations. The studies just reviewed carry the implication that healthy people who cheerfully engage in helping others and similar prosocial behaviors should not be encouraged to explore their motivation for doing so, lest they run the risk of reducing that motivation.

Self-reflection, critical and otherwise, is at the core of most forms of psychotherapy and self-help endeavors. It would assuredly be counterproductive if these attempts to reduce human distress were to have the effect of making people less helpful or caring by reducing the implicit motivation of their self-perceived altruism. The issue deserves exploration.

INFLUENCES ON SELF-PERCEPTION

The studies on altruism have shown that it is possible to produce changes in people's self-perception by inducing them to reflect on their motivations. We shall now explore whether other influences are also capable of changing self-perceptions.

Influence of Other People

There is considerable experimental support for the notions that the behavior of other people influences how we perceive ourselves. These other people can be experimenters' confederates who model script-prescribed behavior or interviewers who ask questions that focus the subject's attention in a particular direction.

Fazio, Effrein, and Fallender (1981), for example, showed that when subjects are asked such questions as, "What would you do if you wanted to liven things up at a party?" they perceive themselves as extraverted, whereas such questions as "What things do you dislike about loud parties?" induce introverted self-perceptions that are reflected in their responses to a self-report questionnaire.

Effect of Self-Presentation

Yet another source of support for the notion that self-perception is influenced by interaction with others comes from three studies reported by Jones, Rhodewalt, Berglas, and Skelton (1981). For their first study these investigators used an elaborate cover story that led subjects to believe that they were being considered for admission to an observer team needed for a study of encounter groups. A part of this selection procedure was an interview with the purported leader of the observer team. The subjects, eager to be accepted for that position, were then induced via a modeling procedure to present themselves in that interview in either a self-deprecating or a self-enhancing manner. In the other two studies the subjects simply were instructed to play the role of a self-deprecating or self-enhancing person who is being interviewed for a job. In all three studies the subjects were given a test of self-esteem after the interview. This test was similar to one they had taken before entering the experiment. The responses showed that the self-esteem of subjects in the self-enhancing condition had increased, whereas that of subjects in the self-deprecating condition had decreased. Jones et al. (1981) refer to this as a carry-over effect.

Explanations for the effect. Although the carry-over effect from this single experience is probably not permanent it poses the intriguing question as to how it is to be explained. What mechanism would account for subjects lowering their initially high self-esteem after playing the role of a self-deprecating individual or raising their self-esteem after pretending to be self-enhancing? Jones et al. (1981) point out that two not entirely compatible theories could be invoked in explanation of this phenomenon. One of these is the theory of cognitive dissonance (Festinger, 1957; Wicklund & Brehm, 1976), the other Bem's (1972) self-perception theory.

An explanation based on dissonance theory would say that the inconsistency between the person's existing self-concept and the behavior in which she or he is engaged creates a discomfort that is reduced by an adjustment in the self-concept. Self-perception theory, on the other hand, would say that a person's self-concept is mutable and at least partly a function of the behavior in which the person has recently engaged. Jones et al. (1981) favor a modification of the latter view. They call it "a biased scanning variant of self-perception theory" (p. 408). This variant assumes "that the self-concept is really a complex set of alternative conceptions with continuously shifting salience" (p. 408). Accordingly the self-concept could be construed as "a momentary subset of a larger library of self-relevant information" (Rhodewalt & Agustsdottir, 1986, p. 47).

To clarify the theoretical issue Jones et al. (1981) conducted a third experiment. It had the same results as the first two. Again, subjects in the self-enhancing condition showed raised self-esteem, whereas that of those in the self-deprecating condition was lowered. This time, however, the investigators had included two further conditions that were designed to test which theoretical view best fit the data. In one of these conditions subjects read a script, and thus had little or no personal involvement in what they said during the interview. The other condition entailed having the subjects make a clear choice as to whether to participate in the interview, thus making them personally responsible for what they were saying.

Conclusion. This experiment led the investigators to conclude that both theories are required to explain the results. They see self-perception theory as accounting for self-enhancing carry-over, whereas the self-deprecating carry-over is better explained in terms of dissonance theory. The reasoning follows.

According to self-perception theory subjects, having behaved in a self-enhancing manner, are strengthened in the self-perception of being confident, self-enhancing individuals. Subjects who presented themselves as a self-deprecating person, on the other hand, encounter a discrepancy between their confident self-concept and their self-deprecating behavior. This discrepancy sets up an uncomfortable state of dissonance that calls for a resolution. Because behavior that has already occurred cannot be recalled so that it can be brought in line with the self-concept, it is the self-concept that must be adjusted by making it more congruent with the recent behavior.

A Model of Self-Concept

The difficulty in explaining the results of Jones et al. (1981) led Rhodewalt and Agustsdottir (1986) to advance and test a model that also invokes both cognitive dissonance and self-perception theory, but does so in a more integrated fashion. According to this model the self-concept (to which they refer as the *phenomenal self*) is conceived "as a latitude of acceptance that incorporates both positive and negative self-referent material, and as latitudes of rejection containing potential positive and negative material not currently stored in self-referent form" (p. 47).

Differential accessibility. This conceptualization and its terminology draw on work done by Fazio, Zanna, and Cooper (1977) in the area of attitude change. From that perspective people carry in their memory a range of attributes, past behaviors, and experiences that underlie their present self-conceptions. As is the case with other material stored in memory, some of it is more readily accessible than the rest. The accessible portion of memory is what Rhodewalt and Agustsdottir (1986) refer to as the latitude of acceptance; that which is not accessible is termed the latitude of rejection. The potentially available self-knowledge is conceived as a continuum that ranges from unfavorable to favorable, and people are seen as differing in terms of the portion of that continuum that is readily accessible for constituting the self-concept.

In terms of this model, changes in a person's self-concept, such as those reported by Jones et al. (1981), reflect changes in the accessibility of available self-referent memory. For self-enhancing subjects access to positive aspects of self is increased by the experience of having presented themselves in the job interview as self-enhancing. Such a shift is relatively easy because self-enhancing memories are already in the subject's latitude of acceptance. Rhodewalt and Agustsdottir (1986) would attribute this phenomenon to the processes postulated by self-perception theory as modified by Jones et al. (1981).

The more difficult, negative shift from self-enhancement to self-deprecation, however, is seen as requiring motivated access to material in the latitude of rejection. This, so Rhodewalt and Agustsdottir (1986) maintain, can best be accounted for by cognitive dissonance theory, presumably because that theory has motivational properties.

Test of model. To test their model Rhodewalt and Agustsdottir (1986) replicated the Jones et al. (1981) experiment using nondepressed and mildly depressed college students as subjects. The reason for choosing depression as a moderating variable was that, unlike the nondepressed, people with elevated scores on a depression inventory can be assumed to have self-deprecating material within and self-enhancing material outside their latitude of acceptance.

The results of this study fitted the theoretical model. As Rhodewalt and Agustsdottir (1986) put it,

> The experimental findings support the proposed relations between behavior and the self. Dissonance processes (i.e., the choice manipulation [whether the subject had made an explicit choice to participate]) mediated the carryover of self-presentation to self-esteem only when subjects portrayed a role for which they should have limited available self-referential knowledge (self-enhancement for depressed subjects and self-deprecation for non-depressed subjects). Differential accessibility (i.e., the self-referencing manipulation [whether the subject acted out a script or behaved spontaneously]) mediated the carryover of self-presentational behavior on self-esteem when the presentation depicted a self for which the subjects had readily accessible self-knowledge (self-deprecation for depressed subjects and self-enhancement for non-depressed subjects). (p. 53)

Malleability and Stability

Regardless of whether one accepts the preceding, rather intricate conclusions regarding the roles of self-perception and cognitive dissonance theories, the findings of Rhodewalt and Agustsdottir (1986), as did those of Jones et al. (1981), touch on the broader issues of the stability versus malleability of the self-concept. As we saw in chapter 4 there is substantial support for formulations that do not consider stability and malleability as incompatible. The conceptualization of differential accessibility advanced by Rhodewalt and Agustsdottir (1986) provides for both of these characteristics of the self-concept in that accessibility may be constrained under one set of conditions and more flexible under others. Quoting these authors once more,

> Current contextual cues, behaviors, and affect serve to increase the relative accessibility of one aspect of the self over others. To the degree that other people and situations provide consistent cues, the individual displays apparent consistency and stability of self-relevant behavior. Nonetheless, within any individual's experience is enough contextual variation and varied social feedback to shift the person's focus among social selves (i.e., academic to parent to athlete) and within self categories (i.e., the thrill of victory and the agony of defeat) (p. 53).

Because it is central to the notion of a self-concept, the question whether it is stable or malleable has occupied many investigators. What begins to emerge from that research is that there are aspects of the self-concept that are stable and others that are malleable. A conceptualization and study by Markus and Kunda (1986) made a further contribution to this issue.

Universe of Self-Conceptions

Markus and Kunda (1986) proceeded from the perspective that the self-concept is not a unitary structure but that it encompasses a wide variety of selves such as the good selves, the bad selves, the feared selves, the hoped-for selves, the ideal selves, and so forth. Markus and Kunda (1986) postulate that to respond to the social circumstances of the moment the individual draws from this "universe of self-conceptions" a subset that they call the working self-concept.

The working self-concept. These investigators conceive of the working self-concept as a temporary, malleable structure, whereas the universe of self-conceptions from which it is constructed is seen as relatively stable. Note the similarity of this conceptualization to that of Rhodewalt and Agustsdottir (1986) who, as mentioned earlier, speak of a person's self-concept as "a momentary subset of a larger library of self-relevant information" (p. 47).

On the basis of the theoretical framework they had proposed Markus and Kunda (1986) offer a resolution for the seeming paradox that the self-concept is both stable and malleable. They propose that whenever people are faced with the totally artificial situation of a paper-and-pencil test designed to assess their self-concept they draw on their relatively stable universe of self-conceptions in generating their responses. From the responses elicited in such artificial situations investigators correctly conclude that the self-concept has stability. Malleability emerges only when the self-concept is investigated in true-to-life situations in which people construct working self-concepts that are appropriate to that situation.

Test of the Formulation

To test their formulation of the working self-concept, Markus and Kunda (1986) employed a situation that in some respects is similar to that used by Asch (1956) in his classical studies on conformity, which were described in Chapter 5.

The study. The subjects for this research were female students at the University of Michigan who had been recruited for a study that was ostensibly concerned with attitudes and opinions. Each of these subjects was brought into a room where she and three student confederates sat in a row behind a long table. The subject was always at the far left. The experimenter then showed the participants a series of 18 posters that displayed three numbered items, such as three colors, three cartoons, or three greeting cards. For each of the posters the participants were to write down the identifying number of the item they liked best.

After all 18 posters had been shown the participants were asked to read out their responses, ostensibly so that they could be recorded on computer-coding sheets. Under the guise of making the task more interesting each of the posters was again displayed as the participants announced their preferences. The real subject always announced her choice first, and her response then determined the responses the confederates would give.

There were two experimental conditions: a *uniqueness condition* and a *similarity condition*. In the uniqueness condition the confederates disagreed with the subject and agreed with each other on all but 3 of the 18 trials. On the remaining 3 trials, to increase the credibility of the procedure, the first confederate agreed with the subject, and the other two disagreed with her and with each other in order. The aim of this manipulation was to make the subject feel unusual and unique by exposing her to the experience of having made choices that differed from those of a fairly unanimous majority.

The situation was reversed for the subjects who had been assigned to the similarity condition. Here all confederates agreed with the subject's choices on all but 3 of the 18 trials. On the three remaining trials none of the confederates agreed with the subject, and two of them agreed with each other. Here the aim was to make the subject feel so similar to the other students as to be nearly a clone of them by exposing her to the experience of having made choices that were the same as those of almost everyone else.

The predictions. The investigators had anticipated that the subjects' working self-concept would vary as a function the uniqueness-similarity manipulation. They did not expect that the young women would simply accept the view of themselves as extremely common or extremely unique, nor that they would simply reject the information this social situation presented. What they did expect was that subjects who had been made to feel extremely unique, perhaps a little odd and peculiar, would seek to retrieve from their memory of various self-conceptions (their universe of self-conceptions) some reassuring examples of past behavior that would reveal their similarity to others. Students made to feel uncomfortably similar to others, on the other hand, were expected to call on self-conceptions that could serve as evidence of their uniqueness. As Markus and Kunda (1986) put it, "subjects led to believe they are extremely unique should attempt to verify their similarity to others, whereas those led to believe they are very similar to others should make every effort to affirm their uniqueness" (p. 860).

Tests and Their Results

Similarity to reference groups. To test their predictions, Markus and Kunda (1986) followed their experimental manipulations with the administration of three measures designed to assess the effect of having been made to feel unique or similar, respectively.

The first of these dependent measures required the subject to rate on a 6-point scale how similar she felt to each of 26 reference groups whose names were projected on a screen. Fifteen of these names represented reference groups to which all or almost all of the subjects belonged (e.g., Americans or women), whereas the rest were groups to which none or almost none of them belonged (e.g., men or UCLA students).

The investigators expected that subjects who had been made to feel unique by the experimental manipulation, the uniqueness subjects, would seek evidence to counter that self-conception by affirming their similarity to others and rate themselves as more similar to in-groups and less similar to out-groups. The similarity subjects, conversely, were expected to do the opposite.

The results of this test revealed a trend in the direction of the investigators' predictions, but the statistical comparison of the two groups failed to reach the usually accepted level of significance. In retrospect this is not surprising. Markus and Kunda (1986) may have expected more of their experimental manipulation than it could deliver. How powerful an influence would the uniqueness situation have had to exert to make a woman undergraduate at the University of Michigan see herself as similar to men at the University of California at Los Angeles? From the viewpoint of lending strong support to the experimenters' predictions the results of the two other dependent measures turned out to be more rewarding.

Self-categorization. For this task the subject was shown 31 slides, each containing a trait adjective. Eight of these were related to uniqueness (e.g., original, independent) and nine to similarity (e.g., average, normal). The remaining 14 slides were included for comparison and contained words from the extroversion-introversion dimension. Each of these adjectives was presented for 4 s. The subject was to respond by pressing either a "me" or a "not me" button.

Counting only the number of words that the subjects endorsed by pressing "me," one finds no difference between similarity and uniqueness subjects on either similarity or uniqueness words. This would suggest that the subjects had not been influenced by the information about their similarity or uniqueness that was presented in the experimental manipulation. Highly significant differences between the two groups of subjects emerge only when one looks at the latencies for these self-categorizations, at how soon after a word had appeared on the screen each subject pressed the response button she had chosen.

Reaction time. Before discussing these results it is useful to recall our presentation (see Chapter 3) of the research methods employed by investigators who construe self as a memory network and therefore employ the tools of memory research in their work (Greenwald & Banaji, 1989; Kihlstrom & Cantor, 1984). Asking people what they remember is relatively nonproductive. What is far more revealing is how long it takes them to come up with an answer to such a question. For that reason students of the self-concept, such as Markus and her associates (Markus & Sentis, 1982; Markus & Smith, 1981; Sentis & Markus, 1979) use reaction-time measures in their study of the self-schema. The more quickly a person can retrieve a given trait-related adjective from memory, the more relevant that term is assumed to be to that individual's self-concept. Implied in this is the formulation that the self-concept is an aspect of or stored in the person's memory.

In line with this tradition Markus and Kunda (1986) compared their uniqueness and similarity subjects in terms of the time lag (latencies) between the appearance of the stimulus words and the subject's "me" or "not me" responses to the uniqueness and similarity adjectives. They expected that having become uncomfortable by being made to feel unique or similar by the experimental manipulation, the subjects would retrieve different sets of self-conceptions into their working self-concepts. Specifically, subjects who had been made to feel unique were expected to seek a reaffirmation of their similarity to others by rapidly endorsing as "me" terms conceptually related to similarity, whereas subjects who had been made to feel similar were expected equally quickly to endorse words that would emphasize their uniqueness.

The results were generally in line with these expectations. The similarity subjects were faster than the uniqueness subjects to respond with "me" to the uniqueness words, whereas the uniqueness subjects were faster than the similarity subjects to respond with "me" to the similarity words. Conversely, on the similarity adjectives the uniqueness subjects were markedly slower to respond "not me" than were the similarity subjects. No such difference was found in the "not me" responses of the two groups to the uniqueness words. There, "All subjects seemed to have difficulty rejecting characterization of themselves as, for example, *special*" (p. 862).

Word association. The third task Markus and Kunda (1986) used to measure the effect of their experimental manipulation was a word association test. Here the subject was shown six words, one at a time, and instructed to write down in 1 min as many words as the stimulus word brought to mind. The first two words were related to similarity (ordinary, conforming); the last two had to do with uniqueness (unusual, individualistic); and two in the middle were neutral (honest, polite). The responses were scored for the total number of words produced, for the number of uniqueness-relevant and similarity-relevant words, and for the number of positive (nice, happy, etc.) and negative (bad, ugly, etc.) expressions.

The two groups of subjects did not differ in the number of associations produced, nor in the number of dimension-related adjectives generated. There was, however, a marked difference in whether the adjectives that the subjects produced were positive or negative in quality. As expected, "when responding to the similarity stimulus words, uniqueness subjects generated more positive and fewer negative associations than did similarity subjects. The opposite pattern was found for uniqueness stimulus words—in response to these, uniqueness subjects generated fewer positive and more negative associations than did similarity subjects" (p. 863). It appears that both groups of subjects, having been made to feel either unique or similar, experienced this state as unpleasant and threatening; this was then reflected in the negative associations they produced to adjectives related to that state.

The results just presented are graphically displayed in Figure 6-1, which shows that, compared with the similarity words, the uniqueness words elicited relatively more positive than negative associations from both the uniqueness and the similarity subjects.

Conclusions

Stable and malleable. The subjects' preference for adjectives that have to do with uniqueness that was manifested on the word association test had also been revealed in the self-categorization task in which the women were loath to respond with "not me" to terms like "special."

This would seem to show that the self-concept, though responsive to the influence of challenging social situations and thus malleable, is possessed of an underlying stability that is strongly defended. The subjects in this study, undergraduates at a selective major university, may well have a self-concept of being

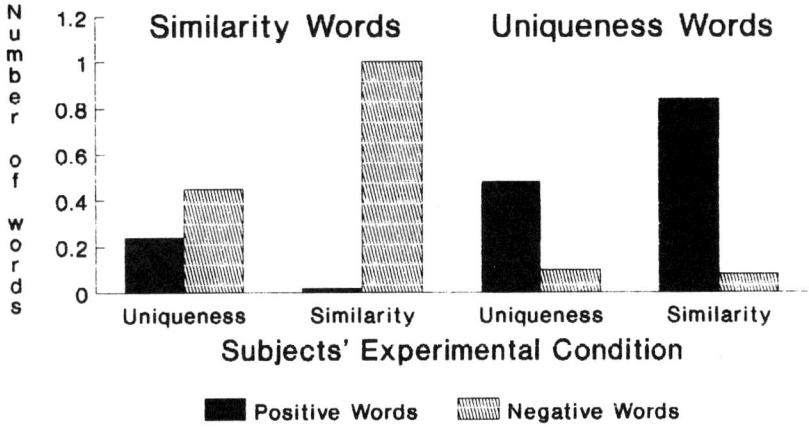

FIGURE 6-1 Associations to types of words by uniqueness and similarity subjects.

Redrawn from Markus, H., and Kunda, Z., 1986. Stability and malleability of the self-concept. *Journal of Personality and Social Psychology, 51,* 858–866. Copyright 1986 by the American Psychological Association. Reprinted by permission.

special, independent, unusual, and individualistic. It would probably take more than a relatively brief session with a group of strangers who all agree with her judgment to make such a student view uniqueness-relevant adjectives in a negative light. One wonders what the results of this study would have been had the subjects been recruited from a social group that emphasizes conformity and obedience while denigrating individualism and independent thought.

What Markus and Kunda (1986) demonstrated is that core aspects of a person's self-concept are relatively unresponsive to the social circumstances of the moment and are not easily altered. A seemingly more superficial aspect of the self-concept, the self-concept of the moment or the working self-concept, however, does respond to the social situation in which the individual happens to be placed, and can thus be viewed as malleable and fluid.

7

Self-Assessment, Self-Efficacy, and Self-Esteem

SELF-ASSESSMENT

Task Choice

Self-perception, as we saw in the previous chapter, deals largely with the question that asks, "What kind of a person am I?" Self-assessment centers on a somewhat different question that might be phrased, "How good am I at doing various tasks?" Investigators of self-assessment, approaching that question as outsiders, have rephrased it to read, "Faced with a choice between two tasks what determines which of them a person is likely to select and what is the basis of this selection?" This question has led to several theories in which self-assessment plays either a peripheral or a central role.

Theories

Motivation. One well-known theory seeks the answer to the question of task choice in the person's motivation (Atkins & Raynor, 1974). According to this view people with a high need to achieve will choose the more difficult of two tasks, rejecting the one in which success is virtually certain. At the same time, these people will reject an extremely difficult task in which the chances of success are exceedingly small.

According to the motivational theory the reason for these choices lies in the affective consequences of their respective outcomes. Success has the positive value of experienced pride; failure the negative value of experienced shame.

Self-Assessment, Self-Efficacy, and Self-Esteem

Following the hedonistic model of motivation, people are seen as seeking to maximize the pride that comes from success and to minimize the shame that follows failure. Accordingly, the higher the probability of success in a given task, the less the pride in success and the greater the shame for failure.

Although motivational theory of task choice does not highlight self-assessment, it is implied in that a judgment of task difficulty is always relative to one's self-perceived level of skill or capacity.

Attribution. An elaboration of the motivational explanation for task choice can be found in the theory advanced by Weiner (1986). In this view the emotional consequences people anticipate from performing a task are a function of the causes to which they attribute success or failure. Accordingly, when the outcome of task performance is attributed to the internal causes of (self-assessed) ability and effort the pride or shame will be far more intense than when it is attributed to the external causes of difficulty or luck.

In the two theories mentioned thus far task choice is seen as primarily influenced by the person's level of achievement motivation or attributional style; self-assessment is involved only by implication. It is central in a theoretical formulation first advanced by Trope (1975, 1979) who refers to his theory as the self-assessment view. In it people's desire for information about their own abilities is the motivation for their preference of one task over another.

Self-Assessment View

The self-assessment view "assumes that people strive to attain a realistic assessment of their weaknesses and strengths in order to be better able to predict and effectively cope with their environment" (Trope, 1980, p. 117).

Diagnosticity. According to this formulation the attractiveness of a task is a function of how much it can tell us about ourselves, the diagnosticity of its outcome. That is to say, the more information we expect a task to provide us about our ability level, the more likely we are to choose that task over one that promises us less information about ourselves.

Uncertainty reduction. From this it follows that the more uncertain we are about our ability, the more likely we are to select tasks that promise to reduce that uncertainty. Uncertainty about one's ability is of course reduced regardless of whether the task one undertakes leads to success or to failure. According to Trope (1980), "the higher the diagnosticity of an outcome, whether success or failure, the higher the attractiveness of the task" (p. 118).

Contradictory predictions. Unlike the hedonistic model of motivation, according to which people prefer tasks that promise to maximize success and minimize failure, the self-assessment model bases task choice on expectations of uncertainty reduction. When two theoretical formulations generate contradictory predictions they present an opportunity to conduct a so-called critical experiment. This was Trope's aim in studies he reported in 1980.

If one wishes to compare the hedonistic with the self-assessment model one has to manipulate the diagnosticities of various task outcomes. In addition, because the predictions of the hedonistic model take a person's achievement motivation into account, that attribute too must be varied if the research is to be relevant to the problem posed. Moreover, inasmuch as the self-assessment model is predicated on reduction of uncertainty that variable must also be manipulated because the task choice of people who are confident in their ability will be different from the task choice of those who lack such confidence. Trope (1980) sought to take all of these variables into account.

Critical experiment. Before the experimental session the achievement motive of Trope's (1980) subjects had been tested. When they later arrived for the study the subjects were told that they were participating in a survey on the attitudes of potential consumers toward a new eye-hand coordination game.

The subjects were then given a booklet that described the game as one that involved tracing a target they would see inside a circle on a television screen. The movement and speed of the target could be controlled by manipulating two handles. The game, so the instructions informed the subjects, had several versions that differed in terms of the speed of the target's movement, the frequency with which it changed direction, and the size of the circle in which it moved.

By varying the instructions the experimenter was able to manipulate not only the perceived difficulty level of the game but also its presumed diagnosticity of success and failure. The latter was accomplished by presenting the subjects with spurious scores obtained by fictitious adult population groups of allegedly high and low eye-hand coordination ability.

For each of the nine different versions of the game the subjects were asked to indicate on 11-point rating scales the extent to which they found that version attractive and the extent to which they might like to play that version. In addition, the subjects were to rate the extent to which they saw the scores in the game as capable of revealing a person's level of eye-hand coordination. It is worth noting that the experiment ended once this information had been gathered so that the subjects did not actually have the opportunity to play the game.

Results. As Trope's (1980) self-assessment formulation had predicted, "[t]he results clearly showed that task attractiveness increased with overall diagnosticity irrespective of whether the task's overall diagnosticity derived from the diagnosticity of success or from the diagnosticity of failure" (p. 127).

Achievement motivation theory would have predicted that people seek to maximize their chances of success by avoiding tasks that might disclose low ability. To judge by Trope's (1980) results, people seem to seek information about their ability regardless of whether a task leads to success or to failure. It is difficult to draw a firm conclusion about this, however, because the judgments of Trope's subjects were based on a written description of a game they had no expectation of playing. Trope (1980) recognized this when he wrote:

> Finally, it is important to note that the generalizability of the present findings may be limited by the fact that this study employed a hypothetical choice situation. It is possible that self-enhancement exerts a stronger influence on preference among real achievement tasks, particularly when performance is expected to be public. Under such circumstances outcomes that diagnose low ability and outcomes that diagnose high ability may have divergent effects upon task preference. It remains for future research to investigate these potentially limiting conditions. (p. 128)

Self-Assessment or Self-Enhancement?

In mentioning self-enhancement Trope (1980) touches on yet another question. It is whether in their choice of tasks people's motive is to find out how well they perform (self-assessment) or to prove to themselves how good they are (self-enhancement).

Individual Differences

When two distinctly different and equally logical viewpoints, such as self-assessment and self-enhancement, vie for acceptance it is rarely a matter of one being right and the other wrong. What is far more likely is that one of these viewpoints holds true for some people under some circumstances, whereas the other viewpoint applies to other people under other circumstances.

The attractiveness and diagnosticity judgments Trope gathered in his 1980 study are difficult to interpret from the viewpoint of these conflicting predictions, but an individual difference interpretation finds support in the fact that the scores of his subjects on the test of achievement motivation moderated the attractiveness of task diagnosticity. Specifically, the positive relationship between task attractiveness and outcome diagnosticity was considerably more pronounced for subjects with high achievement motivation than for subjects with low achievement motivation. Trope (1980) interprets this to mean that, in comparison with individuals with low achievement motivation, those with high achievement motivation have a greater need to reduce uncertainty about their ability. Those for whom achievement is important also find it important to obtain information about their ability and, in pursuit of that information, they seem willing to undertake tasks on which they might fail.

Self-Assessment or Self-Esteem Protection?

Strube, Lott, Lê-Xuân-Hy, Oxenberg, and Deichmann (1986) sought to answer the question whether, in seeking information about themselves, people are primarily guided by a concern for accurate self-assessment or by a desire to enhance or at least protect their self-esteem. Self-esteem, as we shall soon discover, has to do with a person's judgment of his or her own worth.

The tasks among which their subjects were to choose consisted of tests of cognitive ability. These tests varied in their diagnosticity of success, diagnosticity of failure, and level of difficulty. The investigators reasoned that if accuracy of self-assessment was the primary consideration that governed task choice, subjects should select the test that is highly diagnostic of *both* success and failure. Conversely, if subjects are primarily concerned about protecting or enhancing their self-esteem they should choose the test that is good only in diagnosing success but not in diagnosing failure.

Test difficulty. In addition to varying test diagnosticity Strube et al. (1986) varied test difficulty. The more difficult a test, the less likely a person is to do well on it. Test difficulty thus varies the probability of a successful or unsuccessful outcome. This variable was included because, with respect to test difficulty, the self-assessment and self-enhancement models generate different predictions. The self-enhancement model predicts that the preference for easy tasks increases with increasing failure diagnosticity. The self-assessment model, conversely, predicts that the preference for easy tasks increases with decreasing failure diagnosticity.

Summarizing the results of their study Strube et al. (1986) write, "Overall, clearly stronger support was obtained for the self-assessment model . . . , which suggests that the motive to evaluate abilities accurately is a powerful one" (p. 24). The task choice of the subjects in this study was governed largely by an interest in accurate information on which to base their self-assessment. Whether this conclusion can be generalized beyond this study is another matter.

Issue of Generalizability

To put this result in context it is useful to recall that the subjects in this research were college students who had signed up for a study of "personality correlates of cognitive abilities" that had been advertised by announcements posted around their campus. Unlike the typical subjects in psychological research who are students enrolled in the introductory psychology course and who earn course credits for required participation in experiments, these volunteers were paid $4 and presumably came from all over campus. It is very likely that they volunteered for this study because they wanted to know something about their cognitive ability. It is also worth recalling that college students are used to taking tests that are meant to assess their course performance accurately.

These volunteers then entered a study in which they were presented with a choice among various versions of a test of cognitive abilities. These version varied in their diagnosticity of success and failure as well as in their level of difficulty. Given the reason these subjects had elected to participate in this study, it does not seem particularly surprising that, on the whole, they chose the version that promised to give an accurate result even at the risk of the result showing them as having done less well than they might have hoped.

As we shall see in the following chapter, the self-esteem–enhancing and -protecting strategy of choosing a test that promises to give inaccurate results is employed largely by individuals with tenuous self-esteem. The circumstances of subject recruitment for the Strube et al. (1986) study may well have selected self-assured individuals with high self-esteem who wanted to demonstrate to themselves and others their good cognitive abilities. Strube and his colleagues made no claim for the generalizability of their findings. In light of these considerations here outlined others ought to be circumspect before applying to people in general the conclusions these investigators drew from their study of college students.

SELF-EFFICACY

Powerful Construct

Self-efficacy concerns the perception of one's capacities with respect to an action about to be undertaken. Bandura (1986), who introduced the construct of self-efficacy in a highly influential article (Bandura, 1977), speaks of "perceived self-efficacy," which he views as "a significant mediator of psychological functioning" (Bandura, 1984, p. 247).

The perception of self-efficacy (or self-perceived efficacy) plays a central role in psychological functioning. It has been shown to affect the choice of what people will and will not attempt, how much effort they will put into an action, how long they will persevere on a difficult task, and the amount of stress or anxiety they experience while coping with the demands of the environment. A strong sense of self-efficacy not only facilitates good performance, but it also helps one withstand failures. Moreover, people's judgments of their capacities influence their thought patterns and their emotional reactions while they anticipate or actually engage in transactions with their environment (Bandura 1982, 1986). A review of how this powerful construct is assessed and manipulated communicates its essential features.

Assessment, Induction, and Performance

Efficacy Assessment

The assessment of self-efficacy is typically accomplished by displaying or describing a series of tasks of increasing difficulty and asking the person to indicate how many of these he or she expects to be able to complete successfully. For each task so identified, the individual is then asked to rate the degree of confidence he or she has in this expectation. The instrument used for this purpose is a 10-point scale that ranges from "quite uncertain" to "certain." It is the degree of confidence measured in this fashion that represents the person's perception of self-efficacy regarding the task to which this rating applies.

That description makes it apparent that self-efficacy is closely related to, if not identical with, what is commonly called self-confidence. Bandura often eschews terms that are in common usage, like self-confidence, preferring fairly obscure expressions that are not encumbered by the variety of meanings their popular synonyms have acquired over time.

Efficacy Induction

There are at least four sources of information about one's own capacities that one must have to judge one's efficacy. Bandura (1986) lists these sources as enactive attainment, vicarious experience, verbal persuasion, and physiological state.

Enactive attainment. Another of Bandura's obscure terms, enactive attainment, is the direct, personal experience a person has had with a given task that she or he tackled in the past. Previous success with a task raises efficacy judgment; failure reduces it.

Vicarious experience. Vicarious experience involves observing someone else engaging in an action and experiencing either success or failure. This is closely related to observational learning from models that play a prominent role in Bandura's (1986) social cognitive theory.

Verbal persuasion. The least effective of the four ways of inducing efficacy is verbal persuasion. It consists of others expressing judgments, encouragements, and exhortations such as, "You are good at this sort of thing," or "I know you can do it."

Physiological state. Lastly, people can base judgments about their strength, capacity, and endurance on such signs of their physiological state as fatigue, aches, or pains as well as on the autonomic arousal that is construed and experienced as fear.

Any, or a combination, of these four sources of information can be used to induce positive changes in a person's self-efficacy perception. Thus, people can be exposed to carefully managed success experiences; they can be presented with models who demonstrate success: they can be persuaded or encouraged; or their physiological state can be modified by exercise, diet, rest, or chemical means. In the typical self-efficacy experiment the final step, after initial assessment and induction procedures, is to have the participants actually engage in the task or tasks the self-efficacy for which had been targeted for change.

Generalization of Effect

Bandura (1986) cites studies he conducted with various colleagues and students demonstrating that once established with respect to one activity, enhanced self-efficacy tends to generalize to other situations, "especially those in which performance has been self-debilitated by preoccupation with personal inadequacies" (p. 399). As one might expect, such generalization effects are most likely to be found in activities that have a close similarity to those in which self-efficacy was originally enhanced.

Demonstrations of Fear Reduction

Much of the early laboratory work on self-efficacy was conducted with individuals who were afraid of snakes. We shall refer to one series of such studies (Bandura, Reese, & Adams, 1982) to explicate this approach further.

The first of a series of experiments conducted by Bandura et al. (1982) was designed to demonstrate that performance varies in a predictable fashion with changes in self-efficacy. The subjects were three men and seven women whose fear of snakes was so strong that it seriously interfered with their ability to lead normal lives. They had been recruited through a newspaper advertisement in which treatment for snake phobia was offered.

Pretreatment evaluation. To obtain a baseline of the initial level of fear with which to compare later changes, the subjects were observed to see how closely they were able to approach a harmless snake contained in a glass cage. Their graded task was to approach the cage, to look down at the snake, to touch and hold it (first with gloved and then with bare hands), to let the snake loose in the room and return it to the cage, to hold it a hand's width from their face, and finally to have the snake crawl in their lap while letting their arms hang loosely at their sides.

While they were anticipating this performance task the subjects had been asked to indicate on a 10-point scale how much fear they were experiencing. They were also asked to indicate which of the 18 steps on the graded snake-approach task they felt themselves able to perform. For each of the steps thus identified they were then to use the self-efficacy scale mentioned earlier on which they rated their level of confidence in being able to perform that task. Each subject's self-efficacy was expressed in terms of the number of tasks to which he or she had given a confidence rating above 19.

Treatment. The 10 subjects were then equated for fear rating and assigned to one of three conditions that varied in the level of efficacy they were to attain.

High level of efficacy was defined as a subject's judgment of being able to perform the last three items on the performance task—up to and including having the snake crawling around in their lap. Medium level of efficacy meant the judgment of being able to touch and lift the snake inside its cage, whereas low level was equated with the judgment of being able to approach the cage, look down at the snake, and place a hand near it, just short of physical contact.

A combination of enactive attainment and vicarious experience was used for efficacy induction. Each subject thus experienced both exposure to carefully managed success experiences and observation of a model successfully performing the task. Working with a snake that was different in shape and coloring from the one used during pretesting, a female experimenter first demonstrated coping strategies for the 18 graded tasks. The subjects were then helped to master each of these tasks by employing such training devices as breaking the task into smaller units, working jointly with the experimenter, and using protective aids, such as gloves.

When a subject had mastered a task the self-efficacy scale was again administered, and the induction procedure was terminated when the targeted level of self-efficacy (low, medium, or high) had been reached. At that point the procedures used during pretesting were repeated to assess the subject's fear level, and how closely she or he was able to approach the original snake.

Once the needs of the experiment had been met the subjects whose self-efficacy had been brought only to a low or medium level were given additional treatment until all had reached the high level of self-efficacy.

Treatment effects. The analysis of the data from this experiment showed that the higher the level to which a subject's perceived self-efficacy had been brought, the greater was his or her performance accomplishment. These results are depicted in Figure 7-1. Bandura et al. (1982) report that the probability of obtaining this ordering of performance attainments by chance is .01.

Equally impressive are the results regarding the subjects' self-reported fear. Here, the higher the self-perceived efficacy, the lower was the fear, both in anticipation of a task that had just been explained to them and in performance of the task itself. This relationship is reflected in Figure 7-2.

The results of this experiment lend strong support to the investigators' conclusion that perception of self-efficacy predicts how people are likely to behave and how much emotional arousal they will experience on specific tasks.

Although self-efficacy was the manipulated, independent variable in this experiment its causal role in bringing about the behavior change was not clearly established because the subjects had judged their self-efficacy *after* they had mastered a graded task and before embarking on the next one. This makes it conceivable that the self-efficacy judgment with respect to a task was influenced by the subject's experience with just having performed that task.

Self-Assessment, Self-Efficacy, and Self-Esteem

FIGURE 7-1 Mean intrasubject performance attainment at different levels of self-efficacy.

Adapted from Bandura, A., Reese, L., and Adams, N. E., 1982. Microanalysis of action and fear arousal as a function of differential levels of perceived self-efficacy. *Journal of Personality and Social Psychology*, 43, 5-21. Copyright 1982 by the American Psychological Association. Adapted by permission.

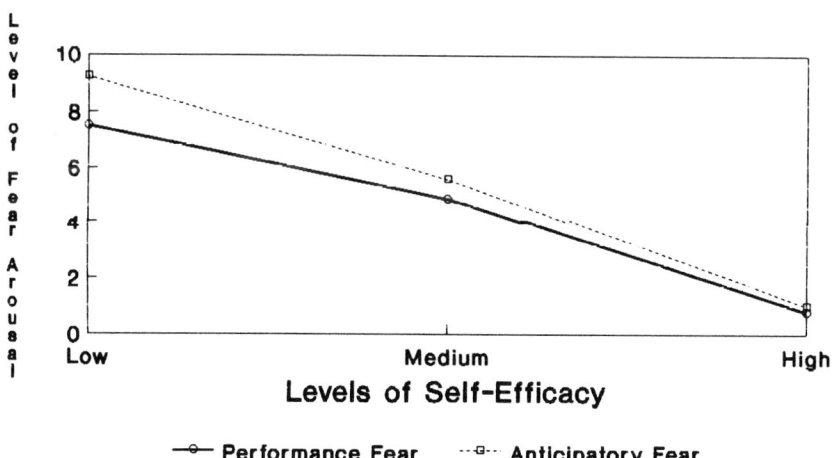

FIGURE 7-2 Mean intensity of fear arousal at various levels of self-efficacy.

From Bandura, A., Reese, L., and Adams, N. E., 1982. Microanalysis of action and fear arousal as a function of differential levels of perceived self-efficacy. *Journal of Personality and Social Psychology*, 43, 5-21. Copyright 1982 by the American Psychological Association. Reprinted by permission.

Vicarious Induction

To eliminate the direct experience with a task that is provided by the enactive attainment procedure, Bandura et al. (1982) conducted a second experiment in which they used only vicarious induction. In this procedure self-efficacy is modified solely by having a model demonstrate a graded series of strategies for coping with a feared task. The subjects thus have no direct contact with the object of their fear when they record their self-efficacy ratings. These judgments could therefore be based only on their observations of actions performed by the model.

The participants in this experiment were 14 women who suffered from an extreme fear of spiders. Except for the difference in the method of induction, the experimental procedures were essentially the same as those used in the snake study.

The results again showed that the higher the level of perceived self-efficacy to which a subject had been brought during the induction phase, the higher was her performance attainment during the posttest, which required actual handling of a spider. Anticipatory and performance fear were again negatively correlated with self-efficacy; the higher the latter, the lower the former. As in the first study, once the requirements of the experiment had been satisfied, all participants were given additional treatment until they achieved complete mastery of their fear. The investigators report that all departed maximally self-efficacious and fearless, but they unfortunately do not provide follow-up information regarding how their subjects fared in their daily lives.

With the potentially confounding factor of direct experience thus eliminated, Bandura (1986) seems justified in attributing the demonstrated reduction in fear and improvement in performance to the increased self-perceived efficacy he and his colleagues had brought about by the procedures they employed in their experiments (Bandura et al., 1982).

Confidence in Performance or in Outcome?

The self-efficacy scale used in the experiments just discussed asks subjects to indicate their level of confidence in being able to perform a given task. Several reviewers of self-efficacy theory have raised the question whether this confidence rating expresses subjects' confidence in their ability to perform the action the task requires or their confidence in arriving at the outcome to which that action presumably leads (Eastman & Marzillier, 1984; Kirsch, 1980; Maddux, Norton, & Stoltenberg, 1986).

Replying to this criticism Bandura (1984) points out that performance and outcome are distinctly different aspects of an action and that the assessment of perceived self-efficacy takes this into account. That assessment, he stresses, entails two steps. First the individuals are asked to identify the tasks they feel themselves able to perform and only for the tasks thus selected are they then asked to indicate their level of confidence in their ability to perform each of them. It is that confidence rating that represents the person's level of perceived self-efficacy, and it is that perception and not expectation of outcome that has an effect on the person's behavior.

An example may help to clarify this issue. Suppose that I live 4 miles from where I work. I know that if I were to walk these 4 miles I could get to my job. That is my knowledge of the outcome. It has nothing to do with self-efficacy, which involves the question whether I see myself as capable of walking that distance and the level of confidence I have in being able to do so. As Bandura (1984) put it, "One cannot conjure up outcomes without giving thought to what one is doing and how well one is doing it" (p. 232).

Widely Effective Intervention

Although modification of self-perceived efficacy was originally developed and tested with cases of fears and phobias (Bandura, 1982) it has since been applied and proven effective with a wide variety of human problems. Responding to a critique by Eastman and Marzillier (1984), Bandura (1984) refers to many studies in which the raised perception of self-efficacy was shown to improve a variety of detrimental or deleterious conditions. Among these are despondency and depression, deficient cognitive skills, lack of perseverance, and low physical endurance. Some particularly impressive demonstrations of the power of self-efficacy induction are cited hereafter. Taken together, these studies provide persuasive support for Bandura's (1984) assertion that perceived self-efficacy is a significant mediator of psychological functioning.

Pain Tolerance

One source of support for this assertion comes from studies that show the direct relationship between high perception of self-efficacy and the ability to tolerate pain. Thus, Holroyd et al. (1984) demonstrated the relationship between reduction of chronic tension headaches and the perception of being able to control them. Manning and Wright (1983) found that the higher their perceived self-efficacy, the longer women were able to tolerate labor pain before requesting medication and the less medication they required. Shoor and Holman (1984) documented that coping with the chronic pain of arthritis is influenced by the patient's percepton of being able to exercise some influence over that pain.

In controlled laboratory studies in which pain is created by asking volunteers to immerse a hand or arm in ice water Litt (1988); Bandura, Cioffi, Taylor, and Brouillard (1988); and Bandura, O'Leary, Taylor, Gauthier, and Gossard (1987) showed that the higher the induced self-efficacy, the longer subjects are able to tolerate the pain. Bandura et al. (1987, 1988) found this effect to be mediated by the release of endogenous opioids, for the stronger the perceived self-efficacy to reduce pain, the greater was the opioid activation.

Smoking Cessation

Self-control. People who wish to stop smoking frequently find that this habit is difficult to break, and many methods have been advocated that are designed to deal with this adamant problem. It is here that perceived self-efficacy is related to what is popularly referred to as "self-control." What people mean by self-control is the ability to exert control over one's own behavior, but as many who have attempted to use self-control have found, such control is difficult to achieve. What seems to be required is not self-control, whatever that might be, but the perceived ability to control oneself—in other words, the perceived self-efficacy of self-control.

Studies of smoking cessation bear this out. For example, Condiotte and Lichtenstein (1981), who offered a behaviorally based smoking cessation program, found that perceived self-efficacy predicted months in advance which participants would relapse, how soon they would relapse, and even the specific conditions under which the first slip would occur.

What is more, perceived self-efficacy at the end of treatment predicted how the participants would handle a relapse, should one occur. The highly self-efficacious participants regained control following a slip. The less self-efficacious would, following a slip, manifest a marked decrease in perceived self-efficacy and relapse completely. Similar results have been reported by DiClemente (1981) and by McIntyre, Mermelstein, and Lichtenstein (1983).

Self-Efficacy and Self-Concept

High Self-Efficacy

Studies on self-perceived efficacy have shown that people who see themselves as capable, who have a high sense of self-efficacy, think, feel, and behave differently from those whose perceived self-efficacy is low. Those with high self-efficacy will see difficult tasks as challenges to be mastered rather than as threats to be avoided. When they encounter difficulty, rather than give up and feel discouraged, they will increase their effort and feel exhilarated. Such people attribute failure to insufficient effort, convinced that had they tried harder they would have succeeded. For this reason, their sense of self-efficacy generally remains unaffected by failure, whereas it is strengthened by success.

Low Self-Efficacy

People with a low sense of self-efficacy, distrust their capabilities and shy away from difficult tasks. In fact, their evaluation of the difficulty level of a task tends to be exaggerated. They will set themselves lower goals than do those with a high sense of self-efficacy; when they encounter difficulties they give up quickly and blame their failure on their own inadequacies. Slow to recover even their initially low esteem of their own capacities, such people tend to feel apathetic, anxious, and depressed. In that manner, perception of self-efficacy is linked to a person's emotions.

Self-Efficacy and Motivation

Self-efficacy is also related to motivation. The person with a high sense of self-efficacy will look for challenges, and work long and hard to meet them. The person with a low sense of self-efficacy will try to avoid challenges, make relatively little effort, and give up trying when difficulties arise. All of this may influence a person's level of education, choice of occupation, and leisure activities; these, in turn, affect whom he or she will have as associates, friends, and a marriage partner. Inasmuch as all of these contribute to a person's self-appraisal, self-perception, and self-esteem, the perception of self-efficacy can well be construed as central to the person's self-concept.

SELF-ESTEEM

Private Matters

Self-esteem, as we pointed out earlier, has to do with one's sense of worth. It is based on a personal evaluative judgment that one makes about oneself, and is thus a private and very subjective matter. If a man were asked the self-concept question, "Who are you?" and he responded that he is a 35-year-old, competent lawyer, the devoted father of two pretty girls, and a registered Republican one could check the veracity of every one of these statements. Could one do the same, however, if he were asked the self-esteem question, "How do you feel about yourself?" Suppose he answered that he does not like himself, feels like an impostor, a failure who is unworthy of the respect his family and friends show him. He was asked how he felt and he answered, but there is no direct way of checking whether he told us the truth because the statements he made do not deal with objective facts, but with subjective feelings. Does he "really" feel that way? Once again we are faced with the question of the validity of statements people make about themselves.

Validity. There are indirect, inferential ways of finding out whether self-esteem statements are valid. For example, we expect that a man who states that he does not like himself and sees himself as a failure reflects these feelings in how he acts, looks, and carries himself. We expect him to be depressed because low self-esteem and depression are correlated. Recall that when Jones et al. (1981)

needed a group of people with low self-esteem they identified them by their high scores on a depression scale.

Aside from the question whether people are telling the truth when reporting on their self-esteem, there is also the more abstruse issue of whether the words people use to describe their feelings correspond to what they actually feel. Given that we have no means for assessing people's feelings other than indirectly by observing their words and actions, this question about the validity of self-esteem statements may well be unanswerable. Conceivably, as Nisbett and Wilson (1977) suggested, people are unable to give a full and accurate report of what is going on inside their heads.

Many scholars who have written about self-esteem (e.g., Epstein, 1973; Harter, 1983; Wylie 1974) struggled with the twin problems of how to define self-esteem operationally and how to establish the validity of self-esteem reports. Inasmuch as one is dealing with people's private, subjective judgments of their worth it may well be necessary to settle for the phenomenalistic definition that self-esteem is what a person reports it to be and to use such reports as data for one's studies. That, indeed, is how most investigators of self-esteem have been proceeding.

Components of Self-Esteem

Global and specific. In responding to the question, "How do you feel about yourself?" a man might say, "Pretty good" and let it go at that. The person who posed the question may be satisfied with such a global answer. To obtain a more specific answer she would have to ask on what that man based his response. He might then say that he sees himself as a well-to-do, successful farmer who is able to fix his own machinery. To that he might add that he is smart, good-looking, popular, honest, law-abiding, and the best poker player in town. In saying all of this the farmer reveals that, in addition to his global self-esteem ("I feel pretty good about myself"), he also has several more specific forms of self-esteem.

For many years theorists, such as Coopersmith (1959), Epstein (1973), and Rosenberg (1979), have debated whether self-esteem is a single, global entity; whether it is represented by several, specific aspects; and whether specific aspects, if they exist, are summed to form the global self-esteem.

As Harter (1983) has pointed out, these possibilities are not mutually exclusive. The issue is best resolved by recognizing that, like our farmer, people can make a self-esteem statement that expresses a global assessment of themselves, but that they are also aware and can speak of specific forms of self-esteem. It is unlikely, however, that global self-esteem is simply the sum of specific self-esteem statements because these may well carry different weights or values. Thus, the farmer's pride in being able to fix his own machinery may contribute more to his overall self-esteem than his knowledge that he is the best poker player in town or vice versa. Why did he mention his mechanical skill, however, and not his competence in driving his truck? Which of the many aspects of a person come to play a role in her or his self-esteem?

Dimensions of Self-Esteem

Historical and cultural relativity. Which aspects of people's life become a part of their self-esteem is very likely a function of their personal values, and of the place and time in which they live. In our own time in North American society, for example, much emphasis is placed on physical appearance, and it is an important aspect of most people's self-esteem. Asked how we feel about ourselves, most of us, like the imaginary farmer, will sooner or later say something positive or negative about our looks. This has probably not always been the case, nor is it necessarily the case in all parts of the world. It is important to keep this relativity in mind as we examine the four categories into which the most frequently mentioned aspects of self-esteem can be grouped. These categories or dimensions are competence, worth, power, and acceptance.

Competence

This dimension includes the attributes most people will think of first when they are asked to talk about how they assess themselves. They will tell about their skills and achievements, what they do well and what they have accomplished. (Eventually they may also report on what they do poorly and where they have failed.) Skill, of course, is found in many areas. There are physical skills, cognitive skills, artistic skills, and interpersonal skills. Achievement also comes in many varieties. It can be in scholarship, artistic performance, business, sports, workmanship, finance, the professions, or waging war. Any of these may enter into someone's self-esteem.

Worth

Once labeled "virtue" (Coopersmith, 1959), this dimension includes such qualitative aspects of the person as her or his moral and ethical standards, physical appearance, and personality traits. In talking about his competencies a man would describe what he is good at, whereas in speaking of his worth he would tell us how good he is and how well he looks. Provided he viewed his worth as positive, he would therefore mention that he is honest and reliable (moral values), outgoing and imaginative (traits), and tall and handsome (physical appearance).

It is noteworthy that we tend to praise people when their competencies are high and to blame them when they are low. We view competencies to be a matter of personal responsibility; people who fall short of our expectations are urged to try harder, study further, or practice longer. In the case of worth, however, we tend to admire rather than praise people for their positive qualities and not to hold them responsible when they lack these. People who do not possess good moral values, have undesirable traits, or have an unattractive appearance are more likely to arouse pity than disappointment. We seem to be saying that these aspects are not qualities that people are responsible for or can do much to change.

Power

This dimension encompasses those aspects of self-perception that have to do with a person's ability to control and influence others (Epstein, 1973). On the basis of her research Harter (1983) adds the sense of control over the direction one's life is taking. The chief executive officer of a large corporation might thus include in her self-image that she is in charge of and responsible for 10,000 employees, and that she alone can decide what she wants to do and when she does it.

Power may well be a derivative of competence and worth. Thus, a woman may owe her powerful executive position to her cognitive and interpersonal competence, and to such aspects of her worth as the traits of dependability, perseverance, and responsibility.

Acceptance

This dimension is a function of how others react to a person, whether they like, respect, or admire her or him. "I am well liked" is a self-esteem statement that falls in this dimension. It too is a dimension that seems be a derivative of others. After all, people are more likely to accept those who have skills that they admire and traits they consider worthy of praise than those who lack skills, have achieved little, and exhibit unappealing traits or appearances.

Tests of Self-Esteem

Earlier we had suggested that one might elicit statements about a person's self-esteem by asking, "How do you feel about yourself?" and requesting more detailed information following a response of a global nature. Investigations of self-esteem, however, rarely employ such an open-ended interview because it takes too much time and is difficult to score. Such research usually makes use of paper-and-pencil questionnaires that can be group-administered and machine-scored (Coopersmith, 1959; Harter, 1983; Helmreich, Stapp, & Ervin, 1974; Rosenberg, 1983).

There is a somewhat circular relationship among such tests and the four, inductively derived dimensions of self-esteem just outlined. The tests are often based on some or all of these dimensions. When the results of such a test are later subjected to a factor analysis, that statistical technique tends to confirm the existence of the dimensions. That is not surprising, of course, for as has often been pointed out, what a factor analysis can bring out heavily depends on what was put in.

A way out of this circularity is to obtain from a large and representative sample answers to open-ended interview questions that have to do with self-esteem. A factor analysis conducted on these answers might then deductively identify the dimensions of which self-esteem is composed. The development of the Piers-Harris Children's Self-Concept Scale (Piers & Harris, 1976) is a rare instance in which that procedure has been used.

Cognition and Affect

As we have seen, self-esteem is an opinion one holds about one's own worth or value. It usually is a firmly held opinion that is maintained over time and relatively resistant to change. Like other opinions that entail matters of worth and value, self-esteem has both cognitive and affective components.

Let us assume that an item on a self-esteem test asks about a man's achievement in his chosen occupation. Like any other item on such a test, whether it deals with competence, worth, power, or acceptance, this one calls for a self-evaluation, no matter how it is worded. People who are taking this test are being asked to indicate what they judge the level of their achievement to be. The question implies a range; most such tests do, in fact, provide a scale (ranging from high or good to low or bad) on which the answer can be recorded.

A self-evaluation calls for a judgment, a cognitive response. In addition, however, and without explicitly asking about it, the question elicits an emotional response. Remember that we phrased the question about global self-esteem as, "How do you *feel* about yourself?" An answer like, "I feel good about myself" communicates positive affect. More specific questions, such as those about a person's competence, though not asking about feelings, elicit these nevertheless. When a woman talks about her skill as a surgeon it is unlikely that she does so without experiencing pride or some other positive emotion. In view of this it is curious that investigators of self-esteem have done little to study the affective aspects of self-esteem (Harter, 1983).

Judging Self-Esteem

Standards

Social comparison. Self-esteem entails evaluative judgments of oneself. To make such judgments one must have a frame of reference, a standard on which the judgments can be based (Marsh & Parker, 1984). Whether I say that I am an average student, a poor salesman, a handsome man, or an excellent chess player, I am invariably implying that I have a basis for judging the qualities of students, the success of salesmen, the physical attractiveness of men, or the caliber of chess players. Implied in any of these judgments is a comparison with other people, what Festinger (1954) called a social comparison.

Standards on which comparisons are based are often expressed in numbers. Thus, students are compared by grade-point averages; baseball players by runs batted in; gamblers by the amount of money they won. Even physical attractiveness or gymnastic skill, though not usually evaluated by quantitative standards, are quantified by points awarded by judges when individuals have entered a contest.

Relative standards. Whether the focus of self-esteem is on competence, worth, power, or acceptance the standards by which we judge ourselves always depend on the reference group being used, on who it is with whom we are comparing ourselves. We encountered this relativity in Chapter 4 in connection with the fishpond problem.

Take a student who knows that she is among the top 2% of her high-school class. With respect to her academic achievement her self-esteem should be very positive. After graduating she enters college where most of her peers are people who had also been in the top 2% of their respective high-school classes. Where once she had little difficulty staying at the top she now must struggle to keep up. What happens to her self-esteem? Again we face the question of stability or malleability. This time, however, we only have indirect evidence on which to base an answer because the stability of self-esteem has usually been explored in the studies investigating the self-concept in general.

Stability of self-esteem. Results of longitudinal research have revealed rather remarkable stability of certain personality characteristics over periods as long as 40 years (Block, 1971; Eichorn, Clausen, Haan, Honzik, & Mussen, 1981). Measures used in these studies often included attributes related to self-esteem. Among these were self-confidence, self-satisfaction, ambition, dependability, and independence as well as interest and pride in cognitive abilities. All were reported to show stability over time.

The judgment of one's own worth, self-esteem, is a central aspect of a person's self-concept. As such people attach great value to their self-esteem and, as we will learn in the next chapter, they seek to enhance it and to defend it against threat.

8

Self-Handicapping

STRATEGY FOR SELF-PROTECTION

We saw in the previous chapter that some people seem to select a task because it serves their need for self-enhancement. A somewhat different conceptualization suggests that task choice may be based on the need to protect one's self-esteem regardless of whether the outcome is success or failure. This strategy, known as self-handicapping, was first described by Jones and Berglas (1978).

Preparation for Success or Failure

Underlying self-handicapping is the hedonistic principle that makes people desire to enhance pride in case of success and avoid shame in case of failure. As in Weiner's (1986) elaboration of the motivational theory of task choice people are seen as attributing outcome to internal or external causes, but in addition they seek to enhance potential success and to discount potential failure by self-handicapping strategies to protect their self-esteem.

Success or failure on a task inevitably tells the individual something about his or her competence. This is what Trope (1980) called the diagnosticity of a task. Jones and Berglas (1978) suggest "that we sometimes do things to *avoid* diagnostic information about our own characteristics and capacities" (p. 200), and they express doubt that "people always want to know precisely who they are and exactly what they are capable of accomplishing at their best" (p. 200).

Examples of self-handicapping. Jones and Berglas (1978) maintain that the diagnosticity of task outcome can be reduced or obscured by various self-handicapping strategies. One example of such a strategy is the student who, facing an important examination, stays up studying most of the preceding night. If she then does poorly on the test she can attribute this to having been tired, thereby weakening the alternative explanation that would impugn her ability and threaten her self-esteem. On the other hand, if she does well on the test it will enhance her self-esteem because she did so well despite having been so tired. Similar strategies involve not exerting maximum effort in task performance or drinking alcohol before or during a potentially diagnostic task. The onus of failure can then be reduced by "I wasn't really trying," or "I was half drunk," which imply that one is capable of far better performance if one but tried or had been sober. The same self-handicapping strategy would enhance the triumph of success because it permits the person to think or say, "I did that well despite the fact that I didn't try very hard [or could hardly see straight]."

What these various strategies have in common is that by externalizing the cause of poor performance and internalizing the cause of good performance individuals protect or enhance their self-esteem. Jones and Berglas (1978) had speculated that self-handicapping strategies would be employed particularly by individuals who have a precarious sense of their own competence.

Test of the Theory

A study conducted by Strube and Roemmele (1985) put this formulation to test. At the same time it examined for which type of individuals each of two views on the determinants of task choice—uncertainty reduction or self-enhancement—is applicable.

Method. Strube and Roemmele (1985) used the Janis-Field Feelings of Inadequacy Scale (Robinson & Shaver, 1973) to assess self-esteem and the Self-Handicapping Scale developed by Jones and Rhodewalt (1980). On the basis of the scores on these tests they then assigned each of their subjects to one of the following four groups:

  A: High self-esteem, low self-handicapping
  B: High self-esteem, high self-handicapping
  C: Low self-esteem, low self-handicapping
  D: Low self-esteem, high self-handicapping

The 34 women and 30 men who participated in this investigation had been recruited for what they thought was a study of personality correlates of cognitive abilities. On arriving at the laboratory and after the administration of the measures of self-esteem and self-handicapping, they were presented with a detailed description of what was purported to be a cognitive abilities test. This description included information about the "extensive development of the test and its four forms."

For each of these forms the subjects were shown the distribution of scores supposedly obtained by individuals with high and low cognitive abilities. By varying the amount of overlap of high and low scores in the distributions for each of the four forms of the "test" the investigators manipulated their presumed diagnostic sensitivity, thereby creating high and low levels of diagnosticity for success and failure.

On the basis of these descriptions the subjects were to rate on 7-point scales the attractiveness of each form and the degree to which they would like to take each of the versions. After that they were asked to indicate which of the four forms of the test they wanted to take. These subjects thus chose a test that they actually expected to be given. After they had made their choice, however, the experimenter terminated the task and explained the need for the deception.

Predictions. Strube and Roemmele (1985) predicted that self-enhancement would be most pronounced in individuals with low self-esteem who showed a tendency toward self-esteem protection. Such persons, they believed, would be more likely to doubt their chances of success and therefore be more afraid of having their incompetence exposed. They should therefore find most attractive a task that has high diagnosticity of success, thus maximizing potential pride, and low diagnosticity of failure, thus minimizing potential shame. These subjects were thus expected to base their choice on the need for self-enhancement. Note that this choice would be roughly analogous to self-handicapping because, having obtained a low score, they could rationalize it by blaming the test's low diagnosticity, saying something like, "It was not a good test."

Subjects with high self-esteem and low self-handicapping needs, conversely, were expected to prefer tasks that are maximally informative, having high diagnosticity for both success and failure. These subjects, in other words, were expected to base their choice on the need for self-assessment. Strube and Roemmele (1985) thus predicted that they would find both self-enhancement and self-assessment, but that each would be exhibited by different types of individuals.

Results. Of the questions the subjects had answered, the one asking which of the test forms they wanted to take is of greatest relevance to the issue of task choice that is here under discussion. Figure 8-1 shows that the results of this aspect of the Strube and Roemmele (1985) study were generally in line with their predictions.

An inspection of Figure 8-1 reveals that the test version chosen by the subjects who were high in self-esteem and low in self-handicapping (Group A) was predominantly the one that was highly diagnostic of both success and failure. The other versions were of relatively little interest to them. Their choice was overwhelmingly determined by a desire for self-assessment, and they showed little need to protect their self-esteem by choosing test versions of low diagnosticity.

In contrast, the low self-esteem, high self-handicapping subjects (Group D) much preferred to take the test that, although highly diagnostic of success, promised to be of low diagnosticity for failure. Alternatively, this group selected

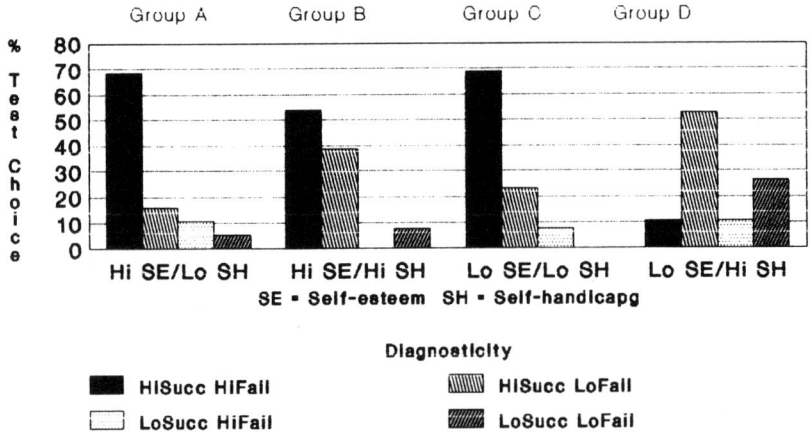

FIGURE 8-1 Diagnosticity, self-esteem, self-handicapping, and test form choice.

From Strube, M. J., and Roemmele, L. A., 1985. Self-enhancement, self-assessment, and self-evaluative task choice. *Journal of Personality and Social Psychology, 49,* 981–993. Copyright 1985 by the American Psychological Association. Adapted by permission.

the version of the test that was of low diagnosticity for both success and failure. That group's need for self-esteem protection by self-handicapping clearly dominated their choice. Unlike the subjects in Trope's (1980) research (see Chapter 7) who, in their abstract choices, valued self-assessment more than self-enhancement, the Strube and Roemmele subjects were willing to forego learning about themselves when the threat to self-esteem was made potent by their choosing a test they expected actually to take.

Turning now to the remaining two groups (B and C) we find that the choices of the subjects with low self-esteem and low self-handicapping (Group C) were very similar to the choices registered by Group A. Both selected the highly diagnostic version of the test in preference over the other versions, although Group C was not quite as unequivocal in its choice as Group A in that 23.1% of the former showed a preference for the version that was highly diagnostic for success but of low diagnosticity for failure. Note that Group C totally rejected the version with low diagnosticity for both success and failure, and made minimal use of the low diagnosticity for success and high diagnosticity for failure.

Group B also had little or no use for these two versions. For that group the version with all-around high diagnosticity was the most attractive, but one also finds that many members of that group selected the version with high diagnosticity for success and low diagnosticity for failure. This shows that for these subjects concern for self-esteem protection was not a negligible determinant of task choice.

Individual differences. On the whole, the results of the study Strube and Roemmele (1985) conducted did demonstrate that self-evaluative task choice is, in part, a function of individual differences. Different considerations guide different people to different choices. At the same time, this study throws light on the use of the self-handicapping strategy. As another look at Figure 8-1 reveals, the test forms most frequently chosen by all four types of subjects were those that were highly diagnostic of either success and failure or of success alone. Test forms of low diagnosticity of success were rejected by all but the low self-esteem, high self-handicapping group. The latter seems to have had an especially pronounced need to prepare a rationale for the failure that their low self-esteem led them to expect.

It stands to reason that in deciding which test of cognitive abilities they want to take most people will select the one with the highest degree of diagnosticity; the one that could tell them whether their abilities are high or low. Only the most insecure individuals would want to take a test that was known to lack the capacity to identify either good or poor performance. It would be better not to take any test at all. If that option had been available to them these subjects would probably have chosen it.

Variables in Self-Handicapping

Gender. The inverse relationship between level of self-esteem and the use of self-handicapping strategies reported by Strube and Roemmele (1985) was also found by Harris and Snyder (1986), but the latter also discovered a gender difference for which Strube and Roemmele had not analyzed their data. Harris and Snyder (1986) reported that the men in their sample who expressed uncertainty about their self-esteem resorted to self-handicapping in preparation for a task ostensibly designed to assess intellectual ability. Unlike the men, women who were uncertain about their self-esteem did not resort to self-handicapping. This gender difference may reflect a cultural bias that makes men more acutely aware of the personal and social implications of failure—hence, more inclined to resort to the self-protective rationale of a handicap when presented with an intellectual evaluation. That similar gender differences in the propensity to use self-handicapping have also been found in other studies (Rhodewalt & Davison, 1986; Shepperd & Arkin, 1989b) seems to lend support to this speculation.

Nature of task. Gender is not the only variable that has been found to play a moderating role in self-handicapping. Shepperd and Arkin (1989a), citing their own and other investigators' studies, enumerate several other variables. Among these are the nature of the task, whether it is introduced as having diagnosticity, and whether it is supposed to reveal something that is important to the subject. It also appears that people will not resort to self-handicapping when they are in an environment where a handicapping condition, such as a distracting noise, is already present. In fact, when such a handicapping condition is present people tend to expend more effort on an intellectually challenging task than when no such condition exists (Shepperd & Arkin, 1989a).

Is Self-Handicapping Intentional?

In studies conducted by Shepperd and Arkin (1989a, 1989b) self-handicapping took the form of choosing to have interfering music played while taking a test that ostensibly predicted academic and career success. In line with the self-handicapping hypothesis subjects who did poorly on that test were then able to blame their failure on the music. This research method makes self-handicapping appear to be a conscious, intentional move that people make before undertaking an evaluative task. There is the question whether this is what Jones and Berglas (1978) meant by self-handicapping strategies when they introduced that concept, giving as examples of self-handicapping the use of alcoholic beverages and the reduction of effort they called underachievement.

Do people really say to themselves, "I'll have a couple of drinks before I take this test so that, if I don't do well, I can blame it on the liquor," or "I won't work very hard on this test so that I have an excuse in case I fail"? Although the use of the term *strategies* seems to suggest just such a scheming approach, it is unlikely that people make such blatantly intentional use of self-handicapping. What is more likely is that the insecure, socially anxious individuals who resort to self-handicapping to protect their uncertain self-esteem do so because this is an approach that paid off for them in the past and that they have thus learned to use whenever they face a challenging task. In fact, Jones and Berglas (1978) offer etiological speculations in which they invoke child-rearing and reinforcement histories, suggesting that their formulation entails a far less conscious, less intentional process than the experimental paradigm of Shepperd and Arkin (1989a, 1989b) was able to explore.

FUNCTION OF SELF-HANDICAPPING

Private and Public Effects

Following the usage found in the literature we have spoken of the self-handicapping strategy as serving the function of maximizing potential pride while minimizing potential shame in the service of protecting self-esteem. Because this terminology entails both internal, private and external, public orientations it bears closer examination.

Pride and shame. Self-esteem, as our earlier discussion revealed, has to do with how a person evaluates himself or herself. It is a personal, inner feeling that is based on the individual's experiences of successes and failures in the world of people and objects. In that sense it is appropriate to speak of the need to maximize potential pride, for pride is one of the feelings that are relevant to self-esteem. I can feel proud about having done well on a task, and I might feel even prouder had I undertaken that task under a self-imposed handicap. Self-handicapping can thus enhance my self-esteem. This can be a very private matter that requires no audience, although impressing others by doing well under a handicap can also contribute to one's self-esteem, especially if these others come forth with applause, admiration, or praise.

What about shame, however? Feeling ashamed is also an inner experience, and repeated experiences of shame will affect one's self-esteem. Unlike pride, however, shame always involves an audience. People do not feel ashamed at having failed a task they undertook in the privacy of their own room. Under these circumstances one may feel angry with oneself or angry at the task, but not ashamed. Only when other people witness or learn about our failure are we likely to feel ashamed. For this reason self-handicapping seems to lack purpose when it comes to undertaking in private a task at which one is likely to fail.

Self-Protection or Impression Management?

Given these considerations it appears important when doing research on the self-handicapping strategy to include the public-private dimension we encountered in our discussion of self-consciousness (see Chapter 5). Kolditz and Arkin (1982) did just that. The basic question these investigators asked was whether self-handicapping is a form of self-presentation, designed to manage the impressions made on others, or whether it is primarily designed to protect and enhance the person's perception of his or her own competence.

Drugs and Test Performance

Following a procedure that had been used in a study by Berglas and Jones (1978), but which had led to somewhat ambiguous results, Kolditz and Arkin (1982) informed their 64 college-age, male subjects that the study in which they were to participate dealt with the effect of two kinds of drugs on intellectual performance. One of these drugs (both of which were in fact placebos) was described as facilitating, the other as disrupting intellectual performance. The performance test, which was described as discriminating at the uppermost levels of intellectual potential, required the solution of anagrams and the completion of progressions.

Three Variables

Their research design permitted the investigators to manipulate three binary variables: The contingency of success, the privacy of the test results, and the privacy of the drug choice.

Contingency of success. This variable involved the subjects' knowledge of how to solve the test problems successfully. To manipulate the contingency of success Kolditz and Arkin (1982) informed all subjects that they would be taking two versions of the test, one before and one after the ingestion of one of the drugs. They then gave each subject the pretest.

This test consisted of two easily solved sample questions, followed by the 20-item test itself. For the contingent condition 16 of these 20 items were soluble, and 4 of them were insoluble; for the noncontingent condition this ratio was reversed: 16 were insolvable and 4 solvable. The test was scored immediately after completion, and all subject were individually told that they had done exceptionally well, having achieved one of the highest scores ever recorded.

The subjects in the contingent group, having worked primarily on easy, soluble problems presumably knew how to approach this test so as to be able to repeat their splendid performance on the posttest. They were certain about their abilities. The subjects in the noncontingent group, on the other hand, who had worked mainly on insoluble problems were left not knowing what they would have to do to repeat their impressive performance on the anticipated posttest. That, presumably, left them uncertain about their abilities.

Privacy of test results. The second variable concerned the manner in which the results of the posttest were to be handled. In the private condition the subjects were assured that neither the experimenters nor anyone else on the college campus would have access to their test scores. They were to place their answer sheets into a large, stamped, and addressed envelope that they themselves were to mail to the out-of-town pharmaceutical company that was ostensibly sponsoring the research. In the public condition the subjects were led to expect that the experimenter would score the posttest in their presence and, as in the pretest, tell them the result immediately.

Privacy of drug choice. This variable dealt with whether the choice of the drug and its dosage was to occur in public or private. The choice was between the performance-enhancing and performance-debilitating drugs, each of which was available at five dosage levels. In the public condition the subject chose and ingested what he presumed to be the drug in the presence of the experimenter. In the private condition the experimenter left the room while the subject made his choice and swallowed the capsule he had selected. To assure complete privacy the subject was instructed to seal the remaining capsules in an envelope that was ostensibly to be mailed to the drug company.

The experiment ended once the subject had made that choice. There was no posttest. Moreover, the experimenter retrieved the envelope with the leftover "medication" to ascertain which capsule the subject had chosen. As the ethical principles for research with human subjects demand, the reason for this deception was explained to all subjects in the course of a thorough debriefing.

Research Design

Recall that the question the experimenters were investigating was whether self-handicapping serves the personal function of protecting one's self-esteem or whether its primary function is the social one of impression management aimed at presenting oneself to others in a favorable light. Underlying this question is the assumption that people are most likely to resort to self-handicapping, whichever its function, when they are uncertain of their ability.

The variable "contingency versus noncontingency of success" had been designed to manipulate the subject's level of certainty about his competence for that certainty depends on knowing what aspect of one's performance led to the successful outcome.

The variable "private versus public posttest results" had been aimed at discriminating between the functions of self-esteem protection and self-presentation because self-presentation can only be involved in self-handicapping if one expects the results of one's efforts to become publicly known.

The variable "private versus public drug choice" was also related to the self-protection versus self-presentation question. Kolditz and Arkin (1982) had reasoned that "when subjects make their drug choice in total privacy, their choice of a performance-inhibiting drug cannot serve as a self-presentation strategy" (pp. 494-495). That strategy can only be served when the drug choice is public and the subject expects that the test results will also be public so that poor performance could be blamed on the debilitating drug.

The combinations of their three variables enabled Kolditz and Arkin (1982) to form eight groups of eight subjects each and to expose each group to a different condition under which to choose between the facilitating and the debilitating drug in anticipation of the posttest. The conditions were as follows:

A: Noncontingent success, public drug choice, public posttest results
B: Noncontingent success, private drug choice, private posttest results
C: Noncontingent success, public drug choice, private posttest results
D: Noncontingent success, private drug choice, public posttest results
E: Contingent success, public drug choice, public posttest results
F: Contingent success, private drug choice, private posttest results
G: Contingent success, public drug choice, private posttest results
H: Contingent success, private drug choice, public posttest results

Predictions and Outcome

Based on the preceding reasoning the investigators predicted that the debilitating drug would be chosen most frequently by the subjects who were uncertain of their competence (noncontingent success), made their drug choice in public, and expected to receive the test results in public. The subjects who would choose the debilitating drug least frequently were expected to be those in the noncontingent success group who made their drug choice in private and expected to receive the test results in private.

These predictions received strong support from the results of the study. The findings for the eight experimental groups are shown in Table 8-1. In this table "contingent pretest success" refers to the condition where most of the problems on which subjects worked had been soluble so that they were able to attribute their success to their own competence. In the "noncontingent pretest success" condition most problems had been insoluble so that, when the subjects were later told how very high their score was, they could have no idea what they had done to achieve this and would therefore remain uncertain of their competence. "Private posttest" and "public posttest" refer to whether or not the subject expected his test score to be available to the examiner. The percentages in the table refer to the proportion of subjects who chose the debilitating drug, and the numerals refer to the mean of the drug choice on a 9-point scale, where 1 represents the maximum dosage of the debilitating drug and 9 the maximum dosage of the facilitating drug.

Self-handicapping before a witness. As Table 8-1 shows, the only condition under which the largest proportion of subjects (75%) chose the performance-encumbering drug was when they were uncertain of their competence, chose the drug in the presence of the experimenter, and expected the experimenter to have access to their test score. This finding leads one to conclude that, under the conditions of this study, self-handicapping was used as a strategy of impression management. It is difficult to conceive of another explanation for the unlikely behavior of college students who, in anticipation of taking a test of cognitive ability, choose to take a drug that was described to them as encumbering their performance. One can imagine one of these subjects, not knowing whether he could repeat his outstanding pretest performance, preparing to be able to say when the experimenter announces the failure he expects on the posttest, "Well, you couldn't expect me to do well. You saw me take that performance-debilitating drug."

Another look at Table 8-1 reveals that the results for all but one of the other conditions follow the logic of this explanation. Subjects who were confident of their ability because they had worked on solvable problems selected the performance-enhancing drug, regardless of whether the choice or the test results were public or private. Even the subjects who had reason to doubt their competence chose the facilitating drug as long as the drug choice was made in private. It seems that there was no point in handicapping oneself when there was no one around who would know about it.

Exception. The only condition in which the result does not fit neatly into this framework is the one in which half of the subjects chose the debilitating drug in

TABLE 8-1 Drug Choice Under Different Experimental Conditions

	Private posttest		Public Posttest	
Pretest success	Private drug choice	Public drug choice	Private drug choice	Public drug choice
Contingent	7.8 0%	5.9 25%	7.5 12.5%	7.7 14%
Noncontingent	8.0 0%	5.0 50%	7.8 12.5%	3.1 75%

Note: In each cell the percentage indicates the proportion of subjects in that condition who chose the debilitating drug. The other number in the cell represents the mean level of the drugs selected, the scale ranging from the maximum debilitating drug (1) to the maximum facilitating drug (9). $N = 63$ (1 subject had to be dropped).
Adapted from Kolditz, T. A., and Arkin, R. M., 1982. An impression management interpretation of the self-handicapping strategy. *Journal of Personality and Social Psychology, 43*, 492–503. Copyright 1982 by the American Psychological Association. Adapted by permission.

the experimenter's presence while expecting the test scores to remain private. Recall that in the "private posttest" condition the subjects were told that after completing the posttest they would place their answer sheets into an envelope that they would mail to the drug company, which would score the test and notify them of the result. Kolditz and Arkin (1982) believe that this manipulation failed to be convincing and that half of the subjects were suspicious about this promised—but not certain—confidentiality, and therefore chose the debilitating drug when the examiner was present.

Further considerations. Two other points deserve mention before we leave the discussion of this intriguing study. The first concerns the assumption that self-handicapping serves not only to protect against the shame or blame of failure, but also to enhance the credit that may accrue from success ("I did that well despite the fact that I had taken the debilitating drug!").

Inasmuch as very few of the confident, success-expecting subjects in the contingent condition chose the debilitating drug, this formulation remained unsupported. It seems that for the subjects in this study avoiding possible blame was more important than enhancing potential credit.

The second point, which Kolditz and Arkin (1982) also made, is that characterizing self-handicapping as an impression-managing, self-presentational strategy "does not mean that it has no influence on attribution of self-competence" (p. 501). While convincing others that our failure was due to external circumstances and not to personal weakness, we may well also be convincing ourselves that we are not at fault. That, however, raises another question. Having taken the debilitating drug in the presence of another person and then doing poorly on a test, why does the person not feel to blame for knowingly having taken that drug in the first place? This question cannot be answered on the basis of this study because Kolditz and Arkin's subjects did not actually take the posttest.

Individual Differences

There is a limit to the number of variables that can be manipulated in any single study, and so it is that Kolditz and Arkin (1982) did not include the recurring question of individual differences in their investigation. Tice and Baumeister (1990), however, made that the main point of their experiments on self-handicapping. They reasoned that the level of an individual's self-esteem plays a role in his or her use of self-handicapping.

Self-handicapping, as pointed out earlier, serves the functions of shifting the blame from internal to external causes in case of failure and of enhancing one's credit in case of success. Moreover, self-handicapping can be used to protect or enhance one's own self-esteem, or it can be employed for the benefit of an audience whose judgment of one's competence is thereby being manipulated. The latter is referred to as impression management or self-presentation.

Self-Handicapping by Inadequate Preparation

We already know that people may resort to alcohol, drugs, or reduced effort to handicap themselves in anticipation of an assessment. The mode investigated by Tice and Baumeister (1990) was inadequate preparation before an evaluation. As had Kolditz and Arkin (1982) before them, Tice and Baumeister (1990) assumed—and the first of their experiments confirmed—that self-handicapping is most likely to be found under conditions where people are uncertain about the outcome of the evaluation because they do not know in what way their performance affects the results.

Paradoxical effect. Lack of preparation before an evaluation can have a paradoxical effect as far as self-handicapping is concerned. On the one hand, inadequate preparation is very likely to lead to poor results, but on the other hand these poor results can then be blamed on the inadequate preparation, thereby protecting one's self-esteem. Note, however, that extensive preparation entails a similar paradox.

Success after extensive practice is not especially impressive, either in terms of one's self-esteem or in the esteem of others. Yet if one fails despite much prior practice one proves oneself incompetent and loses from both perspectives. In deciding on how much to practice before the evaluation it is necessary that one choose between doing well on the impending test (but doing little to enhance one's self-esteem) and doing poorly on the test (but being able to protect one's self-esteem). The choice between practicing much or practicing little thus seems to depend on the level of self-esteem with which the person arrives at this choice. That is what Tice and Baumeister (1990) set out to investigate.

Playing "Roll Up." The task Tice and Baumeister (1990) used in their study was a commercially available game called Roll Up. This entails rolling a metal ball up an incline that is created by two metal rods that must be moved apart to move the ball to the top of the incline and into a hole. If the rods are moved too far apart the ball drops between them, and the player loses. Because practice improves one's performance the investigators used subjects who had little or no prior experience with this game.

After they had completed a test of self-esteem the subjects were told that they were participating in an experiment designed to investigate the effects of practice on different components of a nonverbal intelligence test that could predict postacademic success. Roll Up was presented as one of these components. The participants were told that they would be tested on this task for a 2-min period, given a chance to practice it, and then tested again for another 2 min.

After the first 2-min period (and regardless of the actual quality of their performance) half of the subjects were told that they had scored in the 96th percentile and that this was one of the highest scores the experimenter had seen. These subjects were thus fairly certain of how well they would be doing on the forthcoming, second test. The other half of the subjects was given no feedback regarding their performance. This left them uncertain about how well they would be doing on what they expected to be the real test.

All participants were then given the opportunity to practice the task for however long they wished. They were to let the experimenter know whenever they wanted to stop practicing and take the test a second time. During this practice period the experimenter sat quietly, holding a stopwatch and observing the subject.

Results. The analysis of the data from this experiment revealed the expected interaction between feedback and self-esteem in determining length of practice (self-handicapping). Under the outcome-uncertain condition where subjects had not been given feedback on their performance, those with high self-esteem practiced less than those with low self-esteem. Among the subjects who had received feedback of their success, only those high in self-esteem practiced longer. For some reason, about which the investigators speculate without coming to a conclusion, those low in self-esteem practiced less after hearing of their success than those who had received no feedback. As Tice and Baumeister (1990) conclude, the overall results "support the view that people with high self-esteem are most prone to engage in self-handicapping, particularly under conditions of high performance uncertainty" (p. 451).

Self-Presentation or Self-Protection?

A second experiment that Tice and Baumeister (1990) report in the same article dealt with the issue whether the self-handicapping of high self-esteem individuals under conditions of uncertainty is primarily self-presentational or whether it also serves to protect or enhance their self-esteem. To investigate this they focused on the presence or absence of the experimenter-observer during the practice session.

The method in this second experiment was the same as in the first, except that the subjects were given no pretest—hence, no feedback—and that for half the subjects the experimenter was not in the room while they practiced and (ostensibly) would not know how long they did so.

The results showed that the subjects practiced significantly longer in the private than in the public condition in which those with high self-esteem practiced significantly less than those with low self-esteem. Specifically, those with high self-esteem practiced for an average of 7½ min when they believed they were unobserved, whereas they practiced for an average of only 2 min when the experimenter was watching and timing them. The low self-esteem subjects practiced for an average of 6.4 min in the private condition and an average of 4¼ min in the public condition.

On the basis of these results Tice and Baumeister (1990) conclude that the shorter practice by the high self-esteem subjects in the public condition "was a strategic, self-presentational ploy designed to maximize attributional benefits of performance outcomes. Reduced practice would increase their credit for success and discount the implications of failure" (p. 456). At another point they conclude that "self-handicapping appears to be a self-presentational strategy used by highly confident people in uncertain situations" (p. 461).

The use of the words "ploy" and "strategy" in the passages just quoted again raises the question whether people choose self-handicapping in an intentional, conscious fashion because they recognize that it will help them in how they will see themselves or are seen by others at a later time. Given the fact that taking a debilitating drug or limiting useful practice while being observed should make one feel pretty stupid it would be surprising if high self-esteem individuals consciously weighed the consequences of their decision before choosing the distant advantage. This, like another issue to be raised later, remains to be investigated.

Alternative Explanation

Returning to the conclusion Tice and Baumeister (1990) drew from their study, consider the following situation. A college student who is taking the Introductory Psychology course goes to a psychology experiment in which a psychologist asks him or her to play with a new game that is introduced as a nonverbal measure of intelligence. It calls for moving a metal ball up an incline by manipulating two rods. When the rods are moved too far apart, the ball falls between them, and this is scored as a failure. Before taking the test the student has an opportunity to practice this game in the presence of the psychologist who is watching and timing the performance. Because the game requires considerable skill most of the initial trials result in failure.

Under this public condition many subjects in this study terminated the practice session sooner than did those who were practicing in private. Is self-handicapping for the purpose of increasing credit for success and discounting the implications of failure on a forthcoming test the only explanation for this reduced practice?

Tice and Baumeister (1990) considered the alternative explanation that "practicing in the presence of the experimenter made the subjects nervous or embarrassed, which caused them to stop practicing sooner in public than in private, in order to terminate an aversive experience" (p. 457). They then argued against this explanation, emphasizing that it was primarily the high self-esteem subjects who terminated the practice session early. They point out that on the Janis and Field (1959) scale of self-esteem that they had used, high self-esteem subjects show little concern for the opinions of others. For example, to an item that asks how rattled or flustered they usually get when other people are watching them as they try to win in a game or sport, high self-esteem subjects tend to respond with "very little." Tice and Baumeister (1990) contend that it should have been the low self-esteem subjects and not the high who resorted to shortened practice because the presence of the experimenter made them nervous. They point out that it is the people with low self-esteem who respond to items like the one just cited with "very much."

On the basis of this argument Tice and Baumeister (1990) reject the nervousness explanation in favor of one that centers on self-presentation. A more definitive explanation for their finding could have been attained had these investigators found out how their subjects felt while being watched or asked them why they did not practice longer.

Hypothetical versus actual situations. These investigators' reasoning was based on the assumption that there is no difference between responding on a paper-and-pencil test to questions about competing in front of spectators and actually being observed in a situation like the one Tice and Baumeister (1990) used for their public condition. Without impugning the validity of the Janis-Field test one can speculate that high self-esteem individuals, asked how they would react in a hypothetical situation such as trying to win at a game in front of spectators, would immediately assume that they are winning and respond with the equivalent of "It wouldn't bother me at all." To be certain of one's competence is, after all, the essence of high self-esteem.

These same individuals, placed in a situation in which a psychologist is watching while they are having difficulty mastering what looks like a simple game, might very well be bothered enough to terminate that aversive experience as soon as possible. The more certain one is of one's competence, the more likely one is to be sensitive to appearing inept before another person, particularly one as imposing and enigmatic as a psychologist is to many undergraduates.

Consider now the subjects with low self-esteem. On the Janis-Field scale they would rate themselves as easily rattled or flustered when trying to win a game in front of spectators. They see themselves as incompetent and are sure that they would be losing that game. In the public condition of the Roll Up game they do not expect to be doing well, and their performance confirms it. Moreover, such individuals fail frequently and thus are used to having others witness to their failures. Therefore, although they do not practice quite as long as they do under the private condition, they nonetheless continue their practice for considerably longer than their high self-esteem peers.

Self-handicapping? If this alternative explanation has merit—and the argument used by Tice and Baumeister (1990) fails to refute it—does it mean that this study failed to demonstrate a self-presentational motive on the part of high self-esteem persons? On the contrary, but the self-presentation may have been unrelated to self-handicapping.

Self-presentational considerations, concern about how we appear to others, would be playing an important role if the high self-esteem subjects' premature termination of the practice session were indeed due to their discomfort at being watched while experiencing repeated failure. In that case, the abbreviated practice would have had nothing to do with self-handicapping, a strategy people presumably employ so as to look good or less bad on a test they anticipate taking at a later time.

Unanswered Questions

There are several questions that none of the studies on self-handicapping have asked thus far. One of these is whether subjects who engage in what the investigator interprets as self-handicapping behavior actually use it for that purpose. When they are informed of their test results do subjects refer to the handicap to enhance the credit for success or to reduce the onus of failure?

Following the procedure Berglas and Jones (1978) had employed in their pioneering study, neither Tice and Baumeister (1990) nor Kolditz and Arkin (1982) had their subjects actually take the test they had been led to expect. What is needed to answer some of the questions here raised is a condition in which subjects actually take such a test, followed by feedback on their performance and an elicitation of their reactions. If self-handicapping has occurred, some of the subjects, when told they did poorly, should spontaneously say something like, "Well, no wonder. You saw how little I practiced," or, told they did very well, brag, "Wow and despite the fact that I had taken that debilitating drug."

Another question that remains to be investigated is the subjects' own explanation for choosing the debilitating drug or refraining from performance-enhancing practice. Berglas and Jones (1978) mention some self-report data they had gathered at the end of the first of their two experiments. These they saw as "of little help in confirming the theoretical reasoning about self-handicapping"

(p. 412). Only 2 out of 30 subjects who had chosen the debilitating drug explained their choice as related to defending themselves against anticipated failure. The rest either claimed that the choice was completely arbitrary or that they chose that drug to help the experimenter by making the experiment "work." Having been told that they had done exceedingly well on the pretest, the latter group reasoned that the performance-enhancing drug could do little to raise their near-perfect score and that the debilitating drug was therefore more likely to show the effect for which they thought the experimenter to be searching.

This rather sophisticated reasoning about a ceiling effect suggests that subjects in an experiment (and particularly college students recruited from psychology courses) may generate their own ideas about the purpose of the studies in which they are participating. Experimenters rarely elicit these ideas or take them into account in interpreting their findings. The instructions participants are given may at times contribute to their construing the experiment in ways that distort the results.

Take, for example, the instructions Berglas and Jones (1978) had given their subjects when they presented them with the choice between presumably debilitating and performance-enhancing drugs. The experimenter said (in part): "Select either drug or no drug at all according to your own personal preference, *according to what you will find most interesting*" (p. 409, emphasis added). This reference to "interesting" might well have aroused subjects' curiosity and biased an unknown number of the more venturesome of them to find out what a "debilitating" drug would do to their performance. Their choice of that drug might thus have had more to do with curiosity than with self-handicapping.

Conscious choice? Earlier we had raised the question whether the individuals who had been studied in the various experiments here discussed chose to engage in the self-handicapping behavior in an intentional, conscious fashion with an eye to protecting themselves against potential failure or to increase their credit for potential success.

In the research report that introduced the concept of self-handicapping Berglas and Jones (1978) proposed that "the basic purpose behind such strategic choices is the control of the actor's *self*-attributions of competence and control" (p. 407; emphasis in original). People, they wrote, may "deliberately run the risk of being out of control—through drug abuse, or inadequate preparation, or not trying—to protect their belief in ultimately being capable of control when it is really necessary, when the chips are down" (p. 407). These phrases clearly argue for an intentional, conscious choice on the part of those who engage in self-handicapping. Yet in their theoretical paper that followed the publication of their experiments Jones and Berglas (1978) had offered psychodynamic speculations about the childhood origins of self-handicapping that read as if they viewed the basis for this behavior as being other than conscious. This then is another question about self-handicapping that has to be added to those that remain to be answered.

Until data relevant to these questions become available self-handicapping remains a provocative formulation and all we can say with relative assurance is this: In situations in which they anticipate taking a test in which the result is uncertain high self-esteem subjects (and particularly men) will, when they are being observed, behave in a manner that is likely to handicap them in their test performance. Presumably, the reason for this puzzling, self-defeating behavior is that they wish to externalize the cause of probable failure. That, however, remains a presumption on the part of the experimenters.

Implicit in topics such as self-esteem, self-efficacy, and self-handicapping, which we have been discussing, is the idea that the person is focusing attention on his or her own thoughts, feelings, condition, or action. In the next chapter, we turn our attention once again to an explicit discussion of self-attention or its synonym, self-focused attention.

9

Self-Attention, Self-Prediction, and Self-Regulation

SELF-ATTENTION

Attention

Like other words that psychologists inherited from the natural language, attention means different things to different people. We shall here follow Berlyne (1970), who recommended that the term *attention* be employed only to denote the selection and processing of specific aspects of the stimuli available at the moment. Berlyne referred to this as *selective attention*. This selection can be peripheral, as by physical orientation such as eye movements, or central, as in the cognitive processing of one but not another incoming message (Broadbent & Gregory, 1964).

Among the multitude of stimuli potentially available to persons at any given moment are of course those that pertain to themselves.

Interchangeable terms. Self-focused attention "refers to attention directed internally toward thoughts and feelings as opposed to outwardly toward the external environment" (Ingram, Cruet, Johnson, & Wisnicki, 1988, p. 967). Thus defined, and as Wicklund and Hormuth (1981) proposed, self-focused attention is the same as objective self-awareness (Duval & Wicklund, 1972) and private self-consciousness (Carver & Scheier, 1981). It is not unusual to find these three expressions used interchangeably (e.g., Berkowitz, 1987). We have already devoted space to self-awareness and self-consciousness in Chapter 5 and the justification for discussing self-focused attention under a separate heading is to explore a literature that has evolved under that rubric.

Self-Focused Attention

Trait or State?

Different investigators of self-focused attention have approached that topic from two different perspectives, each of which invites a different research strategy. Not surprisingly, this has occasioned considerable debate and much confusion.

From one of these perspectives self-focused attention is viewed as a traitlike individual difference variable; consequently, people can manifest more or less of that characteristic. When this perspective is taken, research participants are assumed to arrive at the laboratory with much or little self-focused attention. One step in the investigator's research strategy therefore is to measure that characteristic to relate it to whatever other variable is to be examined. The measure often used for this purpose is the private self-consciousness subscale of the SCS developed by Fenigstein et al. (1975) and mentioned in Chapter 5.

The other viewpoint regarding self-focused attention is that it is a state that arises under certain conditions. The research strategy that follows from this stance is to expose the participants to an experimental condition that is designed to induce self-focused attention. The procedure typically used for this purpose is to have the participant work on a task in the presence of a mirror (e.g., Baldwin & Holmes, 1987; Berkowitz, 1987) or a television camera (Ingram et al., 1988). Here too it is the private self-consciousness subscale of the SCS (Fenigstein et al., 1975) that tends to be used to check whether the manipulation had the desired effect.

Perspectives on Self-Focused Attention

Trait Perspective

Success and failure. If self-focused attention is a traitlike characteristic, it ought to affect how a person reacts to success and failure. Because they pay more attention to their own contribution to the outcome of a task, people with a high level of self-focus presumably experience more pleasure from succeeding than someone with a low level of self-focus. Conversely, the high self-focus person should experience more displeasure than the low self-focus person after having failed at a task. Studies conducted by Scheier and his colleagues (Scheier & Carver, 1977; Scheier, Carver, & Gibbons, 1979) confirmed these assumptions.

Because high self-focus entails attention to such internal events as thoughts and feelings, whereas low self-focus finds expression in attention to external events one might expect a person with high self-focused attention to blame failure on him or herself, whereas someone with a low self-focused attention would be likely to blame the failure on something in the environment. Again there is research that supports this expectation (e.g., Duval & Wicklund, 1973; Fenigstein & Levine, 1984; Ickes, Wicklund & Ferris, 1973).

State Perspective

Expectations of failure. People's level of self-focused attention has been shown to influence their behavior when they expect to fail at a task. Kernis, Zuckerman, Cohen, and Spadafora (1982), approaching their study from the state perspective, employed the typical mirror-present, mirror-absent method to manipulate self-focus, but they did not measure self-focus either before or after the experiment. To vary their subjects' expectations regarding the outcome of their task they gave one group instructions that placed the onus of expected failure on the subject, whereas another group was led to believe that their failure would be due to the difficulty of the task. The dependent variables were the subjects' persistence in working on the task and their self-reported interest in it.

The results showed that self-focused attention moderated the effect of the expectancy manipulation. In only the condition of high self-focused attention did the presence or absence of an external reason for expected failure determine the degree of persistence at the task. Subjects with an external reason for failure persisted longer and found the task more interesting than subjects who had not been furnished with that reason.

An unexpected result of this study was a gender difference. Male subjects persisted on the task longer in the external than in the internal expectation condition whereas the opposite was true for the female subjects who persisted longer in the internal than in the external expectation condition. We shall return to the issue of gender differences in self-focused attention after we have examined another study on the effects of success and failure.

Third Perspective?

Self-focus as self-regulation. Greenberg and Pyszczynski (1986) proposed that people focus their attention on themselves in reaction to an experience, such as failure, that carries implications for their self-concept. Viewed in this fashion self-focused attention is neither a pervasive trait nor a temporary state but a self-regulatory mechanism in the sense of the control theory advanced by Carver and Scheier (1981). We shall discuss that theory later in this chapter. For the moment it will suffice to know that in control theory a person seeks to reduce a perceived discrepancy between a personal standard and a current state. For a given individual the personal standard might be to succeed, and the current state might be experiencing failure. Greenberg and Pyszczynski (1986) proposed that such a disruption of the balance between the personal standard and the current state may result in self-focus.

The two experiments these investigators reported lent support to their formulation. In the first experiment subjects were given the task of solving anagrams, most of which, for those in the failure condition, were unsolvable. This was followed by the administration of a measure of self-focused attention, the Self-Focus Sentence Completion task (Exner, 1973). The failure induction was the same in the second experiment, but here self-focus was assessed by asking the subjects to spend 2 min writing down whatever thoughts came to mind. These thought samples were gathered before and after the anagram test and again after the subject had finished reading a 10-page excerpt from a novel. The thoughts were later analyzed for self-focused content, such as statements about how the person was feeling, self-evaluations, self-disclosures, or references to physical or personality traits.

The results of both experiments revealed "a general tendency for greater self-focus immediately after failure than immediately after success" (Greenberg & Pyszczynski, 1986, p. 1043). Following the delay and distraction of reading the story, however, the failure-induced increase in self-focus had dissipated, lending support to the authors' contention that their results are "consistent with a self-regulatory perspective on self-awareness processes" (p. 1043). As they explain, "Individuals self-focus more after failure than after success because self-regulatory needs are greater at that time" (p. 1043).

Trait, State, or Self-Regulatory Mechanism?

As we pointed out at the beginning, the design with which investigators approach their research often depends on the perspective from which they view self-focused attention. This makes it impossible to resolve whether self-focused attention is or is not a traitlike, individual-difference characteristic. Neither Kernis et al. (1982) nor Greenberg and Pyszczynski (1986) had assessed the self-focused attention of their subjects before they exposed them to their experimental manipulations. This leaves open the possibility that the trait perspective is correct and that these investigators' subjects arrived at the laboratory differing in the disposition to respond with self-attention to the mirror presentation or failure experience.

Is Self-Focus Exclusive?

Duval and Wicklund (1972, 1973) had introduced self-focused attention in connection with their studies of self-awareness. To them it represents an increased tendency to "focus on the self to the *exclusion* of other parts of the environment" (1973, p. 20, emphasis added). This notion of exclusiveness was challenged by Hull and Levy (1979) and by Carver and Scheier (1981) who wrote, "self-focused attention does not invariably interfere with perception" (p. 94).

Self-referent encoding. A resolution of this disagreement was proposed by Hull, Van Treuren, Ashford, Propsom, and Andrus (1988) who substitute the term "self-referent encoding" for self-focused attention because it "more accurately captures the nature of the cognitive processes invariantly associated with self-consciousness" (p. 464).

In a series of experiments that examined the cognitive processes involved in self-conscious behavior Hull et al. (1988) had shown that feedback of success or failure affects self-referent memory, which, in turn, affects subsequent self-perceptions. They also demonstrated that individual differences in the way people encode self-relevant material are associated with individual differences in self-consciousness. Both of these differences influenced their subjects' emotional reactions to the success or failure feedback, but individual differences in self-referent encoding (what others have called self-focused attention) appeared to be the dominant variable.

Self-Focus and Gender

We mentioned earlier that Kernis et al. (1982) had found differences between their male and female subjects in the conditions under which they persisted on a difficult task. This difference was independent of the mirror-induced self-focused attention, and the authors sought to attribute it to the tendency of male subjects to be more concerned than female subjects about the implications of performance outcomes to their self-esteem. If this were the case, and because a threat to self-esteem appears to evoke self-regulatory efforts, and because (as we just saw) such efforts have been shown to involve self-focused attention, we should expect to find gender differences in self-focused attention.

Such differences have indeed been found. Like Greenberg and Pyszczynski (1986), Ingram et al. (1988) came to the study of self-focus through an interest in depression. Because it is well established that depression is more frequently diagnosed in women than in men and inasmuch as depression has been linked to self-focused attention, Ingram and his colleagues sought to investigate whether there is a relationship between self-focused attention and gender. The clinical concept of depression need not concern us here so that we will review only that part of this research that concerns the gender differences in self-focused attention.

In the first of three studies they reported, Ingram et al. (1988) "examined the issue of sex differences in reactions to self-focusing stimuli to determine whether men and women might differ in their propensity to self-focus" (p. 968). To this end they used the presence or absence of a large (86 cm × 62 cm) mirror to manipulate self-focus. Like others they employed the private self-consciousness subscale of the SCS by Fenigstein et al. (1975) as a measure of self-focused attention after the subjects had been exposed to the mirror manipulation.

The subjects in this study were 20 male and 20 female college students who, as is nearly always the case in research of this kind, participated in partial fulfillment of requirements for their introductory psychology course. They were told that the purpose of the study was to collect data on several characteristics of college students.

After signing a consent form, the subject was left alone "for several minutes to allow possible self-focusing to take place" (Ingram et al., 1988, p. 969). For subjects in the experimental group the room contained the previously described large mirror. In the control condition an art poster was in the same place that the mirror had occupied. Both mirror and poster had attached to it a note that read "Save for Experiment 17" to give the impression that it had nothing to do with the ongoing study. After the experimenter had reentered the room, the subject was given the private self-consciousness test, debriefed, and dismissed.

Critical comments. Before we look at the results of this study several comments are in order. It is unfortunate that the investigators do not report specifically how long their subjects were in the presence of the mirror. For anyone wishing to repeat this study, being left alone "for several minutes" is not very helpful. Nor does this vague statement reveal whether all subjects were left alone for the same length of time. Note, furthermore, that the subject had not been given a task to perform while the experimenter was out of the room. A task that is to be performed at the table on which the mirror rests increases the likelihood that the subject looks at the mirror. In the present study the mirror (or the art poster) "was situated on a table and leaned against a wall in the experimental room" (Ingram et al., 1988, p. 968), but without a task on which to work on the table a subject might easily have sat looking at the door and not at the mirror. The subject, who presumably thought that she or he was simply waiting for the next phase of the experiment, may thus not be exposed to the mirror at all. In addition to these oversights there is again the absence of a pretest of self-focused attention that we commented on before. Like Greenberg and Pyszczynski (1986) these investigators apparently also assumed that all subjects arrive at the laboratory with the same level of self-focus so that any differences on the posttest could be attributed to the mirror manipulation. The use of a control group does little to attenuate this problem inasmuch as random assignment can easily fail to randomize when there are only 10 subjects in each condition. Lastly, there is the investigators' unusual explanation for their choice of the private self-consciousness subscale as a measure of self-focused attention. They state that they employed that scale because of "the general lack of state self-focused attention measures" (p. 968), although an instrument designed specifically to assess self-focused attention (Exner, 1973), which they employed in the third study of this series, had been available for many years.

Gender differences. Given the questions just raised about this study it may be pointless to examine its results. We do so nonetheless because these results were replicated in a second study that included certain improvements over the first.

That first study revealed that in the mirror-absent (control) condition there were no significant differences in the scores on the test for self-focused attention between female and male subjects, nor were there any significant differences between the mirror-present and mirror-absent conditions for the male subjects. That is to say that the self-focus scores of the male subjects were not affected by the mirror manipulation. Conversely, the female subjects in the mirror-present condition had significantly higher self-focus scores than the female subjects in the mirror-absent condition.

Ingram et al. (1988) sum up the results of this study as providing "preliminary evidence for a sex-linked self-focusing reactivity effect. Specifically, the data suggest that men were not influenced to increase their level of self-focusing by the presence of the mirror. For women, on the other hand, the mirror manipulation produced the enhanced self-focusing effect: Women in the self-focus condition scored significantly higher than women in the non-self-focus condition" (p. 969).

Replication. As mentioned, the second study in this series replicated these findings. There, however, the manipulation designed to affect self-focus was potentially more powerful than the mirror-poster one used in the first study. This time the subjects in the self-focusing condition were seated in front of a television monitor that displayed their own image via a live feed from a video camera positioned immediately behind the monitor so that when the subjects looked at the screen, they looked directly at themselves. Moreover, the subjects were told that the purpose of the study was to examine how television viewing affects task performance, and those in the self-focus condition were instructed to view themselves on the television monitor and to pay attention to themselves for approximately 3 min, after which the examiner would ask them some questions about themselves.

The research design also included a group that viewed a tape of a same-sex stranger engaged in working on some written problems and a control group that spent the same amount of time in the room with the video equipment turned off. Although the results again showed that male and female subjects reacted to the self-focusing manipulation in a markedly different manner, they also included two unexpected findings. Here is how Ingram et al. (1988) report their results (their reference to an "external" condition is to watching a stranger's television image):

> When confronted with self- or external stimuli, male subjects responded by *decreasing* their self-focused attention in both situations. Female subjects responded in almost the exact opposite fashion. For women, both manipulations *increased* self-focusing, most notably in the self-focus condition. Although the increase in self-focused attention in the external focus condition was unanticipated (and hence the label *external* is obviously a misnomer for these subjects), the heightened self-

focusing in the self-focus condition is consistent with theory-derived expectations. The fact that female subjects increased self-focusing in a condition not specifically intended to promote self-awareness suggests not only a readiness in women to engage in self-focused attention, but perhaps also a greater range of stimuli that can induce this process. (p. 970; emphases in original)

The suggestion that the increased self-focus of the female subjects who had watched another woman on a television screen reflects their greater readiness to self-focus under a variety of conditions calls for further research. Again, it is unfortunate that Ingram et al. (1988) did not have a preexperimental measure of self-focused attention because, if their speculation has merit, these should have shown the female subjects to have higher initial scores than the male subjects. It is worth noting that the investigators' speculation suggests that they are willing to consider self-focused attention to be, at least in part, a dispositional variable and not simply a state that can be induced by situational conditions.

Source of the difference. If, as this research suggests, men and women do indeed differ in self-focused attention, regardless of whether it is viewed as a reactive state, a disposition, or a combination of these, the question arises how this difference comes about.

Ingram et al. (1988) provide some data from their third study that may point to an answer. That study investigated the relationship between depression and self-focused attention. We shall not concern ourselves with its details, except to note that it included the administration of the Bem Sex Role Inventory (S. L. Bem, 1974). This inventory is designed to assess the degree to which people of either gender perceive themselves as possessing the psychological attributes our society associates with masculinity (e.g., confident, aggressive) and femininity (e.g., considerate, sensitive). This instrument is said to identify "feminine" attributes in men and "masculine" attributes in women, as well as to define a group of people who possess attributes of both genders whom Bem (1974) labeled *androgynous*.

Instead of comparing the self-focus scores of men and women, as they had done in the first two studies, Ingram et al. (1988) now compared the scores of feminine, masculine, and androgynous subjects regardless of their biological sex. They did this by examining the relationship of scores on the Self-Focus Sentence Completion Scale (Exner, 1973) and the scores on the Bem Sex Role Inventory (S. L. Bem, 1974). This revealed that the feminine group that had been exposed to the video manipulation previously described had significantly higher self-focus scores than any of the other groups who did not differ from one another.

Aside from again demonstrating the effectiveness of the video manipulation, the results of this study strongly suggest that the male-female differences in self-focused attention that were found in the previous studies are in part, if not largely, a function of psychosocial rather than biological factors. At least in the cultural milieu in which all of these studies were carried out looking at one's reflection, whether in a mirror or on a television screen, has a different effect on women than on men, possibly because this culture places a differential emphasis on the external appearance of men and women. A cross-cultural replication of a self-focus study might test this speculation.

SELF-PREDICTION
Do People Know Themselves?
Check on Validity of Self-Reports

The research on every topic we have explored thus far, whether self-focus, self-esteem, self-perception, or self-awareness, relies heavily on what the subjects report about themselves on the various questionnaires and rating scales used by the investigators. The results of that research and the conclusions drawn from it thus depend on the validity of these instruments, on the validity of what people say about themselves, on how well they know themselves. We have previously touched on this source of difficulty in conducting research on unobservable constructs such as self-esteem and self-handicapping. Now we turn to a self-related topic where the accuracy of what people say about themselves can be checked against an observable criterion, where the validity of self-statements can be tested. The topic is self-prediction.

Self-assessment. When people say how they are likely to behave at some future time one can assume that they have conducted a self-assessment because, unless they are guessing, that prediction is based on their knowing their own predilections, dispositions, interests, skills, and capacities. The validity of such a self-assessment can be investigated by asking people to make specific predictions about their behavior and later checking these predictions against observations of the behavior in which they actually engaged. That was the approach Osberg and Shrauger (1986, 1990) employed in an ingenious set of studies.

Potential Pitfalls

Any study that seeks to investigate whether the predictions people make about their behavior will in fact come true must guard against several pitfalls if it is to produce nontrivial results.

Base rate. The first of these pitfalls concerns the base rate at which the behavior being predicted tends to occur. It would, for example, be meaningless to demonstrate that, having predicted that I will brush my teeth tomorrow morning, I do indeed engage in that behavior on the morning of the next day. Toothbrushing has such a high probability of occurrence or base rate in my repertoire that my predicting it will rarely if ever prove wrong. Conversely, my eating kangaroo meat has such a low base rate that my predicting that I will not be doing so within the next 6 months is almost certain to come true. A self-prediction study must avoid predictions of this kind. As Osberg and Shrauger (1986) state it, "Events that have very high or very low base rates of occurrence are more predictable than those with base rates that lie more in the middle range" (p. 1045).

Self-fulfilling prophesy. A second potential pitfall against which to guard is that of the self-fulfilling prophesy. Assume that in a psychological experiment on predicting your own behavior you rate it highly likely that in the next 2 months you will eat a type of food you have never eaten before. After making this and several other predictions you are told to return 2 months later for the second part of the experiment.

A week after the session in which you made your predictions a friend takes you to a restaurant. In addition to the usual fare of steak, chicken, lobster, and fish the menu features a Greek specialty with which you are not familiar. Recalling your prediction, and in line with the notion of the self-fulfilling prophesy, you order and eat *cheli tis skaras*, which turns out to be broiled eel. Your "prophesy" has been fulfilled.

Two months after the original session you return to the investigator's laboratory and report that you ate a dish you had never eaten before. This could lead the investigator to the spurious conclusion that you correctly predicted your behavior when, in fact, it was the prediction that led you to behave the way you did.

False reporting. When an investigation of self-prediction is based on the subjects' self-report there is, of course, the further problem of the veracity of these reports. To appear consistent or discerning, some subjects might be inclined falsely to claim that they had eaten an unfamiliar food or to classify as unfamiliar a food that they had eaten before simply because they had made a prediction to that effect.

Guarding Against Pitfalls

Osberg and Shrauger (1986, 1990) were aware of these potential hazards to the validity of their data. To deal with the base rate problem they analyzed predictions made for behaviors with high base rates separately from those with low base rates. The self-fulfilling prophesy and possible misrepresentations were more difficult to guard against. To minimize their subjects' desires to make their predictions appear accurate or their behavior consistent with their predictions they disguised the purpose of their study and of the follow-up session. They seem to have been successful in this for when asked, only 13 of their 264 subjects reported that they had been aware that the focus of the study was the accuracy of self-predictions.

That, however, leaves unresolved another aspect of the self-fulfilling prophesy hazard. It is that making a prediction about a certain behavior may highlight that behavior for the person who made the prediction, making the behavior more likely to occur. A person who had not considered going on a diet, for example, may be more likely to start a dieting program once he or she has predicted doing so within the next 2 months.

One way of reducing this source of error would be to interpose a longer period between the prediction and the assessment of its accuracy because the longer that period, the less likely it is that the prediction influences the behavior. In research for which college students are subjects, however, extended delay before the follow-up session is rarely possible because most studies have to be completed during the term in which the students signed up for the experiment.

Basis and Accuracy of Self-Predictions

The studies Osberg and Shrauger (1986, 1990) conducted addressed several questions having to do with self-prediction. The first study explored what information people use as the basis for making self-predictions. Three subsequent studies, published in the same article, examined the accuracy of these predictions, how that accuracy might be enhanced, and how the qualities of a prediction relate to its accuracy.

Basis of Predictions

For the first study subjects were asked to predict the likelihood of their engaging within the next 2 months in behaviors such as those listed in Table 9-1 and to identify the information on which they had based these predictions. It emerged that this information fell into the following five categories.

Personal base rate. Of the 960 responses the investigators had obtained from their subjects 41% fell into this category. Here the person's prediction is based on the frequency with which the event or behavior has occurred in the past. Subjects would explain their predictions in such words as, "I predicted that because I've done this a lot in the past," or "I said it wouldn't happen because it's never happened to me before."

Circumstances. The next highest proportion of responses (29%) was assigned to this category. It was used when, to make their prediction, subjects had assessed the likelihood of encountering conditions that would affect the probability that they would behave in that particular manner. For example, in explaining why he predicted that he would not fall in love within the next 2 months a

TABLE 9-1 Life Events Questionnaire

1. Become very upset with or had an argument with a very close friend.
2. Gone an entire night without sleep.
3. Gone to services at a church or synagogue.
4. Been a patient in a hospital or infirmary because of some physical problem.
5. Gone into finals with a grade of C or below in at least one course.
6. Introduced yourself to someone you are attracted to.
7. Started to play a new sport or physical activity you had not done before.
8. Gone on a diet.
9. Offered advice to a friend concerning his or her romantic relationship.
10. Attended a concert for which an admission was charged.
11. Skipped class because you simply didn't feel like going.
12. Met someone new with whom you would like to have a romantic relationship.
13. Agreed with someone or said something you didn't mean or feel so as not to hurt their feelings.
14. Treated someone to a meal in a restaurant or a night out.
15. Will not have had enough money to pay an important bill.
16. Will at some point feel generally dissatisfied with the way your life is going.
17. Said something in class which the instructor or another class member criticized or disagreed with.
18. Been to a party or social gathering where you felt badly enough about the way you behaved that you worried about it the next day.
19. Made a joke or humorous comment in a group of at least five people which they laughed at.
20. Will have felt forced to tell someone important to you something negative about themselves which you did not want them to hear.
21. Will have refused to do something that other people wanted you to do even though you thought it might cost you their friendship.
22. Will have written a paper, done a project, or done an exam that you felt was the best you had ever done.
23. Will have changed your plans regarding what you will mainly be doing in the summer (going to school or working, type of work will be doing).
24. Found yourself refereeing an argument between friends or members of your family.
25. Went to a class unprepared for the discussion because you had not done the required reading.
26. Had to have some dental work done.
27. Changed your hairstyle or type of haircut.
28. Will have been unable to sleep for at least an hour after going to bed because you were thinking about some important decision or event.
29. Gotten high on some type of drug besides alcohol.
30. Begun to work particularly hard on some activity in which you currently lack confidence.
31. Will have been in a situation in which your performance was poorer than usual because you were anxious.
32. Go into final exams with a grade of A in at least one course.
33. Will have ended a romantic relationship.
34. Bought a phonograph record.
35. Will have had some type of sexual experience which you have not had previously.
36. Have fallen in love.

TABLE 9-1 (continued)

37. Will have read at least one book that was not assigned or recommended for a course.
38. Have had period of a day or more when you could get very little done because you feel too down and discouraged.
39. Will have had sexual relations.
40. Become intoxicated.
41. Will have gone out and partied when you should have been studying for exams.
42. Eaten your main meal of the day alone.
43. Had an argument with one of your parents that was serious enough for you to be concerned about it the following day.
44. Met someone new whom you expected to be a close friend for years to come.
45. Eaten a type of food you have never had before.
46. Been awakened from your sleep by an unpleasant dream.
47. Gone to a movie.
48. Been rejected by a group of people who were important to you.
49. Participated in a group sports activity.
50. Fretted or worried on and off for at least three days about something someone said that angered or upset you.
51. Had a sexual experience that was frustrating or unsatisfying.
52. Parents or family members will have complained to you about some important aspect of your behavior of which they disapprove.
53. Will have learned that someone who you thought liked you said something unfavorable about you.
54. You will have become jealous of someone else's good fortune.
55. You will have begun to smoke cigarettes or increased your cigarette smoking.

From Osberg, T. M., and Shrauger, J. S., 1986. Self-prediction: Exploring the parameter of accuracy. *Journal of Personality and Social Psychology, 51,* 1044–1057. Copyright 1986 by the American Psychological Association. Reprinted by permission.

subject said, "I'm already in love, and I don't expect that to change." Or the reason for giving a low probability to having an argument with a close friend might have been given as, "All my close friends are back home and I won't be seeing them for a while."

Personal dispositions. Eighteen percent of the explanations were based on the subject's knowledge of his or her own personal qualities or dispositions. "I am basically a shy person, so I predicted that I wouldn't tell a joke before a group in the near future" is an example of a statement in this category as is, "I am strongly opposed to drugs so I predicted that I wouldn't use them."

Intention. This was a rarely used category; only 5% of the responses fell into it. Here a subject would explain a prediction by pointing out that he or she had already made plans to engage in a specific behavior, such as going to a movie.

Population base rate. To be placed in this category a response would have had to allude to the frequency of the behavior or event in the general population. "Everybody does that from time to time" or "That rarely happens to anybody" exemplify statements of that nature. As it turned out, hardly any responses (1%) took that form.

Accuracy of Predictions

Once these categories had been established, Osberg and Shrauger (1986) employed them in their second study that was devoted to finding out the kind of information on which their subjects had based their accurate self-predictions. For this purpose the subjects first rated the likelihood of each of the 55 items shown in Table 9-1. After that they were asked to indicate the basis of each prediction by choosing no more than two items from the following list of alternatives.

- A: I thought about how frequently it has happened to me in the past. (Personal base rate)
- B: I thought about whether or not I'm the kind of person who would do that. (Personal disposition)
- C: I thought about how likely it was to happen to anyone. (Population base rate)
- D: I thought about, based on the future circumstances of my life, whether it was likely to happen. (Circumstances)
  Leave blank—None of the above.

The subjects returned 8 to 9 weeks later to report whether or not the events they had predicted had in fact taken place.

Results

When they related the accuracy of their subjects' predictions to the four categories of information (personal base rate, personal dispositions, population base rates, and circumstances) Osberg and Shrauger (1986) found only moderate associations. Statistically significant relationships only emerged when the items were separated according to the frequency with which the subjects reported them as having occurred—that is, by the base rate of the behaviors.

With that approach the analysis showed that for high base-rate behaviors accuracy was associated with predictions based on subjects' personal base rate. The only other significant statistic involved predictions based on circumstances, but here the association was negative. In other words, particularly for high base-rate items, these predictions were *wrong* more often than would be expected by chance.

Individual differences. These disappointing results were based on the entire group of 62 subjects. It is possible that some of these subjects made highly accurate predictions, whereas others predicted wrongly. Had this been the case, the significance levels of the results could have been diluted. This speculation receives some support from a further data analysis that Osberg and Shrauger conducted and in which they took individual subject characteristics into account.

At an earlier time approximately two thirds of their subjects had completed the SCS of Fenigstein et al. (1975). From our earlier discussion it will be recalled that this scale distinguishes between private self-consciousness and public self-consciousness. People high in private self-consciousness are those who predominantly attend to their own thoughts and feelings, whereas people high in public self-consciousness largely attend to the impression they are making on others.

When Osberg and Shrauger (1986) related the accuracy of self-predictions to subjects' public and private self-consciousness they found that high levels of public self-consciousness were associated with reduced accuracy in self-prediction. Conversely, people with high private self-consciousness tended to give more valid self-reports. It seems that the more one concerns oneself with the reactions of others, the less one is likely to know about oneself—hence, the less able one is to make accurate predictions about one's own behavior.

Enhancement of Self-Prediction Accuracy

Following their two preliminary studies Osberg and Shrauger (1986, 1990) next sought to determine whether the accuracy of subjects' self-predictions could be enhanced by directing them to attend to a specific source of information. The sources to be used were personal base rate, personal dispositions, and population base rate.

For this study the subjects were given a written description of the information source relevant to the experimental group to which they had been assigned. They were then instructed to rate the likelihood of occurrence of each of the 55 items in their Life Events Questionnaire (Table 9-1) with that information source in mind. The subjects in the personal-disposition group, for example, were instructed to ask themselves, "Based on my own personal qualities or attributes, or the kind of person I am, how likely is this event to happen to me?" They were repeatedly exhorted to focus on their personal qualities and urged to consider their likes and dislikes, and strengths and weaknesses in arriving at their judgments.

The personal base-rate and the population base-rate groups were given similar instructions. There was also a control group that made predictions without having been given instructions about the type of information to which they were to attend.

Results. The accuracy of the predictions was again assessed from the self-reports the subjects furnished in a follow-up session some 2 months later. As before, an item was scored as correct when it had been predicted to occur and did, or if it had been predicted not to occur and did not. The data showed that the group that had been instructed to focus on personal dispositions had made the highest number of correct predictions. Their mean accuracy score was 40.7 out of a possible 50. The personal base-rate group was next with a mean of 39.6, followed by the control subjects (mean = 38.2) and the population base-rate subjects (mean = 36.5).

These results indicate that in attempting to predict one's own behavior it is best to focus on one's personal qualities or attributes; on the kind of person one sees oneself to be. Almost as effective, however, is to try and recall one's own past behavior and to base one's predictions on that.

Self-Perception Theory

There are reasons to believe that the two foci, personal qualities and past behavior, are closely related, if not the same. Bem (1972), in proposing his self-perception theory, had suggested that people make statements about their personal qualities or attributes based on recollections of their past behavior. For example, people who know that they have frequently gone to services in a house of worship are likely to label themselves religious. Conversely, people who label themselves religious, regardless of the basis of that label, are very likely to attend religious services frequently because they know that this is what religious people do or are expected to do.

When such individuals are then asked to predict, as they were in the Osberg and Shrauger (1986) study, whether they will be attending religious services within the next 2 months they are not only very likely to assign the occurrence of that event a high probability, but they are also very likely to engage in that behavior. This then results in the accuracy of this self-prediction being very high, regardless of whether the prediction was based on personal base-rate information or personal dispositions.

The above speculations find support in the results of the fourth in the series of studies Osberg and Shrauger (1986) had conducted. There, in addition to making self-predictions, the subjects were asked to indicate how confident they were about each of their predictions. When these predictions were later checked against the subjects' self-reports of their actual behavior the investigators found a highly significant ($p < 0.00001$) association between the certainty with which the subjects had stated their self-predictions and the accuracy of these predictions.

People Know Themselves

Self-prediction, we had pointed out, is a measure of the validity of self-assessment because people must assess themselves to be able to make predictions about their behavior. What can one conclude about the validity of self-assessment from the results of the studies conducted by Osberg and Shrauger (1986)?

It would seem that the college students who served as subjects in these studies were able to assess themselves quite well. They were remarkably accurate in predicting their own behavior, particularly when in so doing they drew on their knowledge of themselves and of their past behavior. The accuracy of these predictions was especially high among individuals with the keen attention to self-relevant information that characterizes high private self-consciousness. It thus appears that people who pay attention to their own thoughts, feelings, experiences, and reactions, and who consider these when asked to make predictions about their own behavior, make these predictions confidently and with considerable accuracy.

SELF-REGULATION

Historical Antecedents

It is not a novel notion to propose that people check their own thoughts and behavior and regulate these so as to keep them in line with standards they have somehow internalized. Contemporary theorizing about self-regulation thus has antecedents in Freud's (1933) postulation of a tripartite personality in which ego is the regulating agent and superego the repository of the internalized standards to which the impulses of the id are expected to conform.

A form of self-regulation is also implied in Festinger's (1957) theory of cognitive dissonance, which holds that whenever there is a discrepancy or incompatibility between two or more psychological processes, such as belief and action, we experience tension that motivates our seeking to resolve the dissonance. A similar process underlies Piaget's (1952) concepts of assimilation and accommodation that are called into play to reduce a discrepancy between a new experience and the existing schema. In parallel with these psychological processes of self-regulation one finds Cannon's (1929) physiological concept of homeostasis, the body's tendency to maintain the conditions of its internal environment at an optimal level by various forms of self-regulation.

Control Systems

These physiological and psychological processes of self-regulation have their analogue in the automatic control systems that are the subject matter of the science of cybernetics (Wiener, 1948). The most widely known example of such a control system is the thermostat that monitors and regulates room temperature. In winter the occupant sets the desired temperature, and whenever the thermostat senses that warmth of the room has fallen below this standard, it causes the furnace to come on. Once the temperature has again reached the set standard so that the discrepancy has been eliminated, the thermostat sends another signal that causes the furnace to turn off.

Four requirements. To function properly a thermostat must possess four capabilities. It must have a means by which the desired temperature, the reference value, set point, or standard can be set. In addition, it must have a way of sensing the current room temperature and the means to compare this with the standard. Lastly, it must be able to send to the furnace a message that initiates appropriate action. Note that to carry out these functions, a thermostat must have a source of energy. In this case it is a low-voltage electric current. We shall have more to say about this analogy in a moment.

TOTE unit. Miller et al. (1960) suggested that the cybernetic control system could serve as a model for conceptualizing how humans plan and regulate their behavior. As the basic element of such self-regulation they proposed the TOTE (Test-operate-test-exit) unit.

According to this conceptualization, the person's plan or goal serves as the standard with which the present state or the outcome of an action is compared (test). If this test finds a discrepancy between plan and outcome, an action designed to reduce the discrepancy is initiated (operate), followed by another comparison (test). This feedback cycle continues until the discrepancy has been eliminated. At that point the sequence comes to an end (exit). Because such a self-regulating system serves to reduce or eliminate a discrepancy between state and standard, it is technically referred to as a *negative feedback loop*.

Self-Regulation and Motivation

A homely example of a TOTE unit and the operation of a negative feedback loop is a young man, dressing for a date, who is putting on his necktie in front of a mirror. His plan is to get the tie on "just right"—that is, in conformity with the accepted standard of fashion. Looking in the mirror he sees that the narrow end of the tie is longer than the wide end (test). He undoes the tie and reties it (operate), checks the mirror again (test), and, satisfied with the result, turns away to put on his jacket (exit). Were one to wonder about his motivation for his behavior and ask what made him retie his necktie, he would probably say something about not wanting to look like a slob when he meets his date.

Self-regulation and affect. The question of motivation has been raised about self-regulation in general. Duval and Wicklund (1972), in the context of their theory of objective self-awareness, attributed this motivation to negative affect. They postulated that the person experiences negative affect whenever the automatic comparison of the self with standards of correctness reveals a discrepancy. They predicted "that a person who is objectively self aware, and whose actual self is discrepant from the standard of correctness, would attempt to change his [or her] present state toward agreement with the standard" (p. 10). Once that agreement is reached, they reasoned, the person would find relief from the discrepancy-induced, unpleasant negative affect and thus be reinforced for reducing the discrepancy. The negative affect, in other words, is here seen as motivating the discrepancy-reducing action. For the young man retying his necktie, the negative affect might have been anxiety about his date's reaction. In this formulation negative affect is analogous to the low-voltage electrical current that drives the action of a thermostat.

Models based on analogies. Not everyone agrees that it is necessary to postulate a motive source of energy, a drive, for human self-regulation. Merely because the thermostat requires an energy source to function is not a good reason to assume that self-regulation must also have an identifiable source of energy. Like other models of human behavior and mental processes that were based on analogies to such inventions in engineering as the steam engine, the hydraulic elevator, the telephone switchboard, and the modern computer, the thermostat ultimately falls short as a source for a model because it is an electro-mechanical instrument and not a living organism.

Control Theory

Carver and Scheier (1981) took issue with the drive-reduction formulation proposed by Duval and Wicklund (1972) and offered instead a model of self-regulation that is squarely based on cybernetic control theory. According to the theory they put forth, self-regulation entails a process that is schematically depicted by the flow chart in Figure 9-1.

The process begins at the lower left-hand corner of the diagram as the person perceives his or her current state. That state can be a physical sensation, a behavioral act, or a cognitive process such as a plan being contemplated or an attitude being held. The perception of that current state is then compared with the person's knowledge of the standard, with what the state ought to be. This standard may be the individual's personal goals and values, which may or may not be consonant with the rules, laws, and expectations of his or her society. This process of comparison is symbolized in the flow chart by a "comparator." It is the equivalent of the test part of the TOTE unit. The comparison between state and standard entails a binary judgment. If state and standard match, the process ends, but if they do not match action is initiated to reduce this discrepancy. When completed that action will have resulted in a new state that becomes the object of perception, and the cycle starts over again and is repeated until the state matches the standard.

Life as the energy source. The operation of the self-regulating system just described follows that of the room thermostat in every respect, except one. It

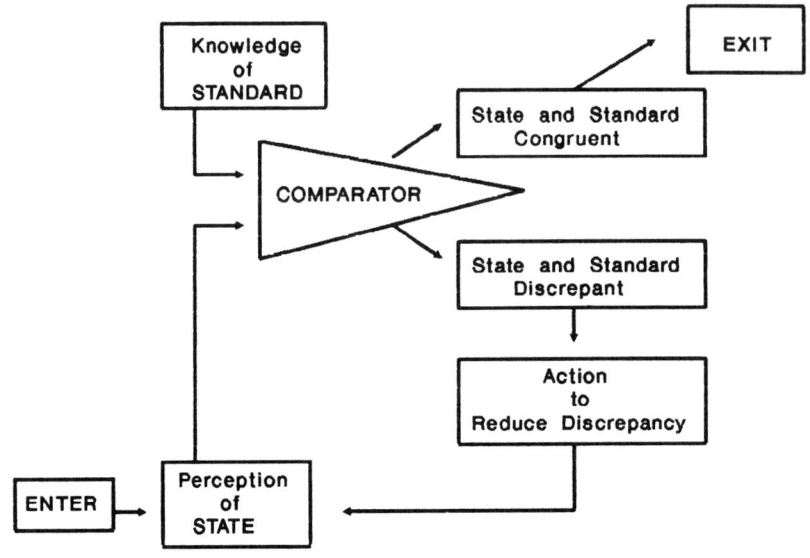

FIGURE 9-1 Schematic flowchart of self-regulation.

From Carver, C. S., and Scheier, M. F., 1981. *Attention and self-regulation: A control-theory approach to human behavior.* New York: Springer Verlag. Copyright 1981 by Springer Verlag. Reprinted by permission.

lacks the source of energy for performing the various functions—energy that the thermostat derives from the transformer or battery to which it is attached, and that the person in the Duval and Wicklund model obtains from the need to reduce the negative affect.

Carver and Scheier (1981) explicitly disavow the residue of Hullian drive-reduction theory (Hull, 1943) that leads one to invoke an energy source for a model of self-regulation. These theorists assume instead (Carver & Scheier, 1981, p. 341) that the goal-setting, discrepancy-reducing tendencies are normal consequences of the way human beings are organized; they are self-regulatory systems. Self-regulation, Carver and Scheier assert, is a natural part of being human and one does not have to postulate a special energy source to explain what makes people function the way they do. In offering their cybernetic model of self-regulation they thus knowingly depart not only from Hullian drive-reduction theory but also from Skinnerian notions of reinforcement (Skinner, 1953).

Conceptions regarding self-regulation in general and control theory specifically are theoretical formulations that help one think about the proccesses that might be going on inside a person who modifies his or her attitudes or actions after exposure to new information. The results of studies we cited in our discussion of self-focused attention, such as the one by Greenberg and Pyszynski (1986), can be explained in terms of a self-regulatory feedback loop. Self-regulation will also be a helpful frame of reference to keep in mind as we look at self-monitoring in Chapter 10.

10

Self-Monitoring

FROM FOCUS ON OTHERS TO FOCUS ON SELF

Thus far the self-related topics we have been discussing have dealt primarily with self-focused concerns in the sense that self-awareness, self-perception, self-efficacy, self-esteem, self-assessment, and so forth all had to with the person's view of himself or herself. Only when we spoke of public self-consciousness did we see that for some people an awareness of themselves in relation to others can affect their own behavior. With self-monitoring we now take up a topic where the central focus is on the self-regulation that can come with the perception of others' reactions to oneself.

From Attention to Action

We have had repeated occasion to mention the SCS of Fenigstein et al. (1975), which differentiates between private and public self-consciousness. People who score high on private self-consciousness tend to endorse such items as, "I often examine my inner feelings," whereas those who score high on public self-consciousness check such an item as "I always wonder what other people think of me." One of the differences between these two response tendencies lies in the focus of people's self-attention. Those high in private self-consciousness focus primarily on their own reactions, whereas the primary focus of attention of those high in public self-consciousness is primarily on the reactions others have to them.

This difference in attentional focus raises the question whether there is a difference in the social behavior between those who score high in private self-consciousness and those who score high in public self-consciousness. Will a woman who agrees with the statement, "I always wonder what other people think of me" do anything to influence what others think of her? To investigate this question Snyder (1974) developed a scale that defines the construct he called self-monitoring.

Self-Monitoring Scale

The verb, to monitor, connotes not only observation, but also regulation and control; not only attention but also action, which is exactly what Snyder's use of that term is meant to impart. Unlike the SCS of Fenigstein et al. (1975), which deals primarily with the focus of a person's self-attention, the items on Snyder's (1974) Self-Monitoring Scale are designed to assess how the respondent behaves in social situations.

A person who scores high on the Self-Monitoring Scale—a high self-monitor—would accept as true such statements as the following:

"I can make impromptu speeches even on topics about which I have almost no information."
"I guess I put on a show to impress or entertain others."
"In different situations and with different people, I often act like very different persons."
"I may deceive people by being friendly when I really dislike them."
"I would probably make a good actor."

A low self-monitor, on the other hand, would reject these statements as false and endorse as true such statements as the following, which a high self-monitor would reject:

"I find it hard to imitate the behavior of other people."
"In a group of people I am rarely the center of attention."
"I am not particularly good at making other people like me."
"At a party I let others keep the jokes and stories going."

Altogether there are 18 such items on the revised version of the original 25-item Self Monitoring Scale (Gangestad & Snyder, 1985).

High self-monitors. Persons whom this scale identifies as high self-monitors characteristically assess the interpersonal situation in which they find themselves and control the social image they display so as to suit the occasion. They thus practice a form of impression management.

Low self-monitors. In contrast to high self-monitors, low self-monitors do not constantly assess the social climate, but are more concerned with their own feelings, attitudes, and beliefs. They value agreement between who they are and what they do. Thus, they will honestly express what they are thinking and feeling, even at the risk of disagreeing or offending those around them.

Which is better? Reading these descriptions and the items that define a person as a high or a low self-monitor, it is easy to succumb to a value judgment and a preference of one of these social orientations to the other. Snyder (1987), however, takes pains to point out that neither of these approaches to interpersonal situations is inherently "better" than the other.

Depending on one's choice of words, the high self-monitor can be described as an opportunistic, manipulating, unauthentic, dishonest chameleon or as a flexible, realistic, adaptable person who copes well with the diversity of roles that are called for by an increasingly complex society. By the same token, the low self-monitor can be depicted as a genuine, forthright, honest, open, steady, predictable individual who is always true to his or her principles and values. Yet the same person can also be said to be an opinionated, rigid, stubborn, and inflexible bore.

Snyder (1987) cautions against making value judgments and stresses that each orientation represents a different approach to life, each with its own assets and liabilities. He seeks to be value neutral in his own definition of the two poles on the dimension of self-monitoring when he writes,

> The prototype of the high self-monitor is someone who is particularly sensitive to cues to the situational appropriateness of his or her social behavior and who uses these cues as guidelines for monitoring (that is, regulating and controlling) his or her expressive behavior and self-presentations. By contrast, the low self-monitor is less attentive to social information about situationally appropriate self-presentation and does not possess a highly developed repertoire of self-presentational skills. His or her expressive self-presentations seem, in a functional sense, to be controlled by inner attitudes, dispositions, and values, rather than to be molded and shaped to fit the situation. (Snyder, 1987, p. 14)

Acting reprehensibly. Support for the contention that high self-monitors are no more immoral than low self-monitors can be found in a study of Jones, Brenner, and Knight (1990). These investigators instructed their subjects to play the role of a reprehensible person who responds to such moral dilemmas as the one posed by whether to conceal the need for major repairs when attempting to sell a car. Later the subjects learned from audience feedback that they had succeeded or failed in their role-playing task. In line with Snyder's (1974) formulation of self-monitoring, scores on a measure of self-esteem revealed that high self-monitors felt good about themselves when they had succeeded in their portrayal of a morally reprehensible person, whereas low self-monitors felt good about themselves when they had failed. In their responses to a postexperimental questionnaire, however, both high and low self-monitors indicated that they viewed as immoral and inappropriate the person they had been asked to portray. As Jones et al. (1990) observe, high self-monitors do not like self-serving manipulators any more than low self-monitors do.

Self-Monitoring and Related Dispositions

To be of any value a psychological test must be capable of telling related constructs apart. A test designed to assess fear, for example, must not confuse fear with anger or vice versa. Campbell and Fiske (1959) referred to this as discriminant validity. In the case of the Self-Monitoring Scale related constructs are a need for approval, the tendency to exploit others to one's own advantage, and extraversion. How do these constructs and measures designed to assess them relate to self-monitoring and the Self-Monitoring Scale?

Need for approval. The Social Desirability Scale of Crowne and Marlowe (1960) is frequently employed to measure the need for approval by others. Persons with that need tend to answer items on psychological questionnaires in what they believe to be the "right," socially acceptable direction. That tendency, however, is not the same as the ability to present oneself in a wide variety of social situations in such a way as to gain the approval and acceptance of others, which is what the Self-Monitoring Scale is supposed to measure. To demonstrate its discriminant validity scores on the Self-Monitoring Scale should therefore be independent of scores on the Social Desirability Scale. Validity studies have shown that there is but a low positive correlation between these two scales (Jones & Baumeister, 1976).

The difference between social desirability and self-monitoring can be illustrated by the item on the Self-Monitoring Scale that a high self-monitor would accept and that reads, "I may deceive people by being friendly when I really dislike them." Because it describes an inclination most people would view as undesirable that statement is not likely to be checked as true by someone who has a high score on the Social Desirability Scale.

Exploitation. The impression management practiced by the high self-monitor must also be differentiated from the tendency to manipulate and exploit others for one's own benefit, a proclivity that is at times referred to as Machiavellianism (Christie & Geis, 1970). The two seem closely related. In fact, "A white lie is often a good thing," which is an item from Christie's "Mach" scale that is used to assess Machiavellianism, has the same implication as the self-monitoring item, "I can look anyone in the eye and tell a lie with a straight face (if for a right end)."

Nevertheless, there is a difference between Machiavellianism and self-monitoring. Machiavellians focus on themselves; high self-monitors focus on the other person. This was illustrated in an unpublished study of unstructured conversations (cited in Snyder, 1987) in which individuals with high scores on the Mach scale made preponderant use of first-person singular pronouns (I, me, mine), whereas those with high scores on the Self-Monitoring Scale tended primarily to employ second- and third-person pronouns (you, yours, he, she). As Snyder (1987) puts it, "Although both types may be motivated, at times, to get their own way, the tools of their trades differ. The high self-monitor relies on techniques of impression management, and the Machiavellian on more exploitative tactics of manipulation" (p. 26).

Extraversion. The outgoing, active, sociable, cheerful qualities that characterize the extravert (Eysenck, 1970) would also seem descriptive of the high self-monitor who would probably *disagree* with such items on Snyder's scale as, "In a group of people I am rarely the center of attention," or "At a party I let others keep the jokes and stories going." How closely are extraversion and self-monitoring related?

Investigators such as Lippa (1978) have reported a slight statistical association between extraversion and self-monitoring, and a factor analysis of the Self-Monitoring Scale conducted by Briggs, Cheek, and Buss (1980) isolated not only an extraversion factor but also two other factors that they identified as other-directedness and acting ability. Briggs et al. (1980) as well as Miell and Le Voi (1985) have questioned whether what the Self-Monitoring Scale measures is best conceptualized as a unitary factor, which is what Snyder (1974) proposed. We shall return to the issue of conceptualization at a later point.

Snyder (1987) maintains that there is a difference between extraverts and high self-monitors. He points out that extraverts present their sociable, gregarious, and outgoing characteristics across a wide range of social situations, even in those where a reserved demeanor would be more appropriate. High self-monitors, on the other hand, alert to the nuances of their social environment, employ their self-presentational skills to play different roles with different people in different situations.

On the whole Snyder (1987) concludes from his review of the relevant research that the findings on the relationship between self-monitoring and related constructs "usually have been trivial and statistically insignificant" (p. 24).

Origins of Self-Monitoring

Heritable predisposition. Snyder and Gangestad (1986) have summarized a substantial body of research that attests to the robust nature of the Self-Monitoring Scale and supports the construct that scale was designed to measure. What is it that makes one person a high, another a low self-monitor?

Available research suggests that the self-monitoring tendency is unrelated to an individual's social class, economic status, region of origin, and religion. A person's environment, in fact, appears to play only a facilitating, enhancing role in the development of that tendency. A person's biological-genetic background, on the other hand, does seem to contribute to a predisposition for his or her characteristic manner of relating to the social environment.

Study of twins. The best method available for investigating the contribution of genetic factors to a given human characteristic is to compare the concordance of this characteristic in monozygotic (identical) and dizygotic (fraternal) twins. Concordance expresses the probability of the characteristic under investigation being manifested by both twins in a pair.

Gangestad (1984) conducted a study of 149 pairs of monozygotic and 76 same-sex dizygotic twins. Based on this study and on work by Dworkin (1977), Snyder and Gangestad (1986) report that it has been estimated that the monozygotic twins "are nearly always, if not always" (p. 128) concordant for self-monitoring, whereas dizygotic twins "are concordant at better than a chance rate, but at a rate substantially less than [monozygotic] twins" (p. 128).

As is true of other personality variables, such as sociability (Buss & Plomin, 1984), for which there is evidence of contributions by biological-genetic factors, people are not born as high or low self-monitors. These factors provide a predisposition that may become actualized by their interacting with the person's experiences in his or her environment.

Two social skills. Self-monitoring, it is worth remembering, involves two social skills. The first is the capacity to attend and be sensitive to the often subtle cues emanating from the social environment; to be able to sense what others expect of you. The second entails the ability to adjust one's own behavior so as to make it fit, to match the expectations of those with whom one is interacting at the moment. It is likely that genetic factors play a greater role in the attentional than in the adjustment aspect of self-monitoring, whereas experiences in the social environment provide the occasions for acquiring and honing the adjustment skill.

Genotype → Environment Effect

Scarr and McCartney (1983) have proposed a helpful framework for understanding the ways in which genetic factors (the genotype) may influence the kind of person a child will become (the phenotype). They refer to their formulation as the genotype → environment effect, and differentiate among evocative, passive, and active influences.

Evocative influence. The evocative influence has to do with the way the people in the young child's environment respond to his or her initially largely innate behavior. In the case of the sensitivity to social cues that is essential if one is to become a high self-monitor, these responses may be joy in and admiration for the infant's ability to tell people apart or to anticipate their behavior (as in reaching toward the parent just before being picked up).

Passive influence. The passive influence stems from the child's biological parents who provide a rearing environment that is, in part, based on their own genetic endowment. If self-monitoring has a genetic component, one or both of these parents may be high or low self-monitors so that they will display this interactive mode and, in terms of Bandura's (1986) social-cognitive theory, provide potent models for the child as she or he is growing up.

Active influence. The active influence represents children selecting and seeking out from the environment those aspects that are most compatible with their genotype. Children who will later be classified as high self-monitors may pick a variety of friends who engage in many different activities. Future low self-monitors, however, would probably prefer a few friends and a limited repertoire of activities. Later on, the former might gravitate toward theatrical productions or play reading groups, whereas the latter develop such largely solitary hobbies as stamp collecting. Career choices too tend to be influenced by such personality variables as self-monitoring. High self-monitors may tend to go into sales and low-self-monitors into librarianship. Such "niche-picking," as Scarr and McCartney (1983) called it, leads to expanded skill development with everyone being comfortable in—hence, rewarded—by the environment in which their genotypic predisposition continues to be adaptive. Ultimately, it becomes impossible to determine the relative contributions of the innate and the acquired.

Self-Monitoring and Social Relations

Choice of Friends

In discussing the origins of self-monitoring we speculated on the influence this orientation might have on people's choice of friends and career. Snyder (1987) cites studies that found high self-monitors to select their friends along lines of the activities in which they engage. There are the friends with whom they play tennis, the friends with whom they attend concerts, and the friends with whom they go to restaurants. Because there often is little or no overlap among these specialized groups high self-monitors tend to live in a rather compartmentalized social world.

Low self-monitors, in contrast, tend to choose as friends those with whom they feel most compatible. With these they engage in a variety of activities that both they and their friends enjoy. High self-monitors, in other words, focus on the external situation (their activity); low self-monitors focus on the internal state (their feelings).

Reaction to Others

Not only the choice of one's friends but also how one reacts to the behavior of other people appears influenced by a person's self-monitoring orientation. Jones and Baumeister (1976) report a study that had as one of its purposes to determine whether there is a relationship between scores on the self-monitoring scale and approval of tailoring one's expressed beliefs to earn a monetary reward.

To test this the investigators had male subjects watch a videotape that showed two men engaged in a discussion of contemporary issues. There were two conditions. In one the discussants agreed with one another, in the other they displayed polite disagreement. One of the discussants was identified for the subjects as the investigators' confederate and they were informed that he had been promised a monetary reward for getting his discussion partner either to like him or to respect him. The subjects were also told that showing agreement with the discussion partner was an ingratiating strategy for gaining affection, whereas displaying autonomy by politely disagreeing was a strategy for gaining respect. After viewing the tape the subjects rated their impression of the confederate.

The main finding of this study was "that high self-monitoring individuals have a relatively negative reaction to those who shape their behavior in line with motivational constraints and a relatively positive reaction to those who resist such constraints. Low self-monitoring individuals, on the other hand, show a general liking for those who are agreeable and for those not operating under an ingratiation motive" (Jones & Baumeister, 1976, p. 670).

This study thus showed subjects with high self-monitoring scores to display more social sensitivity than those with low scores. That is not surprising in view of the fact that self-monitoring requires one to be alert to the cues of the social environment so as to be able to adjust one's behavior to its demands. What is surprising is that the high self-monitors, who know and admit that they themselves tailor their behavior to the demands of the social situation, disliked the confederate who behaved in this very fashion.

Jones and Baumeister (1976) try to explain this seeming paradox by speculating that high self-monitors also dislike their own chameleon-like behavior. If that were the case, however, they would hardly admit to it as readily as when they respond with "false" to such a transparent question on the self-monitoring scale as, "I have trouble changing my behavior to suit different people and different situations."

A more likely explanation of their surprising result is these authors' suggestion that the high self-monitors saw the confederate's behavior as too blatant—hence, ineffective. "The high self-monitoring individual" they write, "may feel that he would respond with greater subtlety to the incentives to elicit liking or respect" (Jones & Baumeister, 1976, p. 670).

Judgment of Relationships

High self-monitors focus on the external situation (what they are doing), whereas low self-monitors focus on the internal state (how they are feeling). That distinction holds true not only with respect to the individuals themselves but also to their judgment of others. This was revealed in a study by Glick, DeMorest, and

Hotze (1988) who asked subjects to assess the compatibility of heterosexual couples.

The subjects (20 male and 20 female college students) were shown a set of ten cards, each of which contained a yearbook-type photograph, a rating of the person's sense of humor and extraversion, and a statement of his or her main area of interest. Five of the cards represented male and five female college-age individuals. The participants were asked to pair these individuals into five compatible couples. After they had completed this task they were asked to respond to the items of the Self-Monitoring Scale.

As the authors had predicted, high self-monitors matched couples on the basis of their similarity of physical attractiveness. Low self-monitors, matched them on the basis of their similarity of personality characteristics and interests.

Choice of Dating Partners

The difference in what high and low self-monitors consider important in "match making" has also been found in their choice of their own romantic partners. Snyder, Berscheid, and Glick (1985) reported two investigations in which they had examined the relationship between self-monitoring and male undergraduates' choice of dating partners.

In the first of these investigations subjects were given 50 file folders on women who had supposedly agreed to go on a blind date with them. Each folder contained a page with a small photograph of a reasonably attractive young woman and a page containing such relatively superficial personal information as her preferences in food, cars, reading matter, activities, and so forth. Each subject was asked to look through as many of these folders as he wished and to select the woman with whom he wanted to have a date.

While the subject was thus engaged an observer behind a one-way mirror recorded the time he spent looking at the page with the photograph and at the page with the personal information. When the investigators related previously obtained scores on the Self-Monitoring Scale to these data they found that high self-monitors had spent proportionately more time on the photograph than on the personal information, whereas low self-monitors spent relatively more time on the personal information than on the photograph.

Reasoning that in ordinary life people rarely select their dates from among 50 potential partners, and that in making real choices people must often compromise between physical attractiveness and personal qualities, Snyder and his colleagues (1985) next investigated the question whether a person's score on the self-monitoring scale bears a relationship to how that compromise is met when the choice is limited to two potential dating partners.

For this investigation Snyder et al. (1985) furnished each of their male research participants with information about two female undergraduates. The subject was to decide with which of these two he wanted to go on a date at a local bar or restaurant. The information on the basis of which the subject was to make his choice consisted of a small yearbook-like photograph and a summary of results from the sociability, other-directedness, and emotionality scales of a fictitious personality inventory.

The photograph of one of the potential dates showed her to be rather unattractive in appearance, but the accompanying personality sketch was very positive, describing her as emotionally stable, highly sociable, outgoing and open, with a good sense of humor and an ability to interact well with others. The photograph of the other woman revealed her as a physically attractive person, but her personality summary indicated that she possessed several undesirable characteristics. It described her as a moody person who was reserved toward strangers and concerned more with herself than with other people.

Dilemma. The decision with which of these two women to go on a date thus faced the subject with a dilemma. The one of attractive appearance had undesirable personality traits, whereas the one with attractive personality traits was physically unappealing. The choice thus required a compromise and that revealed a highly significant difference between the high and the low self-monitoring subjects.

As Snyder et al. (1985) summarize their results, "When forced to sacrifice one feature for another, over two thirds of the high self-monitoring individuals chose the physically attractive partner even though she clearly possessed a relatively undesirable personality. In contrast, 81% of the low self-monitoring participants preferred the partner with the sterling inner qualities even though she was physically unattractive" (p. 1435).

The two investigations reported by Snyder et al. (1985) lend strong support to the notion that in selecting dating partners high self-monitors value and attend to the exterior attributes of good looks, whereas low self-monitors concern themselves with the interior attributes of personality.

What determines the choice? There are several ways of explaining this finding. One is to recall that in a social situation the dominant characteristic of high self-monitors is a concern with making a good impression, whereas low self-monitors focus more on their own feelings, attitudes, and beliefs. These different orientations may find expression in the person's choice of dating partner. The externally oriented high self-monitor may choose the physically attractive date because he believes that her good looks will accrue to his credit in the view of others. The internally oriented low self-monitor, in contrast, may select as a date a person who is sociable, open, and willing to listen to others because that serves his own needs to express his thoughts and feelings.

Similarity attracts. Another and related explanation lies in the well-established finding from research in social psychology that shows the important contribution similarity makes to interpersonal attraction (Berscheid & Walster,

1978; Byrne, 1971). By and large, we tend to find attractive those who are similar to us on a variety of dimensions. The low self-monitor would thus be attracted to the potential date who sounds as if she might have a similar orientation, whereas the high self-monitor with his concern about how he looks to others selects as a date the person whom he assumes to care similarly about her appearance.

Attitudes and activities. The important role similarity plays in interpersonal attraction and the fact that the self-monitoring orientation is one of the dimensions of similarity was further clarified by research that Jamieson, Lydon, and Zannna (1987) conducted. These investigators asked their subjects to indicate the extent to which they found attractive four people about whom they were given information. This information included items detailing the individuals' attitudes about controversial political and moral issues as well as items about their interests in various leisure time activities. The attitudes and activities of the four (fictitious) people each subject was to judge had been constructed so as to be either very similar to or quite different from the previously ascertained attitudes and activities of the subject.

The results of this study showed that low self-monitors were more attracted by similarity in attitude than by similarity in activity interests. The reverse was true for high self-monitors who were more attracted by similarity in activity interests than by similarity in attitude. These findings confirm and expand on similar data that had been previously reported by Snyder, Gangestad, and Simpson (1983), and lend further support to the notion that a person's level of self-monitoring plays an important role in determining whom he or she will choose as friends.

Self-Disclosure

Process of getting acquainted. Yet another aspect of interpersonal relations in which self-monitoring plays a role is in how people act while establishing so-called surface contacts during the first stage of getting acquainted. During this stage two people who have recently met develop evaluative attitudes toward one another. If these attitudes are negative, the two may discontinue the contact at that point, but if the attitudes they form are positive they can provide the basis of a continuing friendship.

One of the major factors in this formation of attitudes is self-disclosure (Altman & Taylor, 1973; Cozby, 1973). As the term suggests, self-disclosure involves revealing to others such intimate, private information as one's background, fears, hopes, beliefs, weaknesses, flaws, or embarrassments.

Reciprocal self-disclosure. In the early stages of interpersonal contact such revelations are usually at a fairly superficial level; nonetheless, they communicate that the recipient of this information is being trusted. Much now depends on whether that information is met with acceptance and understanding and whether the other person reciprocates with self-disclosure of his or her own. Reciprocal self-disclosure forms the basis of mutual trust, an essential ingredient of intimacy and friendship.

Role of Self-Monitoring

What role does self-monitoring play in self-disclosure? As is so often the case with complex human behavior, the answer to this question is, "It depends." It depends, first of all, on whether one is a high or low self-monitor. It depends further on whether one expects to have future occasion to interact with the new acquaintance; and it depends on the context or situation in which the contact with the new acquaintance occurs. Moreover, whether and how a person reciprocates another's self-disclosure depends on the nature of the other's revelations.

Shaffer, Smith, and Tomarelli (1982) conducted a study on the role of self-monitoring in self-disclosure reciprocity. The research design was similar to that Shaffer and Tomarelli (1989) later used in their investigation of the relationship of public and private self-consciousness to self-disclosure, which was discussed in Chapter 5.

Subjects who had previously been given Snyder's (1974) Self-Monitoring Scale were recruited for a two-part study entitled "Making New Acquaintances" and told that the investigators were interested in how people become acquainted and get to know one another. As far as the subjects were concerned the focus of the study was on getting acquainted with another person who, unbeknownst to them was the investigators' confederate. The subjects were also led to believe that they would meet that person again in a purported second phase of the study (that in reality was not to take place).

Once the subject and the confederate were alone in the room, the confederate volunteered private information on four very personal topics. The level of intimacy of this information was either low or high, depending on the experimental condition to which the subject had been assigned. The results showed that high self-monitors were more likely than low self-monitors to reciprocate the confederate's self-disclosures in a fashion that imitated their level of intimacy and content, as well as the emotionality with which they had been presented. Low self-monitors, in fact, generally failed to engage in reciprocal self-disclosure.

Instrumental hedonism. Seeking to explain these results Shaffer et al. (1982) speculated that the high self-monitors had been motivated by "instrumental hedonism." This concept had been used by Danheiser and Graziano (1982) to explain the finding that in a competitive game with a partner with whom they expect a future interaction high self-monitors display more cooperation than low self-monitors.

Danheiser and Graziano (1982) construed the high self-monitors' cooperation as a self-presentational strategy that they employ in the expectation that it would "pay off" when that partner is encountered again. In other words, that strategy was intended to be the instrument for bringing about a favorable (hedonistic) experience—hence, instrumental hedonism.

Shaffer et al. (1982) viewed the reciprocal self-disclosure of their high self-monitors in the same light. They assumed that these subjects were currying the confederate's favorable opinion, support, and cooperation, in hopes that this would help them in the expected future interaction with that person. Low self-monitors, on the other hand, were assumed to care less about future benefits so that they felt freer to present their true feelings on each discussion topic.

For instrumental hedonism to be the explanation for the self-disclosures of high self-monitors it is necessary that they anticipate a future occasion at which they can reap the reward of their strategy. How would they behave in the absence of that anticipation? Shaffer, Ogden, and Wu proceeded to answer that question in a study reported in 1987.

The research strategy was much the same as the one that had been employed in the earlier study (Shaffer et al., 1982). High and low self-monitors interacted with a confederate in a session ostensibly designed for getting acquainted. With some subjects the confederate self-disclosed on a very intimate level; with others the revelations were more superficial. In addition, one group of subjects was told "that they would be working closely with their partners on an unspecified decision-making task after completing the initial acquaintanceship phase of the experiment" (p. 81). A control group was given no such expectation.

As in the earlier study, "[w]hen participants thought that they would be interacting with their new acquaintances in a second phase of the experiment, the high self-monitors disclosed more intimately and with more emotion to intimate than to nonintimate acquaintances, whereas low self-monitors failed to show this disclosure reciprocity effect" (p. 91). The experimental manipulation of the anticipation of future interaction, however, showed that instrumental hedonism could not be used to explain these results for when they did not anticipate meeting their partner again, both high and low self-monitors displayed disclosure reciprocity.

Situation and disposition. In explaining these results Shaffer et al. (1987) remind the reader that high self-monitors are situationally guided. That is, they are sensitive to the cues of a social interaction and monitor their behavior so as to adjust it to what they deem to be the demands of the situation. Low self-monitors, on the other hand, are dispositionally guided. Their behavior in a social interaction is largely a function of their own mood, feelings, standards, and ideas to which they are much more attentive than are their stylistic counterparts.

Shaffer et al. (1987) cite data gathered with a postexperimental questionnaire to support the conclusion that the prospect of future interaction with one's partner, particularly one who discloses intimate material, "was at least a mildly stressful point of concern for all participants" (p. 93). This stress, they reason, led the situationally guided high self-monitor to be even more attentive to situational cues when deciding how or what to disclose, whereas the dispositionally guided low self-monitor relied even less on situational cues, and attended more closely to his or her personal thoughts and feelings as the basis for self-presentation. In the relatively low-stress condition, when the participants did not anticipate meeting their partner again, both low and high self-monitors relied on the well-ingrained social norms of politeness that call for reciprocity in a conversation with a stranger.

Whether this explanation is correct must await future explorations. Meanwhile, it seems clear that the extent to which people will engage in self-disclosure depends not only on their level of self-monitoring, but also on whether they anticipate another interaction with the person to whom they are talking at the present time. Moreover, as we shall see in a moment, Ludwig, Franco, and Malloy (1986) showed that self-disclosure also depends on the nature of the situation in which the interaction takes place.

Self-Disclosure in Real Life

In the studies on the effect of self-monitoring on self-disclosure reciprocity discussed thus far the research subjects were students in Introductory Psychology courses who knew from the outset that the purpose of their interacting with the other person was to get acquainted. They had signed up for participation in an experiment entitled "Making New Acquaintances," and when they arrived at the laboratory they were told that the purpose of the study was "to investigate how people become acquainted and get to know one another" (Shaffer & Tomarelli, 1989, p. 766).

These, of course, are not the conditions under which self-disclosure occurs in people's life outside the laboratory. This raises the question of external validity; the question whether the results of studies such as that of Shaffer et al. (1982) can be generalized from the artificial situation of the laboratory to the natural situation of what we like to call "real life."

Ludwig, Franco, and Malloy (1986) set out to investigate this question. They reasoned that such situationally guided individuals as high self-monitors would, by definition, be highly sensitive to the demand characteristics of the laboratory situation, more sensitive, certainly, than the dispositionally guided low self-monitors. On these grounds they disguised their investigation so that the participants did not know that its purpose was to find out how people behave when they are in the process of getting acquainted.

Instead of the ubiquitous students from Introductory Psychology courses who are likely to suspect that the investigator is deceiving them (especially after their course has dealt with social psychology and personality research), Ludwig et al. (1986) used as subjects students enrolled in laboratory courses in biology and experimental statistics.

These students, to whom the Self-Monitoring Scale had previously been administered, were asked to participate in an experiment for which they would be paid $3. (Students in Psychology courses typically serve as experimental subjects to earn course credits [Miller, 1981].) When each subject arrived for the experiment he or she was introduced to another subject (who actually was the experimenter's confederate). Both were then given instructions beginning with, "We are interested in the effects of one person's physiology upon that of another person." After this the subject and the confederate were connected to dummy physiological recording equipment and told, "You are connected to these skin response devices so that we can get a reading of your physiological effects upon each other." The two were then left alone for 10 min during which the confederate self-disclosed at either a high or low level of intimacy.

For the high-disclosure condition the confederates had been trained to maximize their use of self-referent statements, to reveal intimate aspects of themselves as appropriate to the situation, and to speak with enthusiasm. For the low-disclosure condition they had been given the opposite instructions so that they would speak with minimal intonation in their voice, and minimize self-referent statements and intimate information.

Results. Independent judges later scored the subjects' tape-recorded verbalizations for the number of self-referent thought units, the depth of self-disclosure, and the level of emotional investment. The statistical analysis of the data revealed that subjects in both conditions reciprocated the confederate's self-disclosures by offering disclosures at similar levels of self-reference, intimacy, and emotional investment. Inasmuch as the ostensible purpose of this research had been the study physiological responses, self-disclosure reciprocity can be said to be not simply an artifact of the demand characteristics of a laboratory situation in which subjects are instructed to get acquainted with another person.

Failure to replicate. Although the self-disclosure reciprocity during the acquaintance process that had been found in earlier studies was thus confirmed, another seemingly well-established effect was not replicated. Recall that Shaffer and his colleagues had consistently found only the high self-monitors to reciprocate the self-disclosure level displayed by the confederate; the low self-monitors typically remained unaffected by the confederates' verbalizations (Shaffer et al., 1982, 1987; Shaffer & Tomarelli, 1989). This interaction between self-monitoring and self-disclosure was not present in the data of Ludwig et al. (1986). They found that in the condition in which the confederate disclosed at a high level of intimacy and emotionality both low and high self-monitors disclosed at a high level, whereas in the condition in which the confederate disclosed at a low level only the low self-monitors reciprocated at the low level; the high self-monitors tended to engage in high-level self-disclosures under both conditions. The differences in these results are evident in the two graphs in Figure 10-1. The top graph (see Figure 10-1A) shows data reported by Shaffer et al. (1982), and the bottom graph (see Figure 10-1B) depicts those from the study by Ludwig et al. (1986).

Explanation. Ludwig et al. (1986) seek to explain the behavior of the high self-monitors in their study by pointing out that such people have a self-conception of being friendly and outgoing so that, when they are in the presence of a low-key partner who self-discloses at a superficial level of intimacy with little emotional involvement they attempt to make the social situation more compatible with their concept of themselves. This explanation is congruent with the niche picking conceptualization of Scarr and McCartney (1983) discussed earlier as well as with the results of a study by Snyder and Gangestad (1982) that showed high and low self-monitors systematically to choose social situations "conducive to enactment of their characteristic behavioral orientation" (pp. 133-134).

That explanation fails to account, however, for the results of studies such as that of Shaffer et al. (1982) in which high self-monitors reciprocated at a low level of self-disclosure when that was the level at which their partner disclosed. To rationalize that discrepancy Ludwig et al. (1986) suggest that the situational cues to which the high self-monitors were responding in these studies were those of the experimental setting and not those of the confederates' behavior.

As far as the unexpected reciprocation of their low self-monitors is concerned, Ludwig et al. (1986) resort to the speculation that these individuals, whose social behavior is typically guided by their personal moods and feelings, let these inner states be influenced by the behavior of their conversational partner, thus following the pace of disclosure set by this partner. To support this formulation and to explain the difference between their and the Shaffer et al. (1982) findings these authors again cite the difference in the supposed purpose of the experiments that stressed "getting acquainted" in the one case and physiological recording in the other. "Perhaps," they write, "the low self-monitors were unwilling to be appropriate by conforming to the experimental demand to 'get acquainted' and thus did not reciprocate at the same level as projected by their partner" (Ludwig et al., 1986, p. 1081).

SOME METHODOLOGICAL AND THEORETICAL CONSIDERATIONS
Replication in Personality Research

Cell lines and college students. The difficulties Ludwig et al. (1986) had in reconciling their results with those of prior studies highlights a problem that plagues all research on complex human behavior. In a science such as biology it

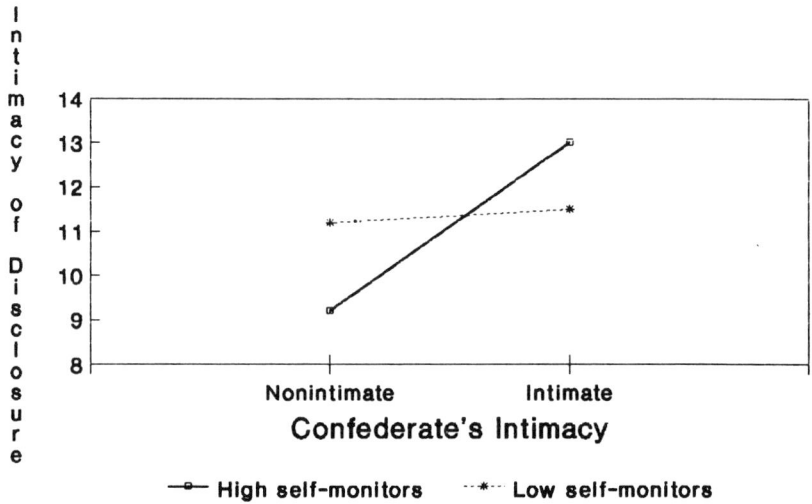

FIGURE 10-1A Self-disclosure intimacy of high and low self-monitors who self-disclosed to an intimate or a nonintimate confederate.

Adapted from Shaffer, D. R., Smith, J. E., and Tomarelli, M., 1982. Self-monitoring as a determinant of self-disclosure reciprocity during the acquaintance process. *Journal of Personality and Social Psychology*, 43, 163-175. Copyright 1982 by the American Psychological Association. Adapted by permission.

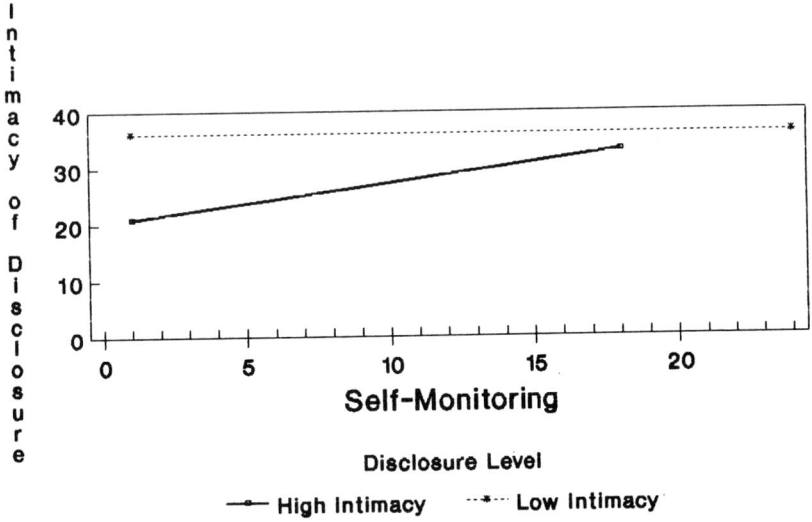

FIGURE 10-1B The effects of self-monitoring on depth of disclosure under conditions of low- or high-confederate disclosure.

Adapted from Ludwig, D., Franco, J. N., and Malloy, T. E., 1986. Effects of reciprocity and self-monitoring on self-disclosure with a new acquaintance. *Journal of Personality and Social Psychology*, 50, 1077-1082. Copyright 1986 by the American Psychological Association. Adapted by permission.

has long been customary to insist that a new discovery reported by one laboratory be duplicated in another before it is accepted as established knowledge. Such replications are facilitated by the fact that the procedures used in the laboratory that made the discovery can be described in great detail so that the identical procedures can be used elsewhere. Moreover, it is possible to have the first laboratory send to the one that seeks to replicate the experiment the very culture or cell line on which the original work had been based. That cell line or culture can then be used in many repetitions and variations of the original experiment for, if carefully maintained, neither will be exhausted.

None of this is feasible in psychological research on human behavior. Minor, but possibly critical, details of the procedure such as the size of the room in which subject and confederate interacted are rarely reported. In biology it does not matter whether the experimenter wore a white coat or a sweater, nor is it necessary to note his or her age, hair style, skin color, dialect, or accent. In psychology such variables may well influence how the subject reacts. Moreover, and this is crucial, the college students who served as subjects in a psychological experiment that is to be replicated cannot be packed in dry ice and transported by air express to another investigator. Who knows in how many ways the students in introductory psychology at the University of Georgia who participated in the study Shaffer et al. published in 1982 differed from the undergraduates at New Mexico State University who were enrolled in biology and experimental statistics laboratories, and served as subjects for Ludwig et al. who published their work in 1986. As for using the same subjects in later versions of the same experiment in the same laboratory, that too is impossible because they are no longer the same subjects. The experience of participating in the first study will have changed their attitudes and expectations toward the second.

Modification of conditions prevents replication. Ludwig et al. (1986) had set out to test whether the "getting acquainted" setting employed in Shaffer's various studies influenced the manner in which high and low self-monitors responded to confederates who displayed different levels of self-disclosure. Even with the obstacles to exact replication just mentioned, it would have been important that they change only that one variable, the setting. Unfortunately, from the viewpoint of comparing their results with those of the earlier studies, Ludwig et al. (1986) also changed the manner in which the communication occurred.

Where Shaffer et al. (1982) had confederate and subject take turns discussing three specified topics, Ludwig et al. (1986) had them freely converse under rather general instructions. Although this resulted in a less artificial, more spontaneous condition it also led to different subjects having unequal amounts of time in which to speak because the time they had available was a function of the time taken up by the confederate's unstandardized verbalizations. Though an attempt was made to control for this by transforming the data before they were analyzed it is conceivable that a subject's self-disclosures were influenced by whether the confederate spoke rarely or often, and for brief or long periods.

Different analyses complicate comparisons. There is one other difference between the Ludwig and the Shaffer studies. It is that they used different statistical procedures to analyze their data. Shaffer et al. (1982) had divided their subjects into groups of high and low self-monitors on the basis of splitting the distribution of subjects' scores on the Self-Monitoring Scale at the median (12). All subsequent comparisons were then conducted on this dichotomy. High and low self-monitors were compared on the intimacy-level and emotional investment of their self-disclosure in the intimate versus nonintimate confederate conditions.

Although Ludwig et al. (1986) also divided their original subject pool into groups of high and low self-monitors on the basis of a median split (11.5), they analyzed their data using the subjects' scores on the Self-Monitoring Scale as a continuous variable. Thus, the principal statistic used by Shaffer et al. (1982) was an analysis of variance, whereas that employed by Ludwig et al. was the Pearson product-moment correlation.

Unanswered Question

The difference in the results of the Ludwig et al. (1986) and the Shaffer et al. (1982) studies is difficult to explain. As Ludwig et al. believe, it may reflect the effect of the different ways in which the experimenters had structured the situation for their subjects: as "getting acquainted" in the work by Shaffer et al. and as an interest in "physiological effects" in the study by Ludwig et al. In view of the fact, however, that in addition to the instructions to the subjects several other aspects of these studies were also different and inasmuch as exact replication is never possible in research on human behavior, one is forced to conclude that the question Ludwig et al. had investigated remains to be answered.

Do People Come in Two Basic Types?

Continuous versus dichotomous variables. As their different statistical analyses reflect, Ludwig et al. (1986) approached self-monitoring as a continuous variable, analogous to height where measures reflect gradations of individual differences. In contrast, Shaffer and his colleagues (Shaffer et al., 1982, 1987; Shaffer & Tomarelli, 1989), following Snyder's (1974; Gangestad & Snyder, 1985) lead, treated self-monitoring as a dichotomy. They spoke of high self-monitors and low self-monitors, analogous to talking of people as either tall or short.

Self-Monitoring

This difference in approach has important theoretical implications. These have been the focus of the research by several investigators (Briggs & Cheek, 1988; Carver, 1989; Gangestad & Snyder, 1985; Miller & Thayer, 1988, 1989).

Different Conceptualizations

Dimensional variables. At issue is how individual differences in self-monitoring and other aspects of human personality are to be conceptualized. Gangestad and Snyder (1985) take the position that there are two kinds of personality variables. The first and more familiar kind consists of the dimensional variables. Here quantifiable characteristics are distributed along a continuum (dimension) and individuals differ in degree. A trait, such as sociability, is an example of a dimensional variable.

Class variables. The second kind of personality variables is less well known and more controversial. They are the class variables. Here individual differences fall into two or more discrete categories (classes), and people can be classified as belonging to one or another of these. Gangestad and Snyder (1985) offer biological sex as an example and argue that in the realm of personality self-monitoring is an instance of a class variable.

A Model

In postulating that self-monitoring is analogous to biological sex Gangestad and Snyder (1985) contend that the behaviors that make up the 18 items on the revised Self-Monitoring Scale are but the surface manifestations of an underlying, latent class variable that is dichotomously distributed. This is not the place to present or examine the genetic explication and statistical analyses Gangestad and Snyder advance in support of the model, but several comments are in order.

According to the proposed model, there are two discrete classes, high self-monitors and low self-monitors. People can be assigned to one or the other of these classes on the basis of their score on the Self-Monitoring Scale. It is noteworthy that these scores distribute along a continuum so that the class assignment depends on how and where this distribution is split.

As noted earlier, the method usually employed in research on self-monitoring is to split the scores at the median, defining the 50% with scores below the median as low self-monitors, those above as high self-monitors. When a sample of research subjects has thus been dichotomized the individuals' scores become irrelevant. Indeed, Gangestad and Snyder (1985) write, "once one knows that an individual belongs to the high self-monitoring class, one should not care whether the person scored 15 or 22" (p. 337).

What then is the difference between a person with a score of 15 and one with a score of 22? When self-monitoring is viewed as a class variable, the difference is not that the person with the higher score is more likely to engage in self-monitoring, but that he or she has a higher probability of belonging to the high self-monitoring class.

This model of discrete classes justifies the median-split approach to the statistical analysis of scores from the Self-Monitoring Scale, but it raises the question whether it makes no difference that some of the individuals in the two self-monitoring groups have a very low probability of belonging there. Is it really appropriate to view people whose scores lie near either side of the median (say 10 and 12 when the median is 11) as equal to those at either end of the distribution of scores (1 and 18)?

Tall or how tall?   For some purposes it may be useful to classify people as either tall or short on the basis of an arbitrary cut-off point, but doing so ignores that there are gradations within each of these classes. Moreover, having assessed each individual to obtain a score or measure on some characteristic, be that height or self-monitoring, one discards many potentially valuable data if one then limits oneself to comparing two categories.

Lastly, it may be well to recall that biological sex, on which Gangestad and Snyder (1985) drew for an analogy, is normally dichotomous only at the chromosomal but not at the hormonal level.

Questions With Dichotomous Answers

True or Probably True?

Related to the question whether dichotomies are suitable for categorizing people is the issue raised by the customary true-or-false format of the Self-Monitoring Scale. This format forces those who are being tested with that scale to judge each item as either true or false.

Take, for example, item 6 of the 18-item version of the scale (Gangestad & Snyder, 1985). It reads: "I would probably make a good actor" (true or false?). As the word *probably* indicates, the respondent is asked for a probability statement. People who have tried being an actor and failed would know quite definitely that, as far as they are concerned, this statement is false. Conversely, those who know from experience that they are good actors would know quite definitely that for them the statement is true. Yet others, who have no experience to fall back on would have to base their answers on a hunch. These different levels of certainty, however, are obscured when the only possible way of responding is to check either true or false. Would one not have a better idea of people's tendency to self-monitor if they were asked to rate the degree to which a given statement applies to them?

Both of these issues—whether self-monitoring is a class variable or a continuous dimension, and how one might improve on the true-or-false choice—have been addressed in several studies (Briggs & Cheek, 1988; Ludwig et al., 1986; Miller & Thayer, 1988, 1989). As discussed earlier, the study by Ludwig et al., which used the entire range of self-monitoring scores, led to results that differed markedly from those reported by investigators who split these scores at their median and analyzed them as representing a dichotomous (class) variable.

True, false, or how true? Miller and Thayer (1989) conducted two studies that directly addressed the issues raised here. In the first of these studies they tested the effect of enabling subjects to respond to the Self-Monitoring Scale in a fashion that is more discriminating than that permitted by the dichotomous true-or-false choice. They did this by giving approximately half of their subjects the traditional true-or-false format, whereas the others received a 5-point Likert-type format. The latter enabled the subjects to indicate the degree to which they disagreed or agreed (from 1 = disagree strongly to 5 = agree strongly) with each of the statements on the scale. The results showed that the Likert and the true-or-false response formats "do not yield precisely similar results" (p. 146) and that the former "demonstrates clearly superior internal consistency relative to that obtained for the true-false response format" (p. 145).

Dichotomous or continuous? Miller and Thayer (1989) also addressed the question whether self-monitoring is a dichotomous or a continuous variable. In so doing they replicated an earlier work by Briggs et al. (1980) that had subjected scores on the Self-Monitoring Scale to a factor analysis. The reasoning for using that statistical method to ascertain which model, the dichotomous or the continuous, is to be endorsed runs as follows. If the scores on the Self-Monitoring Scale distinguish between two classes or types of people (high and low self-monitors) a factor analysis should reveal a single general factor. If more than one factor emerges, self-monitoring would have to be construed as a multifaceted variable.

As the data of Briggs et al. (1980) had earlier, those of Miller and Thayer (1989) supported a three-factor model that proved far superior to a one-factor model. Although the naming of statistically generated factors is always subjective and somewhat arbitrary, it appears that the total score on the Self-Monitoring Scale is a composite reflecting extraversion, other-directedness, and acting ability.

"With the identification of three distinctly separable individual differences" Miller and Thayer (1989) conclude, "it becomes logically impossible to explain how three factors combine to yield two forms of personality" (pp. 153-154). They endorse the view expressed by Briggs and Cheek (1988) who, having conducted their own factor analytic study, stated that "it is misleading to suggest that people in the world come in only two basic types" (p. 674). Miller and Thayer (1989) recommend that the notion of self-monitoring as a class variable be abandoned in favor of formulating it as a continuously distributed variable. That, indeed, is what Snyder (1974) had originally proposed but later abandoned.

Self-Monitoring and Nature of Science

The construct of self-monitoring and the scale Snyder (1974) developed to measure it have spawned a remarkably large number of investigations that demonstrated the ability of that scale to predict not only people's attitudes and preferences, but also how they will behave in and react to a great variety of social situations. The utility of the Self-Monitoring Scale is well established. Whether it is best structured as a true-or-false test and whether the scores should be split so as to make the results dichotomous are questions that remain to be answered. So is the claim, advanced by Gangestad and Snyder (1985), that the scale measures a "genetically explicated, discrete class variable" that exerts an "influence on human social behavior" (p. 338). Questions yet to be answered and conjectures still in need of validation, however, are in the nature of science.

11

Summing Up

At the end of the first chapter we stressed the need for patience in conducting and reading about research on self-related topics. We emphasized the difficulties inherent in research that must often depend on what people are willing and able to offer in self-reports of unknown validity. These difficulties notwithstanding, intrepid investigators whose studies we have examined succeeded in conducting sophisticated, well-executed research that has moved us a step closer to understanding the sense of self. A step closer but not to the point where it would be possible to make definitive statements. For that reason this section represents not a conclusion but a summing up, a status report on where we are and some suggestions of where we should go.

We assert that people do not carry within them a substantive entity such as the one the poet calls "the self." We recognize, however, that people have a sense of self—an awareness of themselves as individuals, separate and different from other individuals. Studies of that awareness have found that it arises gradually during the first 6 months of the second year of life and in the context of the mother-infant relationship. With the individual's maturation and the development of language, this self-awareness expands until, by adolescence, the existence of a fairly elaborate self-concept can be documented. Most of what we know about this development comes from cross-sectional research. More definitive knowledge must await badly needed, but expensive and time-consuming longitudinal studies.

Working with the tools of cognitive psychology and using such statistical methods as factor analysis, investigators have found that people are able to describe the perception they have of themselves—to articulate their self-concept. When they do, their descriptions confirm that personality can be conceived as composed of five dimensions: extraversion, agreeableness, conscientiousness, emotional stability, and culture. As always, the answers people give are a function of the questions they are asked, and new ways of asking new questions are needed to establish the universality of these dimensions.

A recurrent issue in studies on the sense of self is the accuracy of the reports people give about their self-perception. Without answering the philosophical question of how we can ever know what a person is "really" like, it appears that when asked to describe themselves people often produce distortions. Sometimes they flatter and at other times they belittle themselves; however, in either case the distortion protects their self-esteem and one or more of its dimensions of competence, worth, power, and acceptance.

Studies have also shown that it *is* helpful to construe the self-concept as encompassing several dimensions and different levels, but whether and to what extent the self-concept is stable, malleable, or both, and how sensitive it is to environmental influences remains an open question. This uncertainty stems from a difficulty personality psychology shares with other social and behavioral sciences—that of exactly repeating earlier studies. Solving this problem of replication is an important agenda item for studies on personality. One essential step in that direction is to develop and agree on standard units and tools of measurement.

There are two measures that go a long way toward meeting this need, although both are controversial and in need of refinement. One is the SCS of Fenigstein et al. (1975). Its use has demonstrated that it is fruitful to differentiate between public and private self-consciousness. Many personal and interpersonal forms of behavior, including self-awareness, conformity, and consistency of attitudes, correlate with self-consciousness. It has been argued that social dependency is a more exact designation for that characteristic, raising an issue that remains to be resolved.

The other widely and constructively used measure is Snyder's (1974) Self-Monitoring Scale. With it investigators have shown that knowing whether people are mainly concerned with making a good impression or with following their inclinations permits one to predict how they will behave in a great variety of interpersonal situations. It is particularly intriguing to find that the orientation of self-monitoring may have biological-genetic precursors and that hints at a direction future research on the sense of self might profitably take.

In addition to the lack of universally agreed-on measures, research on the sense of self is handicapped by an overreliance on studies conducted in highly artificial laboratory settings with subjects who are mainly volunteer college students enrolled in psychology courses. The few studies that were conducted under the conditions of daily life with samples that represent the general population provide more enlightening results than most of those currently available. Such naturalistic studies are challenging to execute, but much of the work on self-efficacy, conducted with "real people in the real world" stands as an impressive model that others might fruitfully follow.

Summing Up

This then is one perspective on the state of our knowledge about the sense of self. There remain questions to be answered, conjectures to be validated, measures to be developed, and methods to be invented. Being incomplete is the nature of science—that open-ended, self-correcting, constantly growing, sometimes misunderstood, and occasionally abused enterprise—which ultimately may not be able to provide the answers to all our questions. That, however, must not keep us from the thrill of the search.

References

Ainsworth, M. D. S. (1979). Infant-mother attachment. *American Psychologist, 34*, 932-937.
Ainsworth, M. D. S., Behar, M. C., Waters, E., & Wall, S. (1978) *Patterns of attachment.* Hillsdale, NJ: Erlbaum.
Alicke, M. D. (1985). Global self-evaluations as determined by the desirability and controllability of trait adjectives. *Journal of Personality and Social Psychology, 49*, 1621-1630.
Allen, B. P., & Potkay, C. R. (1981). On the arbitrary distinction between states and types. *Journal of Personality and Social Psychology, 41*, 916-928.
Allport, G. W. (1961). *Patterns and growth in personality.* New York: Holt, Rinehart & Winston.
Allport, G. W., & Odbert, H. S. (1936). Trait names: A psycholexical study. *Psychological Monographs, 47*, (Whole no. 211), 1-171.
Altman, I., & Taylor, D. A. (1973). *Social penetration: The development of interpersonal relationships.* New York: Holt, Rinehart & Winston.
Arend, R., Gove, F. L., & Sroufe, L. A. (1979). Continuity of individual adaptation from infancy to kindergarten: A predictive study of ego-resiliency and curiosity in preschoolers. *Child Development, 50*, 950-959.
Asch, S. E. (1955). Opinions and social pressure. *Scientific American, 193*, 31-35.
Asch, S. E. (1956). Studies of independence and conformity: A minority of one against a unanimous majority. *Psychological Monographs, 70*, (Whole no. 416).
Atkins, J. W., & Raynor, J. O. (1974). *Motivation and achievement.* New York: Wiley.
Baars, B. J. (1986). *The cognitive revolution in psychology.* New York: Guilford.
Bachman, J. G. (1970). *Youth in transition: Vol. II. The impact of family background and intelligence on tenth-grade boys.* Ann Arbor, MI: Institute for Social Research.
Bachman, J. G., & O'Malley, P. M. (1986). Self-concepts, self-esteem, and educational experiences: The frog pond revisited (again). *Journal of Personality and Social Psychology, 50*, 35-46.
Bachman, J. G., O'Malley, P. M., & Johnston, J. J. (1978). *Youth in transition: Vol. VI. Adolescence to adulthood—A study of change and stability in the lives of young men.* Ann Arbor, MI: Institute for Social Research.
Baldwin, M. W., & Holmes, J. G. (1987). Salient private audiences and awareness of the self. *Journal of Personality and Social Psychology, 52*, 1087-1098.

References

Bandura, A. (1977). Self-efficacy: Toward a unifying theory of behavior change. *Psychological Review, 84,* 191-215.
Bandura, A. (1982). Self-efficacy mechanisms in human agency. *American Psychologist, 37,* 122-147.
Bandura, A. (1984). Recycling misconceptions of perceived self-efficacy. *Cognitive Therapy and Research, 8,* 231-255.
Bandura, A. (1986). *Social foundations of thought and action.* Englewood Cliffs, NJ: Prentice Hall.
Bandura, A. (1989). Human agency in social cognitive theory. *American Psychologist, 44,* 1175-1184.
Bandura, A., Cioffi, D., Taylor, C. B., & Brouillard, M. W. (1988). *Journal of Personality and Social Psychology, 55,* 479-488.
Bandura, A., O'Leary, A., Taylor, C. B., Gauthier, J., & Gossard, D. (1987). Perceived self-efficacy and pain control: Opioid and nonopioid mechanisms. *Journal of Personality and Social Psychology, 53,* 563-571.
Bandura, A., Reese, L., & Adams, N. E. (1982). Microanalysis of action and fear arousal as a function of differential levels of perceived self-efficacy. *Journal of Personality and Social Psychology, 43,* 5-21.
Barfield, O. (1954). *History of English words.* New York: Doran.
Batson, C. D., Coke, J. S., Jasnoski, M. L., & Hanson, M. (1978). Buying kindness: Effect of an extrinsic incentive for helping on perceived altruism. *Journal of Personality and Social Psychology, 4,* 86-91.
Batson, C. D., Fultz, J., Schoenrade, P. A., & Paduano, A. (1987). Critical self-reflection and self-perceived altruism: When self-reward fails. *Journal of Personality and Social Psychology, 53,* 594-602.
Baumeister, R. F. (1986). *Identity: Cultural change and the struggle for self.* New York: Oxford University Press.
Bem, D. J. (1972). Self-perceptions theory. In L. Berkowitz (Ed.), *Advances in social psychology* (Vol. 1, pp. 1-62). New York: Academic Press.
Bem, S. L. (1974). The measurement of psychological androgyny. *Journal of Consulting and Clinical Psychology, 42,* 155-162.
Berglas, S., & Jones, E. E. (1978). Drug choice as a self-handicapping strategy in response to noncontingent success. *Journal of Personality and Social Psychology, 36,* 405-417.
Berkowitz, L. (1987). Mood, self-awareness, and willingness to help. *Journal of Personality and Social Psychology, 52,* 721-729.
Berkowitz, L. (1989). Frustration-aggression hypothesis: Examination and reformulation. *Psychological Bulletin, 106,* 59-73.
Berlyne, D. E. (1970). Attention as a problem in behavior theory. In D. I. Mostofsky (Ed.), *Attention: Contemporary theory and analysis* (pp. 25-49). New York: Appleton.
Berscheid, E., & Walster, E. (1978). *Interpersonal attraction.* Reading, MA: Addison-Wesley.
Bertenthal, B. I., & Fischer, K. W. (1978). Development of self-recognition in the infant. *Developmental Psychology, 14,* 44-50.
Block, J. (1971). *Lives through time.* Berkeley, CA: Bancroft.
Bowlby, J. (1969). *Attachment and loss: Vol. 1. Attachment.* New York: Basic Books.
Briggs, S. R., & Cheek, J. (1988). On the nature of self-monitoring: Problems with assessment, problems with validity. *Journal of Personality and Social Psychology, 54,* 663-678.

Briggs, S. R., Cheek, J. M., & Buss, A. H. (1980). An analysis of the self-monitoring scale. *Journal of Personality and Social Psychology, 38,* 679-686.

Broadbent, D. E., & Gregory, M. (1964). Stimulus set and response set: The alternation of attention. *Quarterly Journal of Experimental Psychology, 16,* 309-317.

Bronson, G. W. (1972). Infants' reactions to unfamiliar persons and novel objects. *Monographs of the Society for Research in Child Development, 47,* (Whole no. 377.)

Buss, A. H. (1980). *Self-consciousness and social anxiety.* San Francisco: Freeman.

Buss, A. H., & Plomin, R. (1984). *Temperament: Early developing personality traits.* Hillsdale, NJ: Erlbaum.

Byrne, D. (1971) *The attraction paradigm.* New York: Academic Press.

Campbell, D. T., & Fiske, D. W. (1959). Convergent and discriminant validation by the multitrait-multimethod matrix. *Psychological Bulletin, 56,* 81-105.

Campbell, J. D., & Fehr, B. (1990). Self-esteem and perceptions of conveyed impressions: Is negative affectivity associated with greater realism? *Journal of Personality and Social Psychology, 58,* 122-133.

Cannon, W. B. (1929). Organization of physiological homeostasis. *Physiological Review, 9,* 399-431.

Carver, C. S. (1989). How should multifaceted personality constructs be tested? Issues illustrated by self-monitoring, attributional style and hardiness. *Journal of Personality and Social Psychology, 56,* 577-585.

Carver, C. S., & Scheier, M. F. (1978). Self-focusing effects of dispositional self-consciousness, mirror presence, and audience presence. *Journal of Personality and Social Psychology, 36,* 324-332.

Carver, C. S., & Scheier, M. F. (1981). *Attention and self-regulation: A control-theory approach to human behavior.* New York: Springer Verlag.

Cattell, R. B. (1966). *The scientific analysis of personality.* Chicago: Aldine.

Christie, R., & Geis, L. (Eds.). (1970). *Studies in Machiavellianism.* New York: Academic Press.

Condiotte, M. M., & Lichtenstein, E. (1981). Self-efficacy and relapse in smoking cessation programs. *Journal of Consulting and Clinical Psychology, 49,* 648-658.

Conway, M., & Ross, M. (1984). Getting what you want by revising what you had. *Journal of Personality and Social Psychology, 47,* 738-748.

Cooley, C. H. (1902). *Human nature and the social order.* New York: Scribner's.

Coopersmith, S. (1959). A method for determining types of self-esteem. *Journal of Abnormal and Social Psychology, 59,* 87-94.

Cozby, P. C. (1973). Self-disclosure: A literature review. *Psychological Bulletin, 79,* 73-91.

Crowne, D. P., & Marlow, D. (1960). A new scale of social desirability independent of psychopathology. *Journal of Consulting Psychology, 24,* 349-354.

Danheiser, P. R., & Graziano, W. G. (1982). Self-monitoring and cooperation as a self-presentational strategy. *Journal of Personality and Social Psychology, 42,* 497-505.

Davis, D., & Brock, T. C. (1975). Use of first person pronouns as a function of increased objective self-awareness and performance feedback. *Journal of Experimental Social Psychology, 11,* 381-388.

Derlega, V. J., & Chaikin, A. L. (1976). Norms affecting self-disclosure in men and women. *Journal of Consulting and Clinical Psychology, 44,* 376-380.

DiClemente, C. C. (1981). Self-efficacy and smoking cessation maintenance: A preliminary test. *Cognitive Therapy and Research, 5,* 175-187.

Digman, J. M. (1989). Five robust trait dimensions: Development, stability, and utility. *Journal of Personality, 57,* 195-214.

Duval, S., & Wicklund, R. A. (1972). *A theory of objective self-awareness.* New York: Academic Press.

Duval, S., & Wicklund, R. (1973). Effects of objective self-awareness on attributions of causality. *Journal of Experimental Social Psychology, 9,* 17-31.

Dworkin, R. H. (1977, August). *Genetic influences on cross-cultural consistency.* Paper presented at the Second International Congress on Twin Studies, Washington, DC.

Eastman, C., & Marzillier, J. S. (1984). Theoretical and methodological difficulties in Bandura's self-efficacy theory. *Cognitive Therapy and Research, 8,* 213-229.

Eichorn, D. H., Clausen, J. A., Haan, N., Honzik, M., & Mussen, P. H. (Eds.). (1981). *Present and past in middle life.* New York: Academic Press.

Epstein, S. (1973). The self-concept revisited—Or a theory of a theory. American Psychologist, 28, 404-416.

Erikson, E. H. (1959). Identity and the life cycle. *Psychological Issues, 1(1).*

Exner, J. E. (1973). The self-focus sentence completion scale: A study of egocentricity. *Journal of Personality Assessment, 37,* 437-455.

Eysenck, H. J. (1970). *The structure of human personality.* London: Methuen.

Fazio, R. H., Effrein, E. A., & Falender, V. J. (1981). Self-perceptions following social interaction. *Journal of Personality and Social Psychology, 41,* 364-370.

Fazio, R. H., Zanna, M. P., & Cooper, J. (1977). Dissonance and self-perception: An integrated view of each theory's proper domain of application. *Journal of Experimental Social Psychology, 13,* 464-479.

Fenigstein, A., & Levine, M. P. (1984). Self-attention, concept activation and the causal self. *Journal of Experimental Social Psychology, 20,* 231-245.

Fenigstein, A., Scheier, M. F., & Buss, A. H. (1975). Public and private self-consciousness: Assessment and theory. *Journal of Consulting and Clinical Psychology, 43,* 522-527.

Festinger, L. (1954). A theory of social comparison processes. *Human Relations, 7,* 117-140.

Festinger, L. (1957). *A theory of cognitive dissonance.* Stanford, CA: Stanford University Press.

Fiske, D. W. (1949). Consistency of the factorial structures of personality from different sources. *Journal of Abnormal and Social Psychology, 44,* 329-344.

Freud, S. (1933). *New introductory lectures on psychoanalysis.* New York: Norton.

Freud, S. (1953/1974). *The standard edition of the complete psychological works.* J. Strachey (Ed.). London: Hogarth Press.

Froming, W. J., & Carver, C. S. (1981). Divergent influences of private and public self-consciousness in a compliance paradigm. *Journal of Research in Personality, 15,* 159-171.

Funder, D.C. (1991). Global traits: A neo-Allportian approach to personality. *Psychological Science, 2,* 31-39.

Gangestad, S. (1984). *On the etiology of individual differences in self-monitoring and expressive self-control: Testing the case of strong genetic influence.* Unpublished doctoral dissertation, University of Minnesota.

Gangestad, S., & Snyder, M. (1985). "To carve nature at its joints": On the existence of discrete classes in personality. *Psychological Review, 92,* 317-349.

Gergen, K. J. (1985). The social constructionist movement in modern psychology. *American Psychologist, 40,* 266-275.

Glick, P., DeMorest, J. A., & Hotze, C. A. (1988). Self-monitoring and beliefs about partner compatibility in romantic relationships. *Personality and Social Psychology Bulletin, 14,* 485-494.

Goldberg, L. R. (1990). An alternative "description of personality": The big five factor structure. *Journal of Personality and Social Psychology, 59,* 1216-1229.

Greenberg, J., & Pyszczynski, T. (1986). Persistent high self-focus after failure and low self-focus after success: The depressive self-focus style. *Journal of Personality and Social Psychology, 50,* 1039-1044.

Greenwald, A. G., & Banaji, M. R. (1989). The self as a memory system: Powerful, but ordinary. *Journal of Personality and Social Psychology, 57,* 41-54.

Harris, R. N., & Snyder, C. R. (1986). The role of uncertain self-esteem in self-handicapping. *Journal of Personality and Social Psychology, 51,* 451-458.

Harter, S. (1983). Developmental perspectives on the self-system. In P. H. Mussen (Ed.), *Handbook of child psychology: Vol. 4. Socialization, personality, and social development* (pp. 275-385). New York: Wiley.

Helmreich, R., Stapp, J., & Ervin, C. (1974). The Texas Social Behavior Inventory (TSBI): An objective measure of self-esteem or social competence. *Journal Supplement Abstract Service Catalog of Selected Documents in Psychology, 4,* 79. (Manuscript No. 681).

Hetherington, E. M., & Martin, B. (1986). Family factors and psychopathology in children. In H. C. Quay & J. S. Werry (Eds.), *Psychopathological disorders of childhood* (3rd ed. pp. 332-390). New York: Wiley.

Hoffman, M. L. (1981). Is altruism part of human nature? *Journal of Personality and Social Psychology, 40,* 121-137.

Holroyd, K. A., Penzien, D. B., Hursey, K. G., Tobin, D. L., Rogers, L., Holm, J. E., Marcille, P. J., Hall, J. R., & Chila, A. G. (1984). Change mechanisms in EMG biofeedback training: Cognitive changes underlying improvement in tension headache. *Journal of Consulting and Clinical Psychology, 52,* 1039-1053.

Hull, C. L. (1943). *Principles of behavior.* New York: Appleton-Century-Crofts.

Hull, J. G., & Levy, A. S. (1979). The organizational function of the self: An alternative to the Duval and Wicklund model of self-awareness. *Journal of Personality and Social Psychology, 37,* 756-768.

Hull, J. G., Van Treuren, R. R., Ashford, S. J., Propsom, P., & Andrus, B. W. (1988). Self-consciousness and the processing of self-relevant information. *Journal of Personality and Social Psychology, 54,* 452-465.

Ickes, J., Wicklund, R., & Ferris, C. (1973). Objective self-awareness and self-esteem. *Journal of Experimental Social Psychology, 9,* 202-219.

Ingram, R. E., Cruet, D., Johnson, B. R., & Wisnicki, W. S. (1988). Self-focused attention, gender, gender role, and vulnerability to negative affect. *Journal of Personality and Social Psychology, 55,* 967-978.

Jackson, D. N. (1984). *Personality Research Form manual.* Port Huron, MI: Research Psychologists Press.

Jamieson, D. W., Lydon, J. E., & Zanna, M. P. (1987). Attitude and activity preference similarity: Differential bases of interpersonal attraction for low and high self-monitors. *Journal of Personality and Social Psychology, 53,* 1052-1060.

Janis, I. L., & Field, P. (1959). Sex differences and personality factors related to persuasibility. In C. I. Hovland & I. L. Janis (Eds.), *Personality and persuasibility* (pp. 55-68, 300-302). New Haven, CT: Yale University Press.

Jones, E. E., & Baumeister, R. (1976). The self-monitor looks at the ingratiator. *Journal of Personality, 44,* 654-674.

Jones, E. E., & Berglas, S. (1978). Control of attributions about the self through self-handicapping strategies: The appeal of alcohol and the role of underachievement. *Personality and Social Psychology Bulletin, 4,* 200-206.

Jones, E. E., Brenner, K. J., & Knight, J. G. (1990). When failure elevates self-esteem. *Personality and Social Psychology Bulletin, 16,* 200-209.

Jones, E. E., & Nisbett, R. E. (1971). *The actor and the observer: Divergent perceptions of the causes of behavior.* Morristown, NJ: General Learning Press.

Jones, E. E., & Rhodewalt, F. (1980). *Self-Handicapping Scale* (Available from E. E. Jones, Department of Psychology, Princeton University, Princeton, NJ 08540, or F. Rhodewalt, Department of Psychology, University of Utah, Salt Lake City, UT 84112).

Jones, E. E., Rhodewalt, F., Berglas, S., & Skelton, J. A. (1981). Effects of strategic self-presentation on subsequent self-esteem. *Journal of Personality and Social Psychology, 41,* 407-421.

Jöreskog, K. G., & Sörbom, D. (1979). *Advances in factor analysis and structural equation models.* Cambridge, MA: Abt Books.

Jöreskog, K. G., & Sörbom, D. (1984). *LISREL VI: Analysis of linear structural relationships by maximum likelihood, instrumental variables, and least squares methods.* Chicago: National Educational Resources.

Kahneman, D., & Tversky, A. (1973). On the psychology of prediction. *Psychological Review, 80,* 237-251.

Kernis, M. H., Zuckerman, M., Cohen, A., & Spadafora, S. (1982). Persistence following failure: The interactive role of self-awareness and the attributional basis for negative expectancies. *Journal of Personality and Social Psychology, 43,* 1184-1191.

Kihlstrom, J. F., & Cantor, N. (1984). Mental representations of the self. In L. Berkowitz (Ed.), *Advances in experimental social psychology* (Vol. 17, pp. 1-47). New York: Academic Press.

Kirsch, I. (1980). "Microanalytic" analysis of efficacy expectations as predictors of performance. *Cognitive Therapy and Research, 4,* 259-262.

Kolditz, T. A., & Arkin, R. M. (1982). An impression management interpretation of the self-handicapping strategy. *Journal of Personality and Social Psychology, 43,* 492-502.

Lepper, M. R., Ross, L., & Lau, R. R. (1986). Persistence of inaccurate beliefs about the self: Perseverance effects in the classroom. *Journal of Personality and Social Psychology, 50,* 482-491.

Lewinsohn, P. M., Mischel, W., Chaplin, W., & Barton, R. (1980). Social competence and depression: The role of illusory self-perception. *Journal of Abnormal Psychology, 89,* 203-212.

Lewis, M. (1986). Origins of self-knowledge and individual differences in early self-recognition. In J. Suls & A. G. Greenwald (Eds.), *Psychological perspectives on the self* (Vol. 3. pp. 55-78). Hillsdale, NJ: Erlbaum.

Lewis, M., & Brooks-Gunn, J. (1979). *Social cognition and the acquisition of self.* New York: Plenum.

Lewis, M., Brooks-Gunn, J., & Jaskir, J. (1985). Individual differences in visual self-recognition as a function of mother-infant attachment relationship. *Developmental Psychology, 21,* 1181-1187.

Lippa, R. (1978). Expressive control, expressive consistency, and the correspondence between behavior and personality. *Journal of Personality, 46,* 438-461.

Litt, M. D. (1988). Self-efficacy and perceived control: Cognitive mediators of pain tolerance. *Journal of Personality and Social Psychology, 54,* 149-160.

Luchins, A. S. (1942). Mechanization in problem solving: The effect of Einstellung. *Psychological Monographs, 54,* 1-95.

Ludwig, D., Franco, J. N., & Malloy, T. E. (1986). Effects of reciprocity and self-monitoring on self-disclosure with a new acquaintance. *Journal of Personality and Social Psychology, 50,* 1077-1082.

Maddux, J. E., Norton, L. W., & Stoltenberg, C. D. (1986). Self-efficacy expectancy, outcome expectancy, and outcome value: Relative effects on behavioral intentions. *Journal of Personality and Social Psychology, 51,* 783-789.

Manning, M. M., & Wright, T. L. (1983). Self-efficacy expectancies, outcome expectancies, and the persistence of pain control in childbirth. *Journal of Personality and Social Psychology, 45,* 421-431.

Markus, H. (1977). Self-schemata and processing information about the self. *Journal of Personality and Social Psychology, 35,* 63-78.

Markus, H., & Kunda, Z. (1986). Stability and malleability of the self-concept. *Journal of Personality and Social Psychology, 51,* 858-866.

Markus, H., & Sentis, K. (1982). The self in social information processing. In J. Suls (Ed.), *Psychological perspectives on the self* (Vol. 1, pp. 41-70). Hillsdale, NJ: Erlbaum.

Markus, H., & Smith, J. (1981). The influence of self-schemata on the perception of others. In N. Cantor & J. F. Kihlstrom (Eds.), *Personality, cognition, and social interaction* (pp. 233-262). Hillsdale, NJ: Erlbaum.

Marsh, H. W., & Parker, J. W. (1984). Determinants of student self-concept: Is it better to be a relatively large fish in a small pond even if you don't learn to swim as well? *Journal of Personality and Social Psychology, 47,* 213-231.

Marsh, H. W., Relich, J. D., & Smith, I. D. (1983). Self-concept: The construct validity of interpretations based on the SDQ. *Journal of Personality and Social Psychology, 45,* 173-187.

Marsh, H. W., Richards, G. E., & Barnes, J. (1986). Multidimensional self-concepts: The effect of participation in an outward bound program. *Journal of Personality and Social Psychology, 50,* 195-204.

McIntyre, K. O., Mermelstein, R. J., & Lichtenstein, E. (1983). Self-efficacy and relapse in smoking cessation: A replication and extension. *Journal of Consulting and Clinical Psychology, 51,* 632-633.

Mead, G. H. (1934). *Mind, self, and society.* Chicago: University of Chicago Press.

Miell, D., & Le Voi, M. (1985). Self-monitoring and control in dyadic interaction. *Journal of Personality and Social Psychology, 49,* 1652-1661.

Miller, A. (1981). A survey of introductory psychology subject pool practices among leading universities. *Teaching of Psychology, 8,* 211-213.

Miller, G. A., Galanter, E., & Pribram, K. H. (1960). *Plans and the structure of behavior.* New York: Holt, Rinehart & Winston.

Miller, M. L., & Thayer, J. F. (1988). On the nature of self-monitoring. *Personality and Social Psychology Bulletin, 14*, 544-553.

Miller, M. L., & Thayer, J. F. (1989). On the existence of discrete classes in personality: Is self-monitoring the correct joint to carve? *Journal of Personality and Social Psychology, 57*, 143-155.

Monson, T., Tanke, E., & Lund, J. (1980). Determinants of social perception in a naturalistic setting. *Journal of Research in Personality, 14*, 104-120.

Montemayor, R., & Eisen, M. (1977). The development of self-conceptions from childhood to adolescence. *Developmental Psychology, 13*, 314-319.

Nasby, W. (1989). Private self-consciousness, self-awareness, and the reliability of self-reports. *Journal of Personality and Social Psychology, 56*, 950-957.

Nisbett, R., Caputo, C., Legant, P., & Maracek, J. (1973). Behavior as seen by the actor and as seen by the observer. *Journal of Personality and Social Psychology, 27*, 154-165.

Nisbett, R. E., & Wilson, T. D. (1977). Telling more than we can know: Verbal reports on mental processes. *Psychological Review, 84*, 231-259.

Norman, W. T. (1963). Toward an adequate taxonomy of personality attributes: Replicated factor structure in peer nomination personality ratings. *Journal of Abnormal and Social Psychology, 66*, 547-583.

Osberg, T. M., & Shrauger, J. S. (1986). Self-prediction: Exploring the parameter of accuracy. *Journal of Personality and Social Psychology, 51*, 1044-1057.

Osberg, T. M., & Shrauger, J. S. (1990). The role of self-prediction in psychological assessment. In J. N. Butcher & C. D. Spielberger (Eds.), *Advances in personality assessment* (Vol. 8, pp. 97-120).

Peabody, D. & Goldberg, L. R. (1989). Some determinants of factor structures from personality-trait descriptors. *Journal of Personality and Social Psychology, 57*, 552-567.

Piaget, J. (1952). *The origins of intelligence in children*. New York: International Universities Press.

Piers, E. V., & Harris, D. B. (1976). *Piers-Harris Children's Self-Concept Scale*. Los Angeles: Western Psychological Services.

Rhodewalt, F., & Agustsdottir, S. (1986). Effects of self-presentation on the phenomenal self. *Journal of Personality and Social Psychology, 50*, 47-55.

Rhodewalt, F., & Davison, J. (1986). Self-handicapping and subsequent performance: Role of outcome valence and attributional certainty. *Basic and Applied Social Psychology, 7*, 307-322.

Robinson, J. P., & Shaver, P. R. (1973). *Measures of social psychological attitudes*. Ann Arbor, MI: Institute for Social Research, University of Michigan.

Rogers, C. R. (1959). A theory of therapy, personality, and interpersonal relationships, as developed in the client-centered framework. In S. Koch (Ed.), *Psychology: A study of a science* (Vol. 3, pp. 184-256). New York: McGraw-Hill.

Rogers, C. R. (1961). *On becoming a person*. Boston: Houghton Mifflin.

Rogers, T. B. (1981). A model of the self as an aspect of the human information processing system. In N. Cantor & J. F. Kihlstrom (Eds.), *Personality, cognition, and social interaction* Hillsdale, NJ: Erlbaum (pp. 193-214).

Rosch, E. (1975). Cognitive representations of semantic categories. *Journal of Experimental Psychology: General, 104*, 192-233.

Rosch, E., & Mervis, C. B. (1975). Family resemblances: Studies in the internal structure of categories. *Cognitive Psychology, 7*, 573-605.

Rosch, E., Mervis, C. B., Gray, W. D., Johnson, W. D., & Boyes-Braem, P. (1976). Basic objects in natural categories. *Cognitive Psychology, 8*, 382-439.

Rosenberg, M. (1979). *Conceiving the self*. New York: Basic Books. (Reprinted 1986. Malabar, FL: Krieger).

Rosenberg, M. (1983). Self-concept from middle childhood through adolescence. In J. Suls & A. G. Greenwald (Eds.), *Psychological perspectives on the self* (Vol. 3, pp. 107-136). Hillsdale, NJ: Erlbaum.

Ross, A. O. (1977). *Learning disability: The unrealized potential*. New York: McGraw-Hill.

Ross, A. O. (1981). *Child behavior therapy: Principles, procedures, and empirical basis*. New York: Wiley.

Ross, A. O. (1987). *Personality: The scientific study of complex human behavior*. New York: Holt, Rinehart & Winston.

Sande, G. N., Goethals, G. R., & Radloff, C. E. (1988). Perceiving one's own traits and others': The multifaceted self. *Journal of Personality and Social Psychology, 54*, 13-20.

Scarr, S., & McCartney, K. (1983). How people make their own environments: A theory of genotype → environment effects. *Child Development, 54*, 424-435.

Scheier, M. F., & Carver, C. (1977). Self-focused attention and the experience of emotion: Attraction, repulsion, elation, and depression. *Journal of Personality and Social Psychology, 35*, 625-636.

Scheier, M. F., & Carver, C. S. (1983). Two sides of the self: One for you and one for me. In J. Suls & A. G. Greenwald (Eds.), *Psychological perspectives on the self* (Vol. 2, pp. 123-157). Hillsdale, NJ: Erlbaum.

Scheier, M. F., Carver, C., & Gibbons, F. X. (1979). Self-directed attention, awareness of bodily states, and suggestibility. *Journal of Personality and Social Psychology, 37*, 1576-1588.

Schlenker, B. R., & Weigold, M. F. (1990). Self-consciousness and self-presentation: Being autonomous versus appearing autonomous. *Journal of Personality and Social Psychology, 59*, 820-828.

Sentis, K., & Markus, H. (1979). *Self-schemas and recognition memory*. Unpublished manuscript, University of Michigan.

Shaffer, D. R., Ogden, J. K., & Wu, C. (1987). Effects of self-monitoring and prospect of future interaction on self-disclosure reciprocity during the acquaintance process. *Journal of Personality, 55*, 75-96.

Shaffer, D. R., Smith, J. E., & Tomarelli, M. (1982). Self-monitoring as a determinant of self-disclosure reciprocity during the acquaintance process. *Journal of Personality and Social Psychology, 43*, 163-175.

Shaffer, D. R., & Tomarelli, M. M. (1989). When public and private self-foci clash: Self-consciousness and self-disclosure reciprocity during the acquaintance process. *Journal of Personality and Social Psychology, 56*, 765-776.

Shavelson, R. J., Hubner, J. J., & Stanton, G. C. (1976). Self-concept: Validation of construct interpretation. *Review of Educational Research, 46*, 407-441.

Shepperd, J. A., & Arkin, R. M. (1989a). Determinants of self-handicapping: Task importance and the effects of preexisting handicaps on self-generated handicaps. *Personality and Social Psychology Bulletin, 15*, 101-112.

Shepperd, J. A., & Arkin, R. M. (1989b). Self-handicapping: The moderating roles of public self-consciousness and task importance. *Personality and Social Psychology Bulletin, 15,* 252-265.

Shoor, S. M., & Holman, H. R. (1984). Development of an instrument to explore psychological mediators of outcome in chronic arthritis. *Transactions of the Association of American Physicians, 97,* 325-331.

Skinner, B. F. (1953). *Science and human behavior.* New York: Macmillan.

Snyder, M. (1974). The self-monitoring of expressive behavior. *Journal of Personality and Social Psychology, 30,* 526-537.

Snyder, M. (1987). *Public appearance, private realities: The psychology of self-monitoring.* New York: Freeman.

Snyder, M., Berscheid, E., & Glick, P. (1985). Focusing on the exterior and the interior: Two investigations of the initiation of personal relationships. *Journal of Personality and Social Psychology, 48,* 1427-1439.

Snyder, M., & Gangestad, S. (1982). Choosing social situations: Two investigations of self-monitoring processes. *Journal of Personality and Social Psychology, 43,* 123-135.

Snyder, M., & Gangestad, S. (1986). On the nature of self-monitoring: Matters of assessment, matters of validity. *Journal of Personality and Social Psychology, 51,* 125-139.

Snyder, M., Gangestad, S., & Simpson, J. A. (1983). Choosing friends as activity partners: The role of self-monitoring. *Journal of Personality and Social Psychology, 45,* 1061-1072.

Sroufe, L. A. (1979). The coherence of individual development. *American Psychologist, 34,* 834-841.

Sternberg, S. (1969). Mental processes revealed by reaction time experiments. *American Scientist, 57,* 421-457.

Strube, M. J., Lott, C. J., Lê-Xuân-Hy, G. M., Oxenberg, J., & Deichmann, A. K. (1986). Self-evaluation of abilities: Accurate self-assessment versus biased self-enhancement. *Journal of Personality and Social Psychology, 51,* 16-25.

Strube, M. J., & Roemmele, L. A. (1985). Self-enhancement, self-assessment, and self-evaluative task choice. *Journal of Personality and Social Psychology, 49,* 981-993.

Taylor, S. E., & Brown, J. D. (1988). Illusion and well-being: A social psychological perspective on mental health. *Psychological Bulletin, 103,* 193-210.

Thomas, G. C., & Batson, C. D. (1981). Effect of helping under normative pressure on self-perceived altruism. *Social Psychology Quarterly, 44,* 127-131.

Thomas, G. C., Batson, C. D., & Coke, J. S. (1981). Do good Samaritans discourage helpfulness?: Self-perceived altruism after exposure to highly helpful others. *Journal of Personality and Social Psychology, 40,* 194-200.

Tice, D. M., & Baumeister, R. F. (1990). Self-esteem, self-handicapping, and self-presentation: The strategy of inadequate practice. *Journal of Personality, 58,* 443-464.

Trope, Y. (1975). Seeking information about one's own ability as a determinant of choice among tasks. *Journal of Personality and Social Psychology, 32,* 1004-1013.

Trope, Y. (1979). Uncertainty reducing properties of achievement tasks. *Journal of Personality and Social Psychology, 37,* 1505-1518.

Trope, Y. (1980). Self-assessment, self-enhancement, and task preference. *Journal of Experimental Social Psychology, 16,* 116-129.

Turner, R. G. (1980). Self-consciousness and memory of trait terms. *Personality and Social Psychology Bulletin, 6,* 273-277.

Tversky, A., & Kahneman, D. (1974). Judgment under uncertainty: Heuristics and biases. *Science, 185,* 1124-1131.

Waters, E. (1978). The reliability and stability of individual differences in infant-mother attachment. *Child Development, 49,* 483-494.

Waters, E., Vaughn, B. E., & Egeland, B. R. (1980). Individual differences in infant-mother attachment relationships at age one: Antecedents in neonatal behavior in an urban, economically disadvantaged sample. *Child Development, 51,* 208-216.

Watzlawick, P. (Ed.). (1984). *The invented reality: How do we know what we believe we know? (Contributions to constructivism).* New York: Norton.

Webster's New Collegiate Dictionary. (1987). Springfield, MA: Merriam.

Weiner, B. *An attributional theory of motivation and emotion.* (1986). New York: Springer Verlag.

Wicklund, R. A., & Brehm, J. W. (1976). *Perspectives on cognitive dissonance.* Hillsdale, NJ: Erlbaum.

Wicklund, R. A., & Gollwitzer, P. M. (1987). The fallacy of the private-public self-focus distinction. *Journal of Personality, 55,* 491-523.

Wicklund, R. A., & Hormuth, S. E. (1981). On the functions of self: A reply to Hull and Levy. *Journal of Personality and Social Psychology, 40,* 1029-1037.

Wiener, N. (1948). *Cybernetics: Control and communication in the animal and the machine.* Cambridge, MA: M.I.T. Press.

Wylie, R. C. (1974). *The self-concept* (rev. ed. Vol. 1). Lincoln: University of Nebraska Press.

Wylie, R. C. (1990). Mothers' attributions to their young children: The verbal environment as a resource for children's self-concept acquisition. *Journal of Personality, 58,* 419-441.

Indices

Author Index

Adams, N. E., 101, 103, 179
Agustsdottir, S., 86-88, 185
Ainsworth, M. D. S., 10-11, 178
Alicke, M. D., 80, 178
Allen, B. P., 78, 178
Allport, G. W., 4, 178
Altman, I., 162, 178
Andrus, B. W., 135, 178
Arend, R. A., 12, 178
Arkin, R. M., 117, 118, 119, 121, 123-124, 128, 183, 186, 187
Asch, S. E., 12, 79, 89, 178
Ashford, S. J., 135, 182
Atkinson, J. W., 94, 178

Baars, B. J., 4, 69, 178
Bachman, J. G., 41-45, 178
Baldwin, M. W., 54, 132, 178
Banaji, M. R., 91, 182
Bandura, A., 3, 99-101, 102-105, 158, 179
Barfield, O., 23, 46, 47, 51, 55, 179
Barnes, J., 46, 47, 51, 55, 184
Barton, R., 80, 182
Batson, C. D., 81-83, 187
Baumeister, R. F., 1, 2, 124-128, 155, 159, 179, 183, 187
Behar, M. C., 10, 178
Bem, D. J., 18, 26, 85, 146, 179
Bem, S. L., 138, 179
Berglas, S., 85, 107, 113-114, 118-119, 128-129, 179, 183

Berkowitz, L., 56, 131-132, 179, 183
Berlyne, D. E., 131, 179
Berscheid, E., 160, 161, 179, 187
Bertenthal, B. I., 8, 179
Block, J., 112, 179
Bowlby, J., 9, 179
Boyes-Braem, P., 28, 186
Brehm, J. W., 85, 188
Brenner, K. J., 154, 183
Briggs, S. R., 156, 171, 173, 179
Broadbent, D. E., 131, 180
Brock, T. C., 58, 180
Bronson, G. W., 6, 180
Brooks-Gunn, J., 13, 14-15, 183-184
Brouillard, M. W., 105, 179
Brown, J. D., 79-80, 187
Buss, A. H., 57, 67, 69, 132, 145, 152, 156, 157, 173, 180, 181
Byrne, D., 162, 180

Campbell, D. T., 33, 155, 180
Campbell, J. D., 80, 180
Cannon, W. B., 147, 180
Cantor, N., 91, 183
Caputo, C., 73, 185
Carver, C. S., 36, 54, 56, 58-66, 131-134, 149-150, 171, 180, 181, 186
Cattell, R. B., 78, 180
Chaikin, A. L., 63, 180
Chaplin, W., 80, 183
Cheek, J. M., 156, 171, 173, 179
Chila, 105, 182

Christy, R., 155, 180
Cioffi, D., 105, 179
Clausen, J. A., 113, 181
Cohen, A., 133, 135, 183
Coke, J. S., 81, 187
Condiotte, M. M., 106, 180
Conway, M., 80, 180
Cooley, C. H., 36, 72, 180
Cooper, J., 86, 181
Coopersmith, S., 108, 110, 180
Cozby, P. C., 162, 180
Crowne, D. P., 155, 180
Cruet, D., 131, 135, 182

Danheiser, P. R., 163, 180
Davis, D., 58, 180
Davison, J., 117, 185
Deichman, A. K., 98-99, 187
DeMorest, J. A., 159, 182
Derlega, V. J., 63, 180
DiClemente, C. C., 106, 180
Digman, J. M., 34, 181
Duval, S., 131, 133-134, 148-149, 181
Dworkin, R. H., 157, 181

Eastman, C., 104-105, 181
Effrein, E. A., 84, 181
Egeland, B. R., 11, 188
Eichorn, D. H., 112, 181
Eisen, M., 18-19, 185
Epstein, S., 108, 110, 181
Erikson, E. H., 4, 19, 181
Ervin, C., 110, 182
Exner, J. E., 134, 136, 138, 181
Eysenck, H. J., 156, 181

Fallender, V. J., 85, 181
Fazio, R. H., 85-86, 181
Fehr, B., 80, 180
Fenigstein, A., 57, 67, 69, 71, 132, 133, 135, 145, 152-153, 176, 181
Ferris, C., 133, 182
Festinger, L., 85, 111, 147, 181
Field, P., 114, 127, 183
Fischer, K. W., 8, 179

Fiske, D. W., 34, 155, 180, 181
Franco, J. N., 165-170, 173, 184
Freud, S., 4, 147, 181
Froming, W. J., 60-61, 66, 181
Fultz, J., 81, 179
Funder, D., 35, 181

Galanter, E., 20, 27, 148, 184
Gangestad, S., 153, 156-157, 162, 167, 171-172, 174, 181, 187
Gauthier, J., 105, 179
Geis, L., 155, 180
Gergen, K. J., 28, 79, 182
Gibbons, F. X., 132, 186
Glick, P., 159-160, 182, 187
Goethals, G. R., 74-77, 186
Goldberg, L. R., 34, 182, 185
Gollwitzer, P. M., 69, 188
Gossard, D., 105, 179
Gove, F. L., 12, 178
Gray, W. D., 28, 186
Graziano, W. G., 163, 180
Greenberg, J., 133-136, 151, 182
Greenwald, A. G., 91, 182, 186
Gregory, M., 131, 180

Haan, N., 112, 181
Hall, J. R., 105, 182
Hanson, M., 81, 179
Harris, D. B., 111, 185
Harris, R. N., 117, 182
Harter, S., 108, 110, 111, 182
Helmreich, R., 110, 182
Hetherington, E. M., 12, 182
Hoffman, M. L., 81, 182
Holm, J. E., 105, 182
Holman, H. R., 105, 187
Holmes, J. G., 54, 132, 178
Holroyd, K. A., 105, 182
Honzik, K. M., 159, 181
Hormuth, S. E., 131, 188
Hotze, C. A., 159, 182
Hubner, J. J., 38, 39, 186
Hull, C. L., 150, 182
Hull, J. G., 134, 182
Hursey, K. G., 105, 182

Author Index

Ickes, J., 133, 182
Ingram, R. E., 131, 132, 135-138, 182

Jackson, D. M., 57, 182
Jamieson, D. W., 162, 182
Janis, I. L., 114, 127, 183
Jaskir, J., 14, 184
Jasnoski, M. L., 81, 179
Johnson, B. R., 131, 136, 182
Johnson, W. D., 28, 186
Jones, E. E., 73, 85-87, 88, 107, 113-114, 118, 119, 128-129, 154, 155, 158-159, 183
Jöreskog, K. G., 44, 183

Kahneman, D., 27, 79, 183, 188
Kernis, M. H., 133, 134, 135, 183
Kihlstrom, J. F., 91, 183, 184, 185
Kirsch, J., 105, 183
Knight, J. G., 154, 183
Kolditz, T. A., 119, 121, 123, 124, 128, 183
Kunda, Z., 88, 90, 91-92, 93, 184

Lau, R. R., 80, 183
Le Voi, M., 156, 184
Le-Xuan-Hy, G. M., 98, 187
Legant, P., 73, 185
Lepper, M. R., 80, 183
Levine, M. P., 133, 181
Levy, A. S., 134, 182
Lewinsohn, P. M., 80, 183
Lewis, M., 5-7, 9, 13-16, 183, 184
Lichtenstein, E., 106, 180, 184
Lippa, R., 156, 184
Litt, M. D., 105, 184
Lott, C. J., 98, 187
Luchins, A. S., 79, 184
Ludwig, D., 165-170, 173, 184
Lund, J., 74, 185
Lydon, J. E., 162, 182

Maddux, J. E., 104, 184
Malloy, T. E., 165-170, 173, 184
Manning, M. M., 105, 184
Maracek, J., 73, 185

Marcille, P. J., 105, 182
Markus, H., 25-26, 30-31, 88, 90-93, 184, 186
Marlowe, D., 155, 180
Marsh, H. W., 41-43, 46-51, 55, 111, 184
Martin, B., 12, 182
Marzillier, J. S., 104-105, 181
McCartney, K., 157-158, 167, 186
McIntyre, K. O., 106, 184
Mead, G. H., 4, 72, 184
Mermelstein, R. J., 106, 184
Mervis, C. B., 28, 186
Miell, D., 156, 184
Miller, A., 166, 184
Miller, G. A., 20, 27, 148, 184
Miller, M. L., 171, 173, 184
Mischel, W., 80, 183
Monson, T. C., 74, 185
Montemayor, R., 18, 19, 185
Mussen, P. H., 112, 181, 182

Nasby, W., 57, 58, 185
Nisbett, R. E., 73-75, 108, 183, 185
Norman, W. T., 33, 185
Norton, L. W., 104, 184

O'Leary, A., 105, 179
O'Malley, P. M., 42-45, 178
Odbert, H. S., 31, 178
Ogden, J. K., 164, 166, 170, 186
Osberg, T. M., 139-141, 143, 144-147, 185
Oxenberg, J., 98, 187

Paduano, A., 81, 179
Parker, J. W., 41, 42-43, 111, 184
Peabody, D., 34, 185
Penzien, D. B., 105, 182
Piaget, J., 7, 147, 185
Piers, E. V., 111, 185
Plomin, R., 157, 180
Potkay, C. R., 78, 178
Pribram, K. H., 20, 27, 148, 184
Propson, P., 135, 182
Pyszcynski, T., 133-136, 151, 182

Radloff, C. E., 74-77, 186
Raynor, J. O., 94, 178
Reese, L., 101, 103, 179
Relich, J. D., 43, 184
Rhodewalt, F., 85-88, 107, 114, 117, 183, 185
Richards, G. E., 46, 47, 51, 55, 184
Robinson, J. P., 114, 185
Roemmele, L. A., 54, 114-117, 187
Rogers, C. R., 4, 79, 185
Rogers, L., 105, 182
Rogers, T. B., 30, 31, 185
Rosch, E., 28-30, 185, 186
Rosenberg, M., 17, 18, 38, 108, 110, 186
Ross, A. O., 7, 10, 30, 47, 53, 186
Ross, L., 80, 183
Ross, M., 80, 180

Sande, G. N., 74-77, 186
Scarr, S., 157-158, 167, 186
Scheier, M. F., 36, 54, 56, 57, 58-62, 131-134, 149-150, 171, 180, 186
Schlenker, B. R., 70-71, 186
Schoenrade, P. A., 81, 179
Sentis, K., 25, 26, 30, 31, 184, 186
Shaffer, D. R., 63-67, 163-167, 168-171, 186
Shavelson, R. J., 38-41, 186
Shaver, P. R., 114, 185
Sheppard, J. A., 117, 183, 186, 187
Shoor, S. M., 105, 187
Shrauger, J. S., 139-141, 143, 144-147, 185
Simpson, J. A., 162, 187
Skelton, J. A., 85, 107, 183
Skinner, B. F., 104, 187
Smith, I. D., 43, 184
Smith, J. E., 25, 91, 163-167, 168, 170, 180
Snyder, C. R., 117, 182
Snyder, M., 54, 153-156, 158, 160-163, 167, 171-172, 174, 176, 181, 187
Sörbon, D., 44, 183

Spadafora, S., 173, 175, 183
Sroufe, L. A., 10, 12, 178
Stanton, G. C., 38, 39, 186
Stapp, J., 110, 182
Sternberg, S., 26, 187
Stoltenberg, C. D., 104, 184
Strube, M. J., 54, 98-99, 114-117, 187

Tanke, E., 74, 185
Taylor, C. B., 105, 179
Taylor, D. A., 162, 178
Taylor, S. E., 79-80, 187
Thayer, J. F., 171, 173, 185
Thomas, G. C., 81, 187
Tice, D. M., 124-128, 187
Tobin, D. L., 105, 182
Tomarelli, M. M., 63-67, 163-167, 168-171, 186
Trope, Y., 95-97, 113, 116, 187
Turner, R. G., 55, 59, 187
Tversky, A., 27, 79, 183, 188

Van Treuren, R. P., 135, 182
Vaugh, B. E., 11, 188

Wall, S., 10, 188
Walster, E., 161, 179
Waters, E., 10, 11, 12, 178, 188
Watzlavik, P., 79, 188
Webster's New Collegiate Dictionary, 2, 188
Weigold, M. F., 70-71, 186
Weiner, B., 95, 113, 188
Wicklund, R. A., 69, 85, 131, 133-134, 148-149, 181, 182, 188
Wiener, N., 147, 188
Wilson, T. D., 108, 185
Wisnicki, W. S., 131, 135, 182
Wright, T. L., 105, 184
Wu, C., 164, 166, 170, 186
Wylie, R. C., 2, 18, 108, 188

Zanna, M. P., 86, 181
Zuckerman, M., 173, 175, 183

Subject Index

Acceptance
　self-esteem and, 110
Achievement motivation, 97
Altruism, 81-84
　function of, 81
　rewards for, 82
　self-reflection, 84
Analogy
　theorizing by, 149
Androgyny, 138
Attachment, 9-13
　assessment of, 10
　development of, 40
　forms of, 11
　self-recognition and, 13
　stability of, 12
Attention, 131
Attitude, 61-62
　change of, 62, 86
Attraction, interpersonal, 161
Attribution, 26, 95, 113
　of failure, 113
　of traits, 26, 27
　self and others, 26
　style of, 95

Base rate, 139, 145
Behavior
　determinants of, 74
　prediction of, 139
Behaviorism, 4
Bem Sex Role Inventory, 138

Checklist, 32
Coercive communication, 62
Cognition, 4
Cognitive dissonance, 85
　self-regulation and, 147
Cognitive processes, 7
　inferences about, 69
Competence, self-esteem and, 109
Conformity, 60, 89
Constructs, 139
　hypothetical, 2
　theoretical, 45, 56
Control systems, 147
Control theory, 133
　self-regulation and, 149
Correlational studies, limitations of, 46
Cybernetics, 146

Definitions, 53-55
　operational, 46, 69
Depression, 80, 87, 105
　self-esteem and, 107
Diagnosticity of tasks, 95, 96-97, 114-115
Dispositions, 76

Educational attainment, 45
Encoding, 23-24
Experiments
　limits of, 46
　subjects' construction of, 129
Extroversion, 34

195

Factor analysis, 33
False alarm effect, 31

Gender differences
  self-focused attention and, 133, 135, 137
  sources of, 138
Generalizability
  of research results, 99
Genotype
  environment effect, 157-158

Hedonism, 94-95
  instrumental, 163
  principle of, 81, 113
Heuristics, 27
Homeostasis, 147

Identity, 19, 70
  personal, 2
Illusions, 79-80
Impression management, 65, 79-81
Individual differences, 6-7, 26, 38, 56, 58, 97, 117, 124, 144
Individuality, 2
Information processing, 20-21
  self-schema and, 24-25
Introspection, 18, 67

Judgments
  biases in, 79-80
  fallibility of, 27

LISREL, 44

Machiavellianism, 155
Mark-directed behavior, 6-7, 14
Memory, 20-24
  accessibility of, 86
  distortions of, 133
  measures of, 22-23
Mirror studies, 6, 58, 132
  self-focus and, 135
Models
  causal, 44
  theories and, 37-39

Motivation, achievement, 94-97
Multidimensional model, 38-40, 48

Niche-picking, 158

Object permanence, 7
Opinion, 106
Outward Bound, 47-48

Perception, distortions of, 79-80
Personality
  dimensions of, 33-34, 175-178
  terms used in study of, 78
  traits and, 31-32
Personality research, replication in, 169
Personality Research Form, 40
Placebo control, 48
Power, self-esteem and, 110
Prototypes, studies of, 28-30
Psychology, cognitive, 4
Psychotherapy, self-reflection and, 84

Reactance, 62
Reaction time, 23, 29-30
  memory and, 91
Reality, 79
Recall, 21
Recognition, 21-22
Relearning, 22
Replication
  in behavioral science, 42
  in personality research, 169
Retrieval, 24
Rouge task, 8

Schema, 20
Science, requirements of, 3
Self
  history of word, 1-2
  other and, 75
  public and private, 35-36
Self-as-object, 5-6
Self-as-subject, 6
Self-assessment, 54, 94-95
  model of, 98
  self-enhancement and, 97

Subject Index

self-prediction and, 139
  validity of, 146
Self-attention, 131-133
Self-awareness, 1, 53, 132, 175
  objective, 148
  self-concept and, 16
  self-recognition and, 15
Self-concept, 2, 176
  academic, 41-44
  dimensions of, 175
  formation of, 20
  functions of, 2-3
  levels of, 38
  model of, 86-88
  objectivity of, 3
  organization of, 24-25
  origin of, 5
  stability of, 39, 48, 51-52, 88, 92
Self-conceptions, universe of, 90
Self-confidence, 100
Self-consciousness, 2, 53, 58-59
  attitude change and, 63
  conformity and, 60
  correlates of, 58
  critique of, 69
  dependency and, 70
  interpersonal behavior and, 60
  opinion change and, 62
  private and public, 57-59
  self-disclosure and, 63-65
  self-monitoring and, 152
Self-Consciousness Scale, 57, 64, 67, 180, 135, 144
  reliability of, 58
Self-control, 106
Self-deprecation, 85
  depression and, 87
Self-Descriptive Questionnaire, 49
Self-disclosure, 63-64, 165
  reciprocal, 162-163
  self-monitoring and, 163
Self-efficacy, 99-107
  assessment of, 99, 105
  fear reduction and, 102
  generalization of, 101
  induction of, 100, 104

  motivation and, 107
  pain tolerance and, 105
  self-concept and, 106
  smoking cessation and, 106
  questions about, 104
Self-enhancement, 97
Self-esteem, 1-2, 44-45, 54, 107
  cognition, affect and, 111
  components of, 108
  dimensions of, 109
  global, 44-45
  models of, 108
  protection of, 98, 113, 125
  self-handicapping and, 115, 124-125
  self-regulation and, 182
  stability of, 112
  tests of, 110
Self-evaluation, 39, 54, 78
Self-fulfilling prophesy, 74
Self-focus, 55
  measure of, 134, 138
Self-focused attention, 131
  depression and, 138
  gender differences in, 135
  self-regulation and, 133
  state or trait, 132-134, 312
Self-handicapping, 113-114, 117
  conscious choice of, 118, 126, 129
  impression management and, 121-122
  measure of, 114
  self-esteem and, 124-125
  self-presentation and, 119, 128
  variables affecting, 117
Self-knowledge, 2, 73-74, 146-147
  availability of, 86
Self-monitoring, 54, 153, 171
  correlates of, 153-154, 156
  extraversion and, 156
  genetic factors in, 156-157
  impression management and, 153
  Machiavellianism and, 155
  origins of, 156
  self-disclosure and, 162
  self-regulation and, 152
  social desirability and, 155

Self-monitoring (*continued*)
  social judgment and, 159-160
  social relations and, 157, 160
Self-Monitoring Scale, 153, 165, 173
  discriminant validity of, 155
  factor analysis of, 173
Self-perception, 3
  accuracy of, 78-79
  illusions in, 79-80
  influences on, 84
  mental health and, 80
  theory of, 18, 26, 85, 146
Self-prediction, 139-146
  accuracy of, 141-143, 145
  basis of, 141
  self-consciousness and, 145
Self-presentation, 124
Self-recognition, 8-9
  attachment and, 9
  development of, 8
  self-concept and, 15-16
Self-reflection, 81
Self-regulation, 133, 147-149
  affect and, 148
  energy source for, 149-150
  motivation and, 148
Self-regulatory systems, 147-148
  humans as, 149
Self-reliance, 49
Self-reports, 36
  reliability of, 55
  validity of, 3, 55, 139
Self-schema, 20-21, 25
  organization of, 27
  prototypes and, 29-31
  storage, retrieval and, 25-26
Semantic categories, 28
Sociability, 157

Social comparison, 111
Social Desirability Scale, 155
Social norms, 66
Social obliviousness, 70
Socioeconomic status, 45
Strange Situation, 10
Symbolic interactionism, 72

Task choice, 94
TOTE unit, 148
Traits, 17, 31-33, 73
  dimensions of, 35
  factors of, 31
  judgment of, 74
  lay person and, 77
  scale of, 75
  self vs. others, 74
  self-concept and, 34
  states and, 54

Uncertainty, reduction of, 95
Underachievement, 188

Validity
  construct, 52
  discriminant, 49, 155
  self-reports and, 107-108
Values, 149
Variables
  continuous vs. dichotomous, 170-171
  dispositional, 56
  latent, 45
  situational, 56

Worth, self-esteem and, 109

Youth in Transition, 41